SURVIVING THREE SHERMANS:
WITH THE 3RD ARMORED DIVISION
INTO THE BATTLE OF THE BULGE

SURVIVING THREE SHERMANS: WITH THE 3RD ARMORED DIVISION INTO THE BATTLE OF THE BULGE

What I Didn't Tell Mother About My War

WALTER BOSTON STITT, JR.
Edited by Dr. Jessica L. George

CASEMATE
Pennsylvania & Yorkshire

Published in the United States of America and Great Britain in 2024 by
CASEMATE PUBLISHERS
1950 Lawrence Road, Havertown, PA 19083, USA
and
47 Church Street, Barnsley, S70 2AS, UK

Hardcover Edition: ISBN 978-1-63624-428-0
Digital Edition: ISBN 978-1-63624-429-7

A CIP record for this book is available from the British Library

Printed and bound in the United Kingdom by CPI Group (UK) Ltd, Croydon, CR0 4YY
Typeset in India by DiTech Publishing Services

For a complete list of Casemate titles, please contact:

CASEMATE PUBLISHERS (US)
Telephone (610) 853-9131
Fax (610) 853-9146
Email: casemate@casematepublishers.com
www.casematepublishers.com

CASEMATE PUBLISHERS (UK)
Telephone (0)1226 734350
Email: casemate@casemateuk.com
www.casemateuk.com

Front cover image: (National Archives)

Dedication

To my mother, Ada Ruth Crickenberger Stitt, who if she lost her oldest son in the war, would have had memories in the 87 letters she saved.

To Corporal Ellsworth Reavy, Lieutenant Paul E. Baer, and Sergeant John Fasula. As they lost one Sherman tank, they climbed into another. Their bravery cost them their lives. The Allies won World War II because of men and women like them.

To William Megahan, my best friend from eighth grade through high school, who was killed in Saipan. A brave Marine whose comrades came home to tell his father of his bravery and skill.

Contents

Abbreviations

A.A.A. (M.G.)	Anti-aircraft artillery (machine gun)
A.A.A. A.W. (S.P.)	Anti-aircraft artillery auto-weapons (self-propelled)
A.I.R.	Armored Infantry Regiment
A.P.O.	Army Post Office
A.R.	Armored Regiment
C.C.A./B./R.	Combat Command A/B/R
C.G.	Commanding general
C.O.	Commanding officer
E.T.O.	European Theatre of Operations
G.M.C.	Gun motor carriage
K.P.	Kitchen patrol—peeling onions and potatoes, scouring greasy pots and pans, or guarding the garbage cans to make sure his fellow recruits ate all of their food.
M.O.S.	Military Occupational Specialty
M.P.	Military Policeman
O.C.S.	Officer Candidate School
O.D.	Officer of the day
O.T.S.	Officer Training School
P.F.C.	Private first class—the first promotion basic privates received. Next was to corporal.
P.O.W.	Prisoner of war
Pvt.	Private
P.X.	Post Exchange—retail store on Army bases
(R.) O.T.C.	(Reserve) Officers' Training Corps
S.M.G.	Submachine gun
S.S.N.	Specification Serial Number
T.D.	Tank destroyer. The M10 arrived in 1942, the M18 in 1943, and the M36 in 1944.
T.O.&E.	Table(s) of organization and equipment
U.S.O.	United Services Organization
V-mail	Victory Mail
W.A.A.C./W.A.C.	The Women's Army Auxiliary Corps became the Women's Army Corps on July 1, 1943

Prologue

On March 17, 1943, I raised my right hand to swear an oath and became a member of the United States Army. My first official order was to report to the Baltimore and Ohio Railroad Station in Wheeling, West Virginia, to be transported to my induction into the Army at Fort Hayes in Columbus, Ohio.

A 36-hour train ride from Columbus, Ohio, took me to Camp Polk, Louisiana, for the next year. It was from this new address that I wrote my first letter home. This letter, postmarked May 5, was followed in the next 32 months by 87 more. Unbeknownst to me, my mother saved them all, numbered in sequence. This treasure was discovered by my daughter, Beverly, during my move from South Bend, Indiana, to Springfield, Ohio, May 2018.

Beverly read them all and shared her find with me. After reading the first few, I chuckled. When asked how I refrained from disclosing all that was really going on in those letters, my first response was, "When you're eighteen years old, you don't tell your parents everything!" This book is the end result of that conversation. Each letter is printed and followed by much of what was unstated at the time.

Letters home from servicemen overseas were censored. No location, no unit number, no testimonial to your job, just talk that reassured the folks back home that you were alive somewhere.

When you read these letters, you might notice errors in spelling and grammar. Keep in mind, these correspondences were crafted prior to college and seminary, marriage to an English teacher, and writing sermons and articles for publication.

Read on and you'll know more than my parents ever knew as I went on to survive the destruction of three Sherman tanks, the death of three of my crew members, and two wounds. Plus, my beer-drinking prowess!

CHAPTER I

In Training

Camp Polk, Louisiana, March 1943–June 1943

My first free ride on the B&O Railroad was from Wheeling, West Virginia, to Fort Hayes in Columbus, Ohio. On arrival, I was shown a cot for my stay and told to remain close until tomorrow. Later, an urge took me to the latrine, or what the civilian side still regarded as the toilet. The lack of privacy in what I previously knew as a very private place caused me to pause; four fixtures on three walls with no separation was a challenge to my dignity. I returned to the barracks. A call at two in the morning could not be denied, and to my delight, none of the ceramic thrones were occupied.

Day two started with surrender of all civilian clothes, which were packaged in a box and labeled with the recruit's home address. It was in this advanced stage of undress that the recruits headed off to receive physicals. In the area designed for collecting small urine samples were two fellows left over from the previous group, an hour with a bottle in one hand, staring at the wall, and still trying. They were there when group two left. Day one of their World War II career!

Step two was vaccination, which was no problem until I found myself surrendering my arms to needles which some claimed had been purposely dulled. "Feet in the outline" was the next order. Followed by "Pick up the two buckets of sand." This was supposed to reflect what wearing a full field pack would do to your feet. My 9-D shoe size became 9-E.

For the final step, the recruits received clothes. A size 30 waist came out as 32. One can only assume they were anticipating shrinkage when washed. Roll up the sleeves, roll up the pant legs. "Any complaints?"

Day three was the day I found out about Army Axiom #1: Never volunteer. A call for "anyone wanting to be an M.P." elicited my quick response. The badge looked good and I could direct traffic. I found out I could also empty ashes from the barrack's coal burning stoves, bring in coal, and make a round every four hours for the next 24. I learned a hard lesson about Army Axiom #1.

On day four, recruits went to the train yard and hopped on the Troop Transport with bunks stacked three high, one latrine, one water faucet and a conductor who, for 36 hours, swore he had "no idea" where we were going.

One wonders about me because I was still excited. I described my personality as always wondering what was around the next corner!

Who Served?

On September 16, 1940, while the United States was still at peace, President Roosevelt signed the Selective Training and Service Act. This required the registration of men between 21 and 35 who could then be conscripted. At that time military service was limited to 12 months. Some 16 million men registered by the end of 1940. At that time there were 630,000 men in the Army; six months later there were 1.4 million. On August 18, 1941, military service was extended to 30 months and, after war had been declared following the attack on Pearl Harbor on December 19, 1941, to the duration of the war plus six months. At the same time, the age range was increased to those between 18 and 64. The draft continued until 1946 during which time some 36 million men registered, more than 10 million of whom were inducted through 6,000 local draft boards. A significant number of these—around a third, including Walter—volunteered, hoping to choose their branch of service.

Letter #1: May 5, 1943

Dear Mom, Dad, Dick, and Sara:

Well! Finally, I have gotten time to write a few lines. How do you like my new address? Kinda far from home, isn't it? If you look on a map for Leesville, our camp is about 5 miles from there.

This camp is really swell. It is a new one. All the barracks are new and have everything just like home. There is a P.X. [post exchange] and movie on every corner. (I just came from the movie).

If I didn't tell you when I called, my IQ was high enough to apply for Officers' Training School.

We were shipped out of Fort Hayes on Thursday about 12 noon and got here Saturday morning at 2:00. We are still going through a lot of red tape but today was the last (I hope).

When I was classified, the Lieutenant said the best thing to take up in preparation for O.T.S. was gunner in a tank, this way I get training in guns, motor, driving, radio, and a few dozen other things. (When you are reading this letter if you hear a buzzing noise it is just a tank or jeep going by so think nothing of it.)

We get the best of food and everything cost us less. We have all the sugar, coffee, butter, etc. that we want.

Well! There are a million things I want to tell you but I can't think of them and as it is about time for taps, I had better sign off.

With Love
(Little Bit homesick)
Walter Jr.
P.S. Ask me some questions in your letters so I will get wound up and think of something
to say.

This was one of my abridgements. Wheeling to Fort Hayes Columbus, Ohio, to Camp Polk, Louisiana. We shipped out of Fort Hayes on Thursday about noon and arrived Saturday at 2:00 a.m.

My father, a World War I veteran, was upset that I had volunteered to be drafted and advised me to tell the Army I was a student instead of a truck driver. A funny aside is how I got my job as a truck driver. I told my dad if he would lie about my age by one year, I could get a job and he would not have to give me an allowance. I had barely finished my speech when my dad was in the car, honking for me to hurry.

So, when asked, I obeyed my father. As a consequence of saying "I don't want anything with a steering wheel," when confronted with my resume, I became a tanker. The lieutenant must have had a good laugh when he assigned me to be a tanker—tanks have levers for steering. Abridged also was the arrival at Camp Polk. I stood first in line to depart the train, followed orders to jump off the last step when the whistle blew. I promptly lit on the soft ground, pitched forward and landed on my duffel bag. A quick recovery and a dash to the waiting truck. A short ride to another barracks where the bag was dropped off. The food was cold due to a late arrival; however, when you are hungry, a cold meal of meat and potatoes is still tasty. Then it was off to the shower.

Orders for the shower went like this: "Take off your clothes. When I blow the whistle, you and one other recruit will be under the shower. You have thirty seconds to wet each of you, then the water is off! Soap up. In thirty seconds when the water comes on, rinse off and put on your uniform!" It should be noted that soap does not come off that quickly. Everybody groaned but got dressed and was taken to the barracks for a much-appreciated, albeit brief, rest.

Having "a million things to say" was just a filler but not a fact.

The first assignment was to Headquarters Company, Second Battalion, 80th Armored Regiment of the 8th Armored Division. My barracks was directly across the street from where the bugler stood at the microphone. This made it quite easy for me to hear the reveille at 4:30 a.m.

8th Armored Division

The first years of the war showed just how important tanks were. The German Blitzkrieg in western Europe, the fighting in North Africa, and the Axis assault on the Soviet Union emphasized this. To build up this element of the U.S. Army, the 8th Armored Division was constituted as a training command.

From April 13, 1942, it was commanded by Brigadier General William M. Grimes who outlined the mission as, "to provide complete cadres, officers and enlisted men, for new divisions. The primary purpose is to train, organize and prepare these divisional cadres. We are a training division as distinguished from an active division." This continued until March 1943 when the division was transferred to Camp Polk, Louisiana—where Walter joined it—with an altered mission. It was now to become a combat unit.

In September 1943 it was reorganized to the new "light" armored division standard, to ready itself for activation as a combat unit. The reorganization did away with the regiments and balanced the tank, infantry, and artillery components. Three subheadquarters—Combat Commands A, B, and R—allowed role-specific units to be created.

As part of this process, in December of that year, in Texas, 8th Armored took part first in the D Series of exercises and then the Sixth Louisiana Maneuvers in February–April 1944 (as are reflected in Walter's letters 42–54). During the exercises the division lost many trained lower ranks to a War Department levy and had to train replacements, more of which arrived on the return to Camp Polk. Training continued in 1944 and, inevitably, while it waited for movement orders, the division lost some of its personnel to other units—among them Walter, heading to 3rd Armored. Finally, 8th Armored moved to Camp Kilmer, New York in October 1944 and left for the E.T.O. on November 6.

The 8th Armored Division insignia was a cloth badge worn on the shoulder. The U.S. Army Center for Military History explains the design: "The mixture of insignia and distinctive colors of several arms incorporated in the Armored Force symbolize integrity and esprit. It is an interlocked ornament, found in Nordic monuments, composed of three torques: red for Artillery; blue for Infantry; and yellow for Cavalry. The symbols represent the characteristics of Armored Divisions; the tank track, mobility and armor protection; the cannon, firepower; and the red bolt of lightning, shock action." (Noclador/WikiCommons)

"I just came from the movie" was probably something not to write home about. The movie was *How Not to Come Down with a Case of Gonorrhea or Syphilis*, a rather unpleasant film showing images of people afflicted with the ravages of these diseases. Not something to share with the family. The chaplain had his say followed by a doctor. Not letting that lie, a World War I veteran, a colonel, had his own version. "You'll probably have some whiskey with you; pour that on your instrument." The look on the faces of the other speakers should have been recorded. They both did come forward and offer their suggestions as a better choice. The doctor suggested a visit to the prophylactic station before sex for a condom or after sex for a treatment. Chaplain suggested keeping the fly buttoned. This event proved to be a source of hilarious discussion back at the barracks.

The same colonel was observed out in the field rolling his own smokes from a package of Bull Durham. Word came later the colonel was given his honorable discharge after he was observed urinating off the porch at the Officers' Club during a gathering to which wives had been invited.

This short initial letter contained a wealth of information for my family. I was at Camp Polk, Louisiana, which is about five miles from Leesville. My IQ was more than enough to qualify as an officer. I had all the butter I could use (while back home my mother was squeezing packages that looked like lard; inside the sack there was a small red dot, which after much squeezing, looked and almost tasted like butter). The barracks had everything just like home, which translated to running water and toilet facilities. I was going to be a tank gunner and there were also women five miles away, which was important at eighteen years old.

One wonders what my parents told their neighbors and friends about my early Army experiences.

CAMP POLK, LOUISIANA

Dear Mom, Dad, Dick, and Sara:

Well! Finally I have gotten time to write a few lines. How do you like my new address? Kind'a far from home isn't it? If you look on a map for Leesville, our camp is about 5 miles from there.

This camp is really swell. It is a new one. All the barracks are new and have every thing just like home. There is a PX and movie on every corner. (I just came from the movie).

If I didn't tell you when I called, my I.Q. was high enough to apply for Officer's Training School.

We were shipped out of Fort Hayes on Thursday about 12 noon and got here Saturday morning at 2:00. We are still going through a lot of red tape but today was the last (I hope).

When I was classiffied, the Lieutenant said the best thing to take up in preparation for O.T.S. was gunner in a tank, this way I get training in guns, motors, driving, radio, and a few dozen other things (When you are reading this letter if you hear a buzzing noise it is just a tank or jeep going by so think nothing of it).

We get the best of food and everything cost us less. We have all the sugar, coffee, butter, etc., that we want.

Well! There are a million things I want to tell you but I can't think of them, and as it is about time for taps, I had better sign off.

With Love
(Little bit homesick)
Walter Jr.

P.S. Ask me some questions in your letters so I will get wound up and think of something to say.

This was the first letter I sent home after reporting for basic training. It was also one of my longest letters.

Camp Polk, Louisiana

In 1941, Camp Polk—named for the Right Reverend Leonidas Polk, "Sewanee's fighting bishop," who resigned as Episcopal Bishop of the Diocese of Louisiana to become a Confederate general—was built on land that had been taken by the government under its power of eminent domain. Some 250 families were evicted from their farms to provide a training area of around 200,000 acres.

The camp played an important role in the series of huge Louisiana Maneuvers which had started in 1940 and continued to 1944. The camp continued to be used for training throughout the war, and also housed German P.O.W.s.

On June 13, 2023, Fort Polk was renamed to Fort Johnson honoring William Henry Johnson, a hero of the first African American unit to fight in World War I who had been posthumously awarded the Medal of Honor in 2015 by President Barack Obama.

Camp Polk entrance—a 1943 photograph. General George Marshall stayed here when he reviewed the 1941 Louisiana Maneuvers. "I want the mistakes made down in Louisiana and not over in Europe, and the only way to do this thing is to try it out, and if it doesn't work, find out what we need to make it work," he said. (U.S. Army via DVIDS)

Fort Polk in the 1940s. (U.S. Army)

Toilet arrangements in a camp hut. (Jerome Philip Lewis Collection, Veterans History Project, American Folklife Center, Library of Congress)

Letter #2: no date

Dear Family,

As you can see I ran out of ink. And that is not the only thing I need. We are very short on hangers. If you want a list of things to send me here it is:

- Hangers
- Ink
- Camera
- Film (for camera)

After while I will not have be able to write as often. Although we have from 6:00 every night till 5:00 the next morning.

Monday our training starts. We get 13 weeks of it. After 4 weeks we are allowed to leave camp and after 13 weeks we are eligible for a furlough.

Down here they figure every West Virginian can play a mouth organ or guitar and that they all carry guns. Most of the W. Va. fellows lead them on, and tell them about snake soup, etc.

In case I didn't tell you last time there is a camp (South Camp Polk) five miles from here which is full of W.A.C.C.s. They come over for dances, shows, etc. You are allowed to date them if they are the same rank as you.

They just blew the whistle so I have to go. Will write again later.

Walter Jr.

P.S. Don't send candy or anything burdensome.

By Now!

Did I really expect my mother to send me hangers? She did send a Kodak Brownie box camera, but pictures from the camera proved to be very scarce.

Upon arriving at my barracks, I was asked where I hailed from. My "West Virginia" response brought an "Oh no! Not another one from West Virginia." In the barracks were a number of men who had been there for a time. One of these men was a bed-wetter from West Virginia. After the full complement of men arrived, there was an assessment of those who needed to be seen by the professionals, i.e., doctors or teachers. The issues for referral ranged from not being able to read and write, complaints of flat feet, need for treatment of syphilis, and bedwetting. So off went our bed-wetter for treatment. The cure for bedwetting was reported as two bed-wetter partners, one bunk bed with a thin mattress, and one night on the bottom and the next on the top. Somehow the urine shower was grounds for a cure, or so the story goes.

On a regular schedule, we were told to take our mattresses to the rear of the barracks and air them out in the warm Louisiana sun. When the day's activities ended, we came to attention on the company street and were dismissed for the day by an order to "Fall out." With our mattresses out back, there was a mad scramble to grab the best-looking one. Everybody ran except one who could walk slowly back later to get his yellow-spotted charm.

I learned the hard way that not feeling well was not a reason to stay in bed. The first sergeant came looking for me when I missed reveille and found me, a young recruit, lying in bed. Inquiring as to what I was still doing in bed, I told the sergeant I didn't feel well. The first sergeant promptly picked up my mattress and dumped me on the floor. "Sick call is at 0800. Until then, report for reveille." Funny, I never did make it to the sick call later in the day as the anger healed whatever ailed me.

These early days were not easy for new recruits. I found it boring, the hours after hours of repeatedly going over the same commands as we learned how to "left face, right face, about face, attention, at ease, and parade rest." Here, an earlier problem arose. Some recruits had trouble deciding quickly which was "left" and which was "right." Even an exasperated sergeant with colorful language could not effect a quick cure. Attempts were made, like carrying a brick in your left hand. For those whose reaction time to commands was slow, the answer was classification to orderlies or permanent K.P.s.

This letter closed with a mystery. What in the world did I expect my mother to send that would be "burdensome"? How about hangers? The Army did supply hangers and there was an open area to hang clothes in the barracks. During basic training, everything was inspected, even how our clothes were ironed and hung. I wasn't looking to get K.P. because there weren't enough hangers.

Letter #3: dated Wednesday night

Dear Family,
Well here I am again, writing letters after lights out.

Boy! Am I naked, my hair is ½ inch long (that's the cowlick in the back), and I shaved off my mustache. Only officers are allowed to wear mustaches.

I got a slight sun burn Sunday, it's no wonder the temperature is about 100 all day long, and we drill and have classes right out in the open.

Boy! I really like it here. Most of the fellows don't. To me it seems pretty good. We don't have any hills but there are plenty of trees.

Last night the whole 8th division went to a big show. They had W.A.A.C.s [W.A.C.s from July 1943] there who danced with some of the fellows. The show was O.K. till I turned my ankle. Finally I got to the place where I could walk on it, then to top it all off I sprained it again about ½ hour later. They had to carry me to the medical jeep and I got a free ride to the dispensary. The doctor gave me some Epson salts to bath it in and they rode me back to the barracks. This morning I went to get it bandaged and they sent me to the hospital to have my eyes examined (sounds crazy don't it but that's just how damn mixed up it is). When I got back to the barrack again I went to the doc to have ankle bandaged this was about 11:30 and he said to come back at 4:30 I told him to go …. And then went back to my company and began marching. It is now about 2 times as big as it should be but I'll be dammed if I'm going back to the dispensary.

Today I drove a jeep (with a bad ankle). I climbed all over it first like a baby with a new toy. Yesterday I was all over a medium tank (inside & out). Boy! Are those things put together. They have from 2 to 3 inches of steel armor.

If you have not sent it, do not send the camera we are not allowed to have one, so I found out.

Well I only have 3 months and 3 days before my basic training is over. After that I go one maneuvers for about 3 months. Boy! Do they have maneuvers. Some members of the infantry came back they have been gone since Jan. 12th, they have taken no baths or showers except in creeks. (Off the record I saw 4 stiffs come in today).

Well I have to get up at 4:30 so I'll sign off now.

Love

Walter Jr.

P.S. Air mail gets here about one day sooner.

Here is an explanation of my address

Line I- _____

Line II-Headquarters Company

2nd Battalion

80th Armored Regiment

Line III- Army Post Office 258

Line IV-_____

Line V-_____

Line VI-_____

They did me a favor by making me shave off that mustache. It was really scruffy. My next testimony to "liking" Camp Polk was not an opinion shared by many of my fellow trainees, as I indicated. In fact, complaining was a part of the daily barracks discussions. And you would have to have some sympathy for a fellow from West "By God" Virginia who missed being surrounded by hills. My other West Virginia buddies and I wondered how you could go to school for 12 years and not know that Roanoke was not in *West* Virginia. The often-given response to your disclosure about hailing from West Virginia was "Oh, I know somebody in Roanoke!"

My family doctor in 1934 was a very likable 85-year-old practitioner who had known my family for years. Behind his back, he was called the "Epsom salts doctor." Epsom salts for sprains, Epsom salts for upset stomach. You name it, Epsom salts could cure it. So it would come as no surprise to me that warm water and Epsom salts would be the treatment for an injured ankle. Even at Camp Polk, I could not escape the time-honored remedy I had come to know so well. It stretches the imagination that I, a buck private, would tell a doctor, who would have been at least a captain, to "Go to." As we know, "Yes, Sir!" is the more acceptable reply.

There's a story that goes with "classes out in the open." A lieutenant with a pointed stick was going over and over "the action as the bolt goes forward in a Thompson submachine gun caliber 45 M1A1." I went to sleep sitting in the hot sun.

Tank Crew Personal Weapons

The official weapons were:

- The M3 light tank mounted one .45 cal Thompson SMG at the back of the fighting compartment. The later M5A1 had a new turret and the Thompson mounting moved to the top of the radio in the turret bustle. Around 500 rounds of .45 cal ammunition were carried.
- The M3 medium had two mountings for .45 cal Thompson SMGs, one under the bow MGs left of the radio operator's seat, and the other at the back of the fighting compartment. 1,200 rounds of .45 cal ammunition were carried, along with two M2 tripods. These were outside the tank for use when the bow machine guns were dismounted.
- The M4 medium tank (Sherman) mounted one .45 cal Thompson SMG on the top the radio in the rear of the turret, with 600 rounds of .45 cal ammunition. 4,750 rounds of .30 cal, and 300 rounds of .50 cal ammunition were also carried. Two tripods were provided, one for the .50 cal M2HB AAMG and one for a .30 cal M1919A4 MGs.

All of the tanks also carried a number of hand grenades—the M4 medium had 12: 2 × smoke and 2 × thermite grenades in a box on the left side turret wall; 2 × smoke, 4 × M2 fragmentation, and 2 × M3 offensive grenades in a box under the gunner's seat.

Later in the war, the Thompson was replaced by the M3 and M3A1 SMG (the "Grease Gun"), M3 mediums getting one for each crew member. Ammunition quantities were also increased.

On top of this, each crew member also carried a Browning M1911A1 handgun. These are the official issues. Unofficially, of course, there were significant differences—often much more ammunition was carried as well as a range of small arms from M1 carbines to German MP40s.

Startled awake by hearing my name loudly called, I correctly responded, "Yes, Sir."

I promptly denied being asleep, whereupon the officer had me stand up, come forward and explain to the class "what happens when the bolt goes forward." I got it exactly right, but I wasn't out of the woods yet. "I know you were asleep! Twice around the motor pool!" barked the lieutenant. A long jog beats sitting through one more round of "What happens when…"

If anything, I loved being in a tank. I shared the American belief that American steel, American knowledge, and American craftsmanship had built what had to be the world's best. A little over a year later, I would learn otherwise.

I did finally grow out of starting sentences with the word "Boy."

Letter #4: no date

Dear Mom,

Your letter finally arrived, I wrote so many to you before I got one I thought maybe you had forgotten me.

I am really having a time writing to everyone I should. I try to write several letters every night but some night I am too tired or work too late.

On Sundays I got to the Protestant church, there are only two denominations in the Army: Catholic or Protestant. The minister is an Episcopalian (pardon spelling) he believes in salvation by prayer and we pray on our knees (this part is optional, if you kneel you can or vice versa).

In case I didn't tell you it's slightly warm down here. Right now it is 7:00 (1900 army time) and my shirt and pants could be rung out by hand.

So far I have had 3 shots and one vaccination the shots made my arm a little sore but otherwise did not affect me.

There are a lot of people I should write to but I don't know what to say or just how to say it. If anybody you know of expects a letter from me please tell them to write first and then I will now how to write them. (if you get what I mean).

To put it mildly I damn near died waiting for your letter.

Love

Walter Jr.

P.S. It's really a beautiful thing to hear 500 men singing church hymns and praying together. It makes religion more beautiful.

Here is a letter sure to lift the spirits of my mother. I went to church! Ruth Crickenberger Stitt was the pious daughter of a Lutheran pastor. So devout was Ruth that she couldn't bring herself to say words like "poop" or "pee." However, her Victorian upbringing accepted that a male would use words like "damn." I was one to push the envelope.

What a picture! Five hundred (my estimate) men singing lustily in church. I sang in the choir while in the eighth and ninth grade. I liked to sing, but my musical knowledge stopped after I learned the spaces on the treble clef were F-A-C-E.

The former Star-rated Boy Scout went to Scout Camp for a week at least three times and would vehemently deny to anyone but his parents that he was homesick. This letter, with its references to waiting for a letter from home, was a dead giveaway to how homesick I really was. I couldn't admit I was homesick; it just wasn't manly in my mind.

Alas, subsequent letters do not record 500 voices singing church hymns. I had joined most of the other Protestant recruits with a Sunday sleep-in.

Now a more experienced man of the Army, my aversion to using those ceramic facilities with others around had disappeared. Necessity proved a strong motive. This facility was also the only available place to sit down except your bed. So, where else would you go to read the Sunday paper?

Letter #5: postmarked April 20, 1943

Dear Sara,

I want to thank you very much for the pretty card you sent me. The next time I can buy a locket or bracelet from my camp I will send it to you.

Don't forget to write to me, I like to hear from you.

Love

Walter Jr.

P.S. Can you swim and dive yet?

Since the next two letters were to my siblings Sara and Dick, I sent them in the same envelope to save money. Or maybe it was to surprise Sara with a letter she wasn't expecting. Sara would have been eleven years old when I wrote this letter.

Unbeknownst to me at the time was how distressed she was with my leaving for the service. Like she puts it, "News about the war was everywhere you went." At the movies, they started with newsreels from the front. The radio and newspapers carried information about how soldiers were dying. To Sara, I was going off to danger and might never return. We had a good relationship, and I knew she would miss having me around.

My postscript to my sister was about the swimming lessons she was taking at the YMCA. She told me this story, years later, about the day I left for the service. She went to the YMCA for a free swim. Instead of swimming, she went to the showers and cried. She said she stayed in the shower for hours crying. While it might be an exaggeration to the length of time, I can imagine her concern for me.

Letter #6: postmarked April 20, 1943

Dick,

Was glad to hear from you. Thanks for giving my address to Mary & Wes.

How is everything going at school? Still the same old thing? The only part of it I miss is playing basketball. I am getting enough schooling down here. Some days you sit for 8 hours right out in the open under the red hot sun, but we get a break every hour and have 10 minutes to smoke or go the latrine. And another thing the officers are all swell and tell jokes to keep the class interesting.

So far all the tests I have taken on rifles or machineguns I have made S for satisfactory. I made an E for excellent in naming all the parts including bolts & nuts in a rifle.

We took tests in: assembly-disassembly, naming the parts, and finding out which piece of a gun was broken or bent-on scoring. We also took tests on how to do different positions, and how to figure windage.

I can't get a sweater for you in camp, but the cook has one he wears, and he said we could get one in Leesville. But we can't go to Leesville for 2 weeks more.

Buck-Private

Walter

P.S. What happened to the fellows are they dead or something?

It's been over seventy years since I wrote this letter and for the life of me, I can't remember which Mary and who Wes was. Mary might have been my first and oldest cousin, a year older than me. She was quite a character and lots of fun to be around. Her favorite word was "shit." Now her mother, Aunt Helen, being hard of hearing, never knew Mary was using this word until one day, upon arriving home from school, Mary threw her books down and said, "Shit!" Whereupon, Aunt Helen said, "Mary what did you just say?!" This is when Mary learned her mother had a hearing device. It didn't stop Mary from saying her favorite word; it just was used a little more discreetly from her mother.

At 5'9" I played forward on my high school basketball team. I really enjoyed it. However, a failing grade in biology kicked me off the team. The biology teacher felt it was important for knowledge's sake to keep a notebook. One example of his lessons was to watch a film on blood circulation. The film used a cat and cut a vein from which blood poured. Next was cutting the artery which had blood pulsing out. My best buddy, Bill, started saying to the guy behind him, "Get off my back!" After several times, Bill turned around to really have it out with the guy, only to find out the guy had passed out. With such graphic examples, who needs a notebook to remind them what they learned? Thus, the failing grade and loss of a great basketball career in high school.

An interesting side note to this story is I never did do the notebook. As a result, I didn't get my high school diploma, being one credit short at the time of my enlistment. After my time in the service, where I was given two high school credits, I earned my high school diploma in 1946. I received a call from the principal, Phineas Earl King. He wanted me to come and walk across the stage to get my diploma. By this time, I was in college and wasn't at all interested in participating in graduation. Principal King refused to give me my diploma. It wasn't until he had retired that someone found my diploma and sent it to my parents.

Jokes from officers were a stretch. Mostly groaners, easily forgotten and rarely shared. I did brag a little in this letter, as most older siblings do, but I never got below satisfactory in all my training on weapons. The windage was much like what golfers do. Hold a piece of grass up and let it loose. Where it goes shows how the wind is blowing and thus what must be considered when shooting.

Finally, why did my brother want a sweater from me? Leesville was the nearest town and when passes were given, that is where soldiers went. At this time, I wasn't eligible for a pass. After basic training, which was eight weeks, we had the chance to get a weekend pass. While there wasn't a known system for getting a pass, it usually came as an announcement that passes were going to be given. Not everyone took advantage of this for the simple reason they had no money. Being paid $21 once a month meant you had to save some money. Sometimes I was good at saving, sometimes I borrowed money, and mostly I asked my mom to send me $10.

U.S. Army Enlisted Men's Pay

Even though many of Walter's early letters are taken up with requests for money, U.S. servicemen were paid better during World War II than many other country's soldiers and better than many American civilians.

While privates started out on a base pay of $21 a month as Walter says, this figure increased when the United States entered the war on December 8, 1941. From then until May 31, 1942, an enlisted man's pay (under 4 years of service) increased to $31. On June 6, 1942, President Roosevelt signed the Pay Readjustment Act that saw privates' base pay increase to $50 (P.F.C.s received $54, corporals $66, and sergeants $78). On top of these amounts there were allowances for long service (usually 5 percent for each 3 years of service up to 30 years) and for foreign service (20 percent increase on base pay).

Additional amounts were paid to soldiers with dependents—wives, children or family members the soldier supported (the amounts varied; soldiers who were awarded the Medal of Honor, the Distinguished Service Cross, the Distinguished Service Medal, or the Soldier's Medal (an extra $2 a month per medal); and after June 30, 1944, holders of the Expert Infantryman and Combat Infantryman badges were awarded Badge Pay ($5 and $10 per month respectively).

Letter #7: no envelope, no date

Dear Mom, Dad, Dick, and Sara.

As you can see I received your package today. I was worried for a while your last letter said it was coming but I did not receive it for a day later.

In case I didn't tell you before, the weather down here is just like the hottest day in summer every day I am getting a beautiful suntan. And by the way, did I tell you my hair is now ½ inch long?

I don't know yet whether or not I can keep the camera but I am going to take the two rolls full, and then find out.

If you send cookies, send big ones so I can give everyone just one and satisfy them.

I can use some underwear (just the bottoms) if you can get me some. We have a laundry but it takes them a week or more to get your clothes back and you need two or three suites of everything already cleaned. Do not worry about money, when I need some I will send home for it. So far I have stalled off buying anything unnecessary, and I still have about 4 dollars left. We got one supplementary pay of 5 dollars to cover expenses. I bought two packages of writing paper, 3 pairs of socks, and a towel and wash rag, among other things.

Most of the fellows down here drafted and spend half their time griping, but I am having fun and enjoy every minute of it, even if I am so tired I can't talk.

You wanted to know about boys who came from Wheeling. So far the only one I have found is Jim Gilleland (Dick will know him, he played football for Linsly).

There are boys here from every state in the union. I run around with boys from the following states: Penns., N. Jersey, Conn, Iowa, Okla., South Dakota, and Ohio. Some of them call me Walter, but most of them call me Stitt (or pretty close to that). All the boys from the west are farmers. We kid each other all the time about how we talk, etc.

That's about all for now so by-by

Private

Walter Jr.

P.S. to Dad: I worked in the pits on the firing range Sat. for 16 hours, pushing up 6 by 6 targets.

In true fashion, my ability to find joy around me seems impervious to the long, stifling hot days at camp. Everybody griped, and I loved it, and I was getting a tan.

There's an old saying that one should go ahead and sin and recant later. This adage had its Army cousin. Take two rolls of pictures and if caught, use Army Axiom #2: I Didn't Know That.

If you send cookies (*hint, hint*) send big ones so I can give everyone one cookie. During the war, people had to use ration cards for certain items, sugar being one of them. People were only allotted so much each month. Once the ration card was used up, there was no more to purchase until the next month. My mom baking cookies for my platoon and using her ration card for sugar was a big ask. Luckily for me, my mother had several sisters who might have helped with getting the ration supplies for big cookies.

My postscript to my father was because during World War I, he was stationed at Fort Knox in Kentucky during the Asian flu outbreak. His job was to transport the dead bodies from Fort Knox to the trains in Louisville where the bodies were sent on home. Dad never served overseas. Fort Benjamin Harrison was his next and final assignment. His rank was corporal, and his job was the company clerk. I'm sure he understood working in the pits. I also imagine him telling my family what it meant. Working in the pits meant that I was at the firing range in a pit (below ground level) with the assignment of pushing or pulling targets up and down for rifle practice. The targets were 6 by 6 feet. We raised them, they shot at them, we lowered them and phoned the sergeant in charge as to how they hit and scored. When I wasn't raising and lowering, I was sitting on a bench, smoking if I wanted. Unfortunately, sleeping wasn't possible with all the noise. It is here in the story where I can imagine my father raising his eyebrows and sharing my exaggeration of my time spent in the pit. Really? 16 hours? I doubt it, too.

In my recitation of the States represented in my barracks, Jimmy Gilleland, a star athlete at the Linsly Military Institute in Wheeling, was not the only West Virginian. Throughout basic training, Jimmy and I would run into each other. My parents often asked about him and hoped we were hanging out together. They were sure he would have been a good influence on their son.

Unmentioned among those I "ran around with" was a true representation of a West Virginia hillbilly. After a day at the firing range, the talk in the barracks had a lot of excited accounts of ricochets.

"I had one hit just above my head!"

"Man, one really zinged by!"

"One hit the post in front of me!"

All of this got the hillbilly's attention. He hadn't been in the pits, and his query was "What's a ricochet? Are they *pie-soness*?" Our fellow in his southern accent thought a ricochet was a poisonous snake. Later trips to the range were sure to bring out the warning about *pie-soness* ricochets.

I remember underwear, socks, wash rags and towels as being "olive drab." If I got these items from home, they would surely be an obvious misfit.

In this letter, I asked that money not be sent. You sure won't read that often! Army pay was the butt of a joke. "21 dollars a day! Once a month." That amount didn't seem to last long with me.

Letter #8: postmarked April 22, 1943

Dear Mom, Dad, Dick, and Sara,

If you notice a difference in my writing it is because I am so tired. We got back from a 5 mile hike, which we took in a little over an hour, with a pack. Boy! Am I tired.

The time is really passing fast, I can't keep track of what day it is.

This is one year I hope the Easter bunny comes, if he does we'll butcher it. The chow we get is cooked pretty well, but you don't get enough unless you sneak in line again, which I have done quite a number of times.

You wanted a sample of our training so here is an example.

4:45—First Call

5:00—Chow

5:30—Police barracks

6:00–6:30—Physical Training
7:30–8:30—Dismounted drill
8:30–11:30—Weapons Instruction
Chow
13:00–14:30—Training (Films)
14:30–15:30—Instruction (On Film)
15:30–16:30—Road March

This is a typical day, some are worse and some are better. The day does not end at 4:30, after that they have a flock of details.

In case I didn't tell you all classes are out in the open and you get K.P. or detail if the catch you in the shade.

I'm sorry I can't write a longer letter but circumstances forbid it.

Love

Walter Jr.

P.S. Happy Easter

P.S. Jr Am going to take another exam. It is now 7:00 p.m.

Made 100 in a test on Tommy gun today.

Now here is a letter with meat in it, no pun intended for the Easter bunny. My goal at chow was to eat fast and get back in line. They didn't question me about seconds. This might explain my weight gain, or it was just embellishment of the facts to impress my family.

Listed only as "Physical Training" was a lot of strenuous exercise. I gave it my all. I was trying to show off how tough I was. I never mentioned in the letter how my muscles ached. I guess I got it all out complaining in the barracks.

Among the "flock of details" was policing the grounds. A line was formed and we were told to pick up anything that wasn't nailed down. The instruction for this assignment was often given as "Head down and ass up!"

I was taking five-mile hikes with a full field pack in less than an hour. Great for working up a good sweat.

Picture the entire company lined up in two columns on the company street, every man with a full field pack. The first sergeant was an old timer with lots of experience. He walked behind each soldier, smashing his hands onto each field pack. Lo and behold, there was a soldier whose pack made a sound easily recognized as the sound of newspapers being crushed. This ingenious soldier would be placed on K.P.—washing dishes, peeling potatoes, and mopping floors for about a week.

On another occasion, the five-miles-in-fifty-minutes line up was about to depart when a voice called out, "Sergeant, aren't we supposed to have full field packs?" The sergeant sent us all back to get our full field pack, which added another 15 pounds to carry on our hot summer hike. It was not me! Pity the poor soul when he got back to the barracks.

The 100 percent score on the Thompson submachine gun M1A1 was an ironic part of my Army career. My honorable discharge notes my expertise on the Thompson gun. The funny thing is I never fired one after leaving Camp Polk.

Letter #9: no postmark

Dear Family,

I hope you will forgive me for not writing sooner but believe it or not this is the first chance I have had except Sunday, and then the only thing I did was go to church.

We really put in a tough week. Each week the work gets tougher but at the same time it is more fun. About Wednesday I drove a tank. I was commended for my driving and for paying attention to instructions. This week we took up the 45 Thompson Sub Machine gun and 75 mm cannon. I got all S's and E's for satisfactory and excellent in the test. Half the company took a drivers' aptitude test. I made within the first 3 biggest grades.

This Sat. (coming) we get passes to get out of camp and go to town. So far I did not get to take any pictures so I will get some taken in Leesville or Shreveport.

We are now using an obstacle course which would make anything you ever saw before look sick. We climb a 20 ft. incline with ropes and drop off the other side, some fun.

Today I got my first K.P. It was not exactly K.P. but is called D.R.O. (Dining Room Orderly) the ones for this are picked at random. The K.P.s are the ones who do something wrong. D.R.O. lasts one day, K.P. last indefinitely.

He is a list of a few things I could use:

Shoe shine kit (Brown polish)

Chain for dog tags

Furlough

I met Henry Bremson last Saturday. We talked about 45 mins. Before he went to a meeting. He is field director of the Red Cross here. I will probably see him quite a lot as his office is only 100 yards from my barracks.

Hope everyone is well. Tell Cricky to get her private train or her chauffer to bring her down here where it is nice and warm, 120° in the shade, if you can find some shade.

Love

Walter Jr.

P.S. Thanks for the pretty card.

P.S. Jr. may move to Fort Knox in several months. For gunner's training.

There was no way I could ever write the story of how I was "commended for my driving and for paying attention." Disregarding my early stance that I wanted nothing with a steering wheel, I—the former truck driver for Royal Crown—quickly stepped forward to answer the call for anyone who had driven a truck or tractor. There was no way would I miss a chance to drive this iron monster. The driving course was an oval. It began on the level going uphill after the first turn, then a straight line at the top with a watery dip in the middle. The directions from the commander were to get into the tank, put on your head gear and follow instructions. The tanks—either M3A4s or

M4A4s—were powered by Chrysler Multibank engines—five Chrysler engines mounted in a circle.

Upon starting, there were five green lights on the dashboard indicating full power. As each engine failed, a light went red. The tank would run with three greens, but with two, you were done. To shift was four speeds forward.

Inside the tank and ready to move, we were given clear instructions by the commander: "Do not pass." Each tank driver was told when to start driving. I was the fourth tank. With a start on flat ground, I got up to third gear. Around the corner and up the hill, there was a stalled tank. With my knowledge of how to double-clutch, I shifted down to second gear. No surprise here, I passed the stalled tank.

This brought out a loud repeat in the earphone, "I said not to pass." It was too late to stop. I came upon a tank stuck in the muddy ditch; I passed him, as well. By the time I reached the lower level for the second time around the course, the order was changed to "You may pass very carefully." I obeyed this order and was commended for my driving and paying attention to instructions. This was the last time they let me drive. Scoring 100 percent on a gunnery test may have influenced that decision.

It was probably best not to tell my family about the obstacle course training using actual bullets fired from machine guns. We started in a muddy trench. Your path was marked with a wire strand on both sides. Upon the signal, you would slide out of the ditch, hug the ground, and crawl toward the guns that were firing over your head. I had no trouble keeping low.

The course for firing the Thompson submachine gun was an open grassy field. As you walked across the field, targets suddenly popped up in front, at the right, and at the left. Someone later counted bullet holes. It's hard to imagine an enemy soldier lying in the grass, suddenly jumping up to be shot, but at least I was trained to handle that situation.

The first sergeant came to me looking like an undertaker approaching a grieving family. He informed me that a man wanted to see me at the Red Cross office. With some consternation, I entered the office and identified myself, ready for bad news. I almost broke into dance when she said, "Oh go right in, Mr. Bremson has been expecting you."

Henry Bremson was my Sunday School teacher. We had a cold Coke and happy reunion reminiscing about our shared experiences back home. Henry Bremson wasn't with our division in action. His role for the Red Cross was to get notices to soldiers if someone in their family was dying or had died. I was fortunate not to encounter Mr. Bremson for any of these reasons. Upon returning, I did confess knowing Mr. Bremson.

One Sunday before I had enlisted and Mr. Bremson wasn't teaching, his brother-in-law substituted. He had the Sunday School class of teenage boys repeat, "To lose a friend is to die a little," three times. This line became more real as time goes on in the war.

There would be no trip to Shreveport. Too far away. But a trip to Leesville, with my Jewish buddy, Haskell, from New York, proved to be entertaining. The U.S.O. was small, packed with G.I.s, and offered little excitement. Finding a bar meant walking across the street.

This establishment had a list posted on the wall of drinks they could mix. A decision was made to start at the top and work down. Haskell didn't like the first drink because it was too sour and he poured it down the wall of the booth. The next one was better but it contained too much alcohol for Haskell. Not wanting to waste it I took it upon myself to finish it for him. The drink was called a Zombie, full of rum, tequila, vodka, and gin. After consuming two Zombies, another institution seemed like the choice to make. I stood up and fell flat on the floor. I was finally able to get my wobbly legs to work and stumbled to the next bar. This required a walk of at least 100 feet past the store window offering all kinds of trinkets a soldier with two drinks might buy.

I stood in line at the tattoo shop. I sobered up enough waiting in line to bypass getting a tattoo. I felt thirsty and decided to go to another bar for more refreshments. A few hours in town went fast and the bus trip back to camp was probably wise.

"Cricky" was the name all the grandchildren called my grandmother. "Cricky" got her moniker after marrying David Phillip Theodore Crickenberger on November 11, 1886, in Giles County, Virginia. The Crickenberger family could trace their lineage back to the "First Families of Virginia" through the Earlys and Paynes. However, the family also had to claim General Jubal Early, a Civil War General, who was a poor excuse for a general. Supposedly even Robert E. Lee used to call him the "Bad Old Man."[1]

Jubal Early is said to be the source of Al Capp's "General Jubal T. Cornpone" of Li'l Abner cartoon fame. It was a cartoon caricature of Early as a bumbling general. I'm not sure my family bragged to people about this family relative.

My grandmother lived with my family. She had dementia and was in her late eighties. She was usually cold and known to walk away from home. All of us loved Cricky. She had a kind and loving nature. She was much taller than my mom, but this didn't slow my mother down from helping Cricky with all her personal needs. As the dementia took over Cricky's mind, she couldn't

---

[1] History.com Editors, 2009, para. 3.

remember how to walk. So, my very short mother would wrap her arms around Cricky's waist and push her feet along with hers. Trying to get Cricky into a chair, my mom was backing Cricky up when she sat down, pushing my mom into the chair with Cricky in her lap. All mom could do was laugh until one of my siblings came along and rescued her. Ida Octavia Payne Crickenberger, "Cricky", lived until 1950.

I took every rumor to heart, as did most G.I.s. A trip to Fort Knox was one of those.

Interesting to note, I listed being a Dining Room Orderly as my "First" K.P.

Oh, and about the plan of taking pictures in Leesville. Picture a G.I. on his first short leave carrying a Brownie box camera. A lack of pictures from the trip tells the story.

Letter #10: postmarked May 4, 1943

Dear Family,

Well! Here I am in Lake Charles. It is really a pretty place. The houses all have pillars in front. Looks just like the rich homes in Wheeling.

Last night I slept in the lobby of a hotel. I am so sore I feel like a pretzel must feel.

This afternoon I am going swimming and boating.

That reminds me: Please send me my swim suit.

For the last couple of weeks I have been running around with a Mexican boy from Colo. I have fun teasing him about wearing blankets. He says, "Damn it we're civilized."

This morning I had a light breakfast on the U.S.O., they are the only ones who give a damn about soldiers. There is usually a head hostess who talks like a mother and works like a slave to keep everybody happy.

Our first C.O. said we would get a furlough in 13 to 23 weeks after we're here. But our new C.O. won't say.

Tell Dick to find out Anna Mae Norman's address from Fa-Fa, and send it to me. She is probably the one you were talking to at the station.

Thank you for the money. I will make it last me.

Captain Kinsler came over to see me but I was on bivouac and did not get back for several days.

Love

Walter Jr.

P.S. What do want you to know that doesn't take an hour to explain??

Lake Charles was about 67 miles from Camp Polk. The trip started with a bus to Leesville followed by a two-hour bus ride to Lake Charles. Leave was from Friday evening to Sunday evening. Hurrying out of Camp as fast as possible and catching the bus left little time to do much else on Friday, such as finding a room for the night. The fully booked hotel lobby was my room for the weekend.

My family and friends still laugh, with some disbelief, that a friend and I rented bathing suits. Sleeping on the hotel couch was most likely due to trying to save funds for the important things: boating, beer, and a bus ticket back.

I was a people person (still am). I enjoyed interacting with men from different backgrounds. I loved to tease but could also take teasing. My easy-going openness meant I had a lot of what I would call friends. This letter mentions "running around with a Mexican from Colorado."

My brother and I had a number of friends among the large Italian community in Elm Grove, West Virginia, where we lived. Many had nicknames like Fa-Fa Zambito. Then there was NaNa and Balls and Gump. Friends from different ethnic groups were not uncommon in my neighborhood. When World War II started, African Americans in the Army were segregated. While some in the military fought to change this, the Army was not integrated until after 1948.

Women seemed to be on my mind. Why I would want Anna Mae Norman's address, I can't imagine. I was eighteen and hoping to get home on a furlough, which may explain it. At the top of the letter I wrote the name of head hostess, Miss Julie Wren, "who talks like a mother and works like a slave to keep everybody happy," but why do I include her name on a letter to my family? I imagine they wondered the same thing.

Captain Kinsler was a chaplain. He grew up in Grafton, West Virginia, and was a member of the Lutheran Church pastored by my grandfather. Captain Kinsler was sweet on my Aunt Virginia. Family history says she turned down his affections. I'm not sure how he heard I was on base or why he came to visit. Hopefully it wasn't to help him win Aunt Virginia's affections.

This was a postcard of the U.S.O. in DeRidder, Louisiana that I sent to my brother.

Postcard #1: postmarked May 11, 1943

Dear Dick,

I am sending you a shirt as soon as possible. How is T.H.S.? Any excitement around the grove? How is Mary's new store? How is the chip business?

Walter

P.S. Is that enough que[stions] to answer? You can think of something to write now.

My younger brother, Dick, and I were really close. Earlier letters said I would send him a sweater, which probably never happened. Now I was promising him a shirt. This probably didn't happen, either. T.H.S. was Triadelphia High School, which we both attended. Dick was two years younger and a junior. Any excitement around the "grove"—Elm Grove—was an understatement. The Grove was filled with Italians who had lots of emotions, sometimes resolving things with shots or stabs.

Dick's teenage career took a turn for the better when he got his driver's license. He went to work for Bob Muir at Bob's Potato Chips, where I had worked for months. Every Thursday evening, I headed to Bob's garage and started the peeler. From the peeler to the slicer, from the slicer to the bagger, from bagging to weighing, to stapling, to loading for sales. On Saturdays, I headed off to the bars to stock their displays. Pay was not much, but I got all the chips I could eat every Thursday. I swore I would never eat another one! There was a problem, though. Wartime. No tire ration for a potato chip truck. It was deemed nonessential. And then there was a worn-out battery. You could get it started on Saturday by coasting out of the garage into the alley, hoping there was enough momentum that letting out the clutch while in second gear would crank the motor. It didn't always work. Help! Flat tires to change. Dick claimed three in one day. He wouldn't lie. As a side note, Dundee was the biggest competitor in the market. Our dad bowled for Dundee potato chips.

My brother and I laugh about letter writing. I wrote over 80 letters home. He says he never wrote a letter home when he was in the service.

Postcard #2: postmarked May 14, 1943

Dear Family,

I received your package today. Everything was very satisfactory. I will send my package as soon as time allows. (Probably Sat.). Also received money. We have been in the field for several days, now, and time is very precious. There are million and one things I want to tell you, but I can't find the time right now. Tell Dick and Sara to write if they can, I am always glad to hear from them. I am about 20 letters behind in my writing, but I think I can catch up on them this weekend. Am going to Shreveport Sat. & Sun. They have one of best U.S.O.s in the country.

Love to all
Walter Jr.
P.S. Will write long letter soon.

This postcard is filled with optimism and not much logistics for accomplishing all the things I wanted to do. I was going to mail a package (probably the clothing Dick had been waiting for), write 20 letters, and send them a long letter full of the million things I couldn't think to write. While doing all this, I was leaving Saturday for Shreveport by bus for a three hour or more ride, not returning until Sunday.

Now maybe I did all of this because I never did go to Shreveport. It was too far away for a weekend pass. Or was it no money probably keeping me from attending? Or worse yet! Was it K.P.?

Letter #11: postmarked May 18, 1943

Dear Family,
I am so sorry I can't write oftener but when I do get a chance I am so tired I have to force myself.

Today we went on a 50-mile mounted road march in tanks. When we got back my tank was the first and only one to finish the complete trip, the rest had some kind of trouble along the way.

In case I didn't tell you our basic training is over. We are now getting problems and practical applications of what we are supposed to know.

I went swimming in Lake Charles and got a <u>beautiful</u> sunburn. And is it sore!

I have about 20 letters to answer but I can't get around to it. I will try and catch up this week.

Am ready for bed now so I will sign off.

Love
Walter Jr.
P.S. I got the address of that girl in Texas from a newspaper. She is a beauty queen. Her name is Volene Wiggins.
P.S. II We are supposed to get from 12:00 Sat 'til 6:00 Monday morn. off each week, but instead we get off some time Sat. afternoon or evening till 24:00 Sunday.
P.S. III Will send home pictures and so forth, this week.

There was a reason for "I am so tired." I had just gotten back from Lake Charles, where sleep was probably very short. Suntan, swimming, and a local pub with lots of story swapping.

Fifty miles in the tanks provided for training was a trial for the old motors. What's more, there were certain maneuvers which caused the track to leave the sprocket wheel. Putting the tracks back on was not something to look forward to. It didn't take much to end up sitting beside the road waiting on maintenance.

While out in the field, the company commander told me to go down to the kitchen and bring a cup of coffee and creamer on a tray for the general. I promptly did what I was told. Upon returning, the further order was to put it on the tree stump and go tell the general we had coffee for him. This was a big moment for me, a private. I was going to be meeting a general. I walked up to him and gave him my snappiest best salute. Before I could tell him why I was there, he responded, "I haven't had a salute like that in a long time." So, I gave him another one and told him where to find his coffee. Now I had a story to tell my fellow soldiers when back in the barracks.

I had the address of a beauty queen from Texas. The funny thing is I have no knowledge of ever having met Volene Wiggins. I still needed to write 20 letters. I wonder who was to be the recipient of those letters? I think this might have been hyperbole; but perhaps one was intended for Volene!

The last postscript—"I will send home pictures and so forth, this week"— appears to be good intentions that were never accomplished. The only picture found thus far is the one of me lounging on the front steps of the barracks or showing off my different uniforms.

LOUISIANA

Dear Family,

I am sorry I can't write oftner but when I do get a chance I am so tired I have to force myself.

Today we went on a 60 mile mounted road march in tanks. When we got back my tank was the first and only one to finish the complete trip, the rest had some kind of trouble along the way.

In case I didn't tell you our basic training is over. We are now getting problems and practical applications of what we are supposed to know.

I went swimming in Lake Charles and got a beautiful sunburn. And is it sore!

LOUISIANA

I have about 20 letters to answer but I can't get around to it. I will try and catch up this week.

Am ready for bed now so I will sign off.

Love
Walter Jr.

P.S. I got the address of that girl in Texas from a newspaper. She is a beauty queen. Her name is Jolene Wiggins

P.S. II We are supposed to get from 12:00 Sat til 6:00 Monday morn. of each week, but instead we get off some time Sat afternoon or evening till 24:00 Sunday.

P.S. III Will send home pictures and so forth, this week

William Middleton Grimes (1889–1951)

The C.G. of 8th Armored was an experienced general who had been Chief of the Operations Branch on the War Department General Staff. Promoted major general in May 1942, he commanded 8th Armored Division for two and a half years through its period as a training command, its reorganization as a modern "light" division, and almost to the point where it left for the E.T.O.

He handed the division over on October 6, 1944, and became Commandant of the Cavalry School at Fort Riley, Kansas. In his parting comments he said, "During the past two and one-half years since activation the Division has had a major role in the development of armor—ours was a mission to train and produce the cadres for four armored corps and seven of our sister divisions besides furnishing thousands of overseas replacements. Today sees the Division ready to perform its primary mission that for which all of us have waited and trained so hard for so long."

Letter #12: postmarked May 25, 1943

Dear Family,

You should see my dishwater hands. I just got off of K.P. I was picked at random (so far I haven't done anything to be put on K.P.)

There are several rumors going around camp as to where we are going to go for maneuvers: California, South Carolina, and Pennsylvania (a lieut. told me California).

There has been some excitement lately. Three boys were killed. One was a tank commander (like me) but he got careless and was enjoying the ride, and they got two by snake bites on bivouac. Yesterday I was in Lake Charles again and saw my first snake. It was a green water-snake, we tramped it to death.

We are due to be paid this week but when I went to Lake Charles I had to borrow $5.00 from a boy from Cleveland. This month I will not need so much money (I hope) because I have bought about everything I need but cigs.

Hope everyone is well.

Love

Walter Jr.

P.S. Our Chaplain has arranged a party and dance in DeRidder for Thurs. We won't get paid till Sat. or Sun so I will have to borrow $5.00 more.

It's interesting to speculate on the claim that "so far" I had not done anything to deserve K.P. The Army sometimes randomly picked recruits to do K.P. I was the type who never did anything wrong, or that's my story. However, on reading this at home, I'm sure it brought to my mother's mind a day when she was shopping in the largest department store in Detroit and momentarily took her eyes off of her four-year-old son. While tightly holding my hand, a floorwalker, whose job it was to make sure everything was running smoothly in the store, brought me to my mother with the question, "Is *this* your child?" Her positive response got a frosty retort from the floorwalker. "*He* found the switch that turned off *all* the escalators in the store!" Even at four, there was an indication of what could later happen.

The maneuvers never went to any of the places I listed, or even close to those states.

Be sure to write home about all the excitement of young men being killed by accidents or snake bites. I would say "excitement" was not quite how to put this; maybe "anxiety" would have been more appropriate. Every soldier understands they might not survive war, but they must certainly hope a snake bite won't be their demise. Thus, there was a need to kill any snake, even a green snake that wouldn't have harmed me. My parents must have loved this letter. I wonder if my mother censored my letters from my sister.

The tank commander who met his unfortunate end had told the driver to run into a tall pine tree and see if he could knock it down. A limb broke off, fell on the commander, and fractured his skull. Certainly, this was not something to write home about. These sort of training accidents were rare but must have been a real shock to my parents, who assumed their son was only in training and not in combat.

Don't you love subtle hints? "I had to borrow $5, and I will not need so much," followed by, "I will have to borrow $5 more." I never did get to the DeRidder U.S.O., which is just as well. I couldn't dance.

This trip to Lake Charles did not mention swimming or boating. No more rented swimming trunks or boats. A discovery of the excitement of the U.S.O. took precedence. There was a pool table and ping pong tables and local refreshment establishments. Translated: beer and possible young ladies to court!

Letter #13: postmarked May 30, 1943

Dear Family

This morning we had a divisional parade. It was plenty long and plenty hot. There were quite a lot of fellows who fell out.

On Wednesday we had a talk from the General (Grimes). He said we have 8 weeks to go. During this time we will fire all the big guns and go on a 200-mile mounted road march. So that means they will be stricter but life will be easier.

Today the company left for Lake Charles. This week we get from Thur. noon till Mon. morn. I am staying in camp due to financial conditions although some of the fellows who left were in a worse condition.

Aunt Hattie has sent me about 3 or 4 packages. She is about the best aunt a fellow could want. I will mail the package to Dick sometime today.

When I told you about my sunburn I forgot to mention but besides burning my back, I rolled over and also toasted my chest and stomach. Some fun. My hands and face have that beautiful brown, Southern exposure look.

If you still have some hangers left, I could use a few.

Love

Walter Jr.

P.S. It took me 3 days to write this letter. I washed and ironed my clothes. Polished my mess-kit etc.

PS. Jr. Am on the rocks. Don't get paid for another week and 2 days.

A divisional parade in the hot sun was not fun. Fellows falling out meant passing out or getting sick. I didn't mind warm weather; however, parading in a full uniform with a backpack in the Louisiana sun was a test to my enjoyment.

I thought the mounted road march would be easier because we were riding in tanks and not out marching in the hot sun. Inside the tank, you at least had a seat and a whiff of air as the tank rolled along.

Aunt Hattie was my mother's oldest sister. There were four more. Hattie had a bachelor's degree and a master's degree at time when most women never got beyond a high school diploma. She was smart and took delight in her eccentric behavior, which, as the saying goes, "drove her sisters up the wall." But her kind and caring personality was a delight to her nieces and nephews. To them, the fact that she loved to drink wine, her house was a disorderly mess, and a ride in her car meant clothes covered in dog hair was of little concern. Hattie worked for the government in child welfare, trying to make ends meet with a child daycare home. She finally returned to teaching. Although a devout Lutheran and a pastor's daughter, her last and longest stint teaching was at the Catholic School. As she entered her eighties, retiring seemed the way to go. However, the Parish Priest pleaded with her to stay on at least one more year. She did. Eventually old age caught up with Hattie. She had lived in a small town for a long time. It seemed everybody knew her. At least the car mechanic she dealt with did. When her car had to be towed to the shop, the mechanic called Hattie's sister with a plan. "I can fix it, but she shouldn't be on the road! She doesn't stop at stop signs and traffic lights. She drives like people should get out of her way. I'll tell her I can't fix it. Sell it and give her the money." Plan A was readily accepted. Hattie then moved into a retirement home where she surely must have entertained the staff with her conversations, sometimes laced with colorful language.

The packages mentioned were cookies and candy. The package near Christmas was a different story! Hattie also sent me a St. Christopher medal to hang on my dog tags. Christopher was the patron saint of travelers. Knowing how Hattie drove, she could have used one, too.

"On the rocks" meant I was broke again! Some things never seem to change. The Army pay wasn't great. Managing money wasn't my strong suit, either. I liked candy, cigarettes, and beer. Those are things the Army doesn't provide for free, and the pay doesn't go far enough.

Pity poor me. No money, no hangers, no trip to Lake Charles, a sunburn and parading in the hot sun. This letter was postmarked May 30, meaning I was still only eighteen years old.

Letter #14: postmarked June 1, 1943

Dear Family

I hope you are not too surprised to hear from me so often, but after taking a rest last weekend I am caught up enough to write.

Today we went on a 25-mile road march in vehicles. It rained last night and it wasn't so bad riding around.

Life isn't so bad, of late. The Lts. have slacked up and you can kid them without getting them mad.

The only thing I didn't do over the weekend was shave enough. Today a Lt. ask me "Where did you go after you shaved?" I gave him a big broad horse smile and he didn't say anymore.

Give Nova Johnston my congratulations. (I'm not much on that stuff.)

I just got finished playing baseball and I need a shower and a shave so I will sign off.

Love

Walter Jr.

P.S. Received bathing suit today. Thanks!!

P.S. Jr. What grade is Sara in now and when is Dick going to write?

P.S. III By the way!! Is daddy dead? The only thing I hear about him is when he is going to deliver a package.

P.S. IV How about Cricky? She's still the best grandmother in the world.

This letter, written on June 4, would have brought some remarks from the family. "It sure sounds like Walter Jr."

A clue as to how life was going at Camp Polk in June: "not so bad." A 50-mile road trip "wasn't so bad." I learned some officers came out of an enlisted man's background. Others, straight from civilian to officer. Those in the latter group tended to feel their position very strongly and would not be kidded. Knowing which one was which was important.

Kidding a lieutenant went something like this: "Lieutenant, I'm tired. I think I'll take tomorrow off."

The retort would be something akin to this: "You really like K.P. that much?"

Both parties would walk away entertained with the interaction. However, I would only risk this kind of behavior when I knew for certain that Louie (Army slang for lieutenant) was slacked up (was relaxed and not uptight).

Also true to my character was the problem of finding the urge to shave. It came from an equally difficult problem: getting out of bed in the morning! On more than one occasion at early morning roll call, the first sergeant walked up face-to-face and inquired of me, "When was the last time you shaved?" Then, without waiting for an answer, he said, "K.P." Another round of dishwater hands. It's clear my latest attempt to forego further trials by shaving at night didn't work.

Keep in mind, the 8th Armored Division was training eighteen- and nineteen-year-olds. Minute by minute supervision was not possible, which allowed for some foolishness. Take, for instance, this typical situation. A long line of 32-ton tanks driving through a small Louisiana town. The first tank approaches a turn being directed by the M.P. to turn right. The M.P. is getting the impression the tank is getting too close to him. So, he backs up. He does it again as the next tank crowds his space in the middle of the intersection. The next tank then turns but hits the curb, as does the next tank and the last tank. Now, there are only concrete pieces where the curb once was. The tank trainees will enjoy telling the story over and over with much laughter and speculation about the joy of the city.

Nova Johnson was the landlady's daughter who had just gotten married. How to acknowledge this was not part of my "stuff." I liked the women; I just wasn't interested in marriage right now.

In four postscripts, noted with Roman numerals, I addressed the whole family. My sister Sara, my brother Dick, Daddy, and grandmother "Cricky." Sara was in 6th grade and into sending me homemade cards. Dick probably wasn't going to write and was still waiting on his new clothes.

My dad taking the packages to the post office doesn't surprise me. My mom didn't drive. My mom was short, just 4'9". My dad used to say she was two inches taller than a midget. She never appreciated this comment. As the story goes, one day my dad decided he would teach my mom to drive. They were heading straight away when a turn in the road came up. Mom didn't turn and the car ended up in a field. This marked the end of mom's driving.

While dad might have mailed the package, anything I ever got during the war was almost always due to my mom. It goes without saying, the "Thanks" for the bathing suit goes to her. Homesick for sure!

Letter #15: June 8, 1943

Dear Sara,
I was sure glad to hear from you. Here is something confidential; The thing which makes me the most home sick is a letter from you or Dick.

Well! I am glad to hear that you can finally swim. Do you swim like a rock?
[New ink]
I hope it is still summer when I get home so I can take you swimming and dunk you.
If you like warm weather I will take you to Louisiana sometime so you can really sweat.
What are you in the Girl Scouts now? You are about due to go to scout camp aren't you?
Have some work to do now so I will sign off.
Love
Walter Jr.

Then there was this short letter to my sister, Sara. Born in 1931, she was seven years younger than me and a bright student. I get credit from the family for her name. With a great deal of excitement, Sara was born at home. When the doctor left, I was invited into the bedroom to see my new sister and my mother asked me, "What do you think we should name her?"

Remembering my mother's talk of how much she likes her Aunt Sally, I blurted out, "Sara!" Truth be known, the name may have already been decided. However, I am of the opinion it was my choice.

It was natural that my sister would be a Girl Scout and attend camp. My brother and I were in the Boy Scouts. To this day, I can still recite the Scout Law. Boy Scouts are "trustworthy, loyal, helpful, friendly, courteous, kind, obedient, cheerful, thrifty, brave, clean, and reverent." My parents kept us busy, most likely to keep us out of mischief.

Being my baby sister, I loved to tease her with comments like "You swim like a rock" and "I'll take you swimming and dunk you."

Sara never had the privilege of swimming in the Ohio River. As a young man living in Bridgeport, Ohio, I swam in the very polluted Ohio River. Of course, it goes without saying that you kept your arms in front of you, pushing stuff out of your way and keeping your head above water. I often joked that these outings are what gave me immunity to diseases and led to my longevity.

In Elm Grove, West Virginia, we swam in Big Wheeling Creek. My mother decided that Dick and I should babysit five-year-old Sara, so we took her swimming with us. Since she couldn't swim, we put her in a cardboard box to float. As you can well imagine, soon Sara wasn't floating. She was sinking. Luckily, Dick and I had our Boy Scout training and saved her.

Another life-changing incident happened to me at the age of thirteen down at Big Wheeling Creek. A group of us made a makeshift diving board. Uncle Dubois, mom's brother, came down for a swim. He was 33 years old and full of adventure. We all looked up to him. He decided to try out our diving board, not realizing it was shallow water for an adult to dive. He ended up with a broken neck. I ran home to tell my mom. Unfortunately, Dubois never recovered and ended up dying several days later.

These kinds of experiences with their older children was probably why my parents made sure Sara learned to swim at the YWCA.

Letter #16: postmarked June 13, 1943

Dear Dick,

I was glad to hear from you. You answered about 9/10 of all the questions I could think of.

If the paper publishes anything about that last bunch of 4 F's please send it to me. I sent your shirt, you should get it anytime now.

Last week the cooks and some of the non-coms got furloughs so it looks pretty good.

I would have answered your letter sooner but we just came back from a 3 day bivouac, and that is one time when you don't get a chance to write. We went about 50 miles from camp. I rode out in the back of a truck (and slept), and rode back in an M6 G.M.C. (a 37mm cannon mounted on the back of a small truck), that was some ride. I pulled my first guard since I left Fort Hayes I was on from 10 'til 12 (it was fun). My right hand is swollen from mosquito bites there are at least 10 on the back of my hand alone.

I haven't a lot of time to write so tell everyone at the A&P I said hello. Tell Jim Mull to write. Well that's about all for now, so long.

Your needle-bait

Brother

Walter Jr.

P.S. Remember that tooth that I had which was chipped off. Well! I haven't got it now. Here is how the army pulls teeth:

1st They inject two needles for every tooth. One in your jaw and one in the tooth.

2nd Your Jaw is numb

3rd Yank! With no mercy

4th Next 1!!

A letter to my sister on June 8 and now to my brother Dick on June 13. I must have gotten writer's cramp!

I had been at Camp Polk for three months. I was hopeful I would get my furlough soon, a chance to go home. What I hadn't understood was that cooks and non-coms had been at Camp Polk for months before I arrived. Their time for furlough had come. I had a long time to wait.

One of my bragging points was the ability to sleep anywhere. Sleeping in the back of a bouncing truck while sitting on a wooden seat was no small accomplishment.

Dick finally wrote a letter, and he got the long-awaited shirt! While mom wrote about all the good happenings around Elm Grove, Dick gave me the low down on friends and antics that our parents wouldn't be privy to. This was one of the reasons I kept bugging him to write.

My brother was a carry-out person at the local A&P market. He told a story about himself that always got a chuckle. He wheeled a 100-pound sack of animal feed out to a lady's car but was not able to lift it off the cart. She promptly said, "Let me do that," and tossed the sack in the trunk. Dick's hope was that nobody saw what happened.

What would ever prompt wanting a list of Wheeling's 4-Fs? The 4-F means unfit for military service, usually a medical disability. Of course, I was thinking I was coming home for a visit, and I wanted to see what guys were still around. Always planning ahead for a good time.

Jimmy Mull was a classmate of mine from eighth grade through high school. He was 4-F. Asking him to write was like asking for snow in Louisiana in July. At the time of this letter, my heartthrob was Jimmy's wife's sister, Lenore. Jimmy was a stock clerk who eventually owned his own grocery. Maybe this explains part of why I wanted him to write to me.

This was my first encounter with Army dentists. My sign off as "needle-bait" was for all the shots the dentist gave me. That this procedure struck me as odd indicates my civilian experience with dentists. Very little! Raised during the Depression with tight money, the only time you went to a dentist was when all the home remedies failed. Father, mother, and sister ended up with dentures. Dick and I can thank the Army for an introduction to dental hygiene.

Letter #17: postmarked June 23, 1943

Dear Family

Please forgive me for not writing sooner but I have had my hands full. We have been on four road marches and four days on bivouac in the last week and a half.

There's not much happening around here in the way of excitement. Last week a tank ran over a bridge and it took them 2 hours to get the driver and asst-driver out. The gun (50cal) on top of the tank sunk over 6 feet in quicksand before they got it out.

Here some questions you wanted to know.

1. I still owe the girl in Texas a letter from a month ago.

2. My family history on Cricky's side was explained to me. Ruby Rife is a cousin of mine!!!

3. We eat good. We have had pie for 4 meals in the last 2 days. The only thing is, we have pork chops morning noon and night. I hope I never see another pig. Now we start on lamb for a couple of months!!

4. I gained almost 10 lbs.!! I am about the only one in the company who claims he did.

5. I was paid on the 8th. I have saved a little but this month I don't expect to have so many debts! Here is what happened to last month's pay:

a. 6.50 insurance
bonds
b. 1.50 laundry
c. 8.50 pictures
d. 1.20 cigarettes
e. 1.25 shaving toothpaste
25.50

Plus dry cleaning and some more incidental
Have a new dog-tag chain!
Need a furlough!!!
Tell everyone I said hello. Mary V. owes me a letter. Thanks to Eleanor for letters, I haven't time to write many. Like right now I am sitting here waiting for the whistle to blow. We are going on a 2 day road-march.
That's all for now
Walter Jr
P.S. Will write to granddaddy and Cricky later. Hope granddaddy is well. The whistle!!

This letter was dated June 23. I was asking for forgiveness for waiting 10 days to write.

Quicksand? The 50-caliber gun sank over 6 feet. The driver and assistant driver needed to be rescued because the tank ran over a bridge. I guess it was a good thing they built the bridge over the quicksand. I also think this whole story was probably enhanced with each telling. I obviously did not witness this grand extraction. The tank accident and subsequent details of recovery are a typical example of embellishing a story. I was an avid listener to every rumor, or every exciting story passed along in the barracks.

The girl in Texas had gotten my name from a source that suggested writing to servicemen hoping to raise their morale and encourage their determination to help win the war. By the war's end, I still owed her a letter.

You have to hand it to a guy who detailed his expenditures, indicating how he had practiced with such determination to spend his money so wisely. If those reading the letter at home received an "I need money" letter later, this accounting of necessary expenses would certainly have given evidence of my overwhelming need. The monthly pay for a private during World War II was $50.

Ten dollars I never got because it was sent home to my family.

I purchased life insurance to cover my burial if killed. This was optional but most soldiers thought it necessary. After the war, I dropped the insurance. My dad, a Prudential Life Insurance agent, felt I should have kept it because the price was good. No surprise later on, I ended up with a Prudential Life Insurance policy.

Everyone was buying war bonds, and I did, too. The war bonds were meant to help with the war effort. I guess I must have thought serving in the Army wasn't enough help, or it might have been that war bonds could eventually be turned into cash. Guess what I did with mine after the war?

$8.50 for pictures! I wasn't even supposed to have a camera, according to the Army. Shaving, toothpaste, laundry took $2.75. Cigarettes for $1.20.

Now here is the interesting part. Dry cleaning the wool uniform was most likely around $4 and wasn't needed every week. So, what were the incidentals? I spent approximately $10. I'm sure you can guess by now. I needed candy, bus money for leaving base, and of course, a beer or two.

"Pork chops morning, noon, and night. Lamb will be next"? I tended to exaggerate. I also didn't mention getting back in line for seconds, either.

Most of the road marches I mentioned were not on foot. Some were but many, if not most, were by tank. The overnight foot marches required the pitching of a tent. Each soldier had a "shelter-half" which was just half of a tent. I had half of the pegs and half of the necessary poles. The shelter-halves buttoned together, were closed at the ends, and were a tight fit for two men. The shelter-half also served as the wrapper for your blanket. This bed roll was then tied with the ropes from the tent and could be slung over your shoulder. Also, a necessary part of this equipment was your shovel, otherwise known as the "entrenching tool." This tool may not have been designed to do so but also worked as a hammer. In combat, it dug you a foxhole.

Rain was my worst nightmare. I claimed loud and often that I could dig a trench around the tent a foot deep and water still came in. I learned early on, the hard way, not to touch the tent surface when it was wet.

Inspections were another bane of trainees. In came the captain or major, always looking very serious, an indication of their intent to "gig" anyone who did not measure up to the Army's high standards. A "gig" usually got you some

Tents

There were two versions of the shelter tent used by the U.S. Army. The older First Pattern was introduced in 1940. It required two soldiers to divide between them the 10 wooden pegs (the Army called them pins), eight foot-stops and two guy lines, the two poles, and two water-repellent shelter halves which buttoned together, one inside out. The squared-off edge allowed two two-man tents to be attached to each other to make a four-man tent. In 1943 the Second Pattern was introduced. It had an added "V" front section to improve protection from the elements, and both shelter halves had an inside and the buttons of each were staggered to allow them to be combined. In wartime, tank crew often slept on the back of the tank which had been warmed by the engine, or combined shelter halves to create a tent attached to the side of the tank—unless they could find sheltered accommodation in a house or barn.

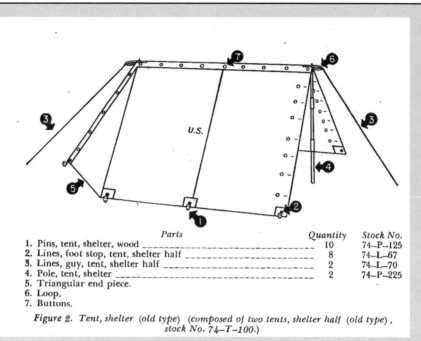

Parts	Quantity	Stock No.
1. Pins, tent, shelter, wood	10	74–P–125
2. Lines, foot stop, tent, shelter half	8	74–L–67
3. Lines, guy, tent, shelter half	2	74–L–70
4. Pole, tent, shelter	2	74–P–225
5. Triangular end piece.		
6. Loop.		
7. Buttons.		

Figure 2. Tent, shelter (old type) (composed of two tents, shelter half (old type), stock No. 74–T–100.)

The old pattern tent created by two shelter halves. (U.S. Army)

Tankers often used a variety of tents and tarpaulins to create a shelter. This M4(105) is making the best of winter conditions at Eupen, Belgium on Christmas Day, 1944, during the Battle of the Bulge. (NARA)

time in the kitchen peeling potatoes. I failed the test after one road march because of my failure to clean my dirty tent pegs! As you can tell, time in the kitchen was not something unknown to me.

This letter contained another Mary reference and I know it wasn't my cousin. Her middle name was Doretha. However, I did thank my younger cousin, Eleanor, for writing. In the summers of my youth, my brother and I would go for an extended stay with my Uncle Ray and Aunt Helen, Mary and Eleanor's parents. Mary was the oldest followed by me, Eleanor, and Dick. There were unfinished houses with just a brick foundation where we would spend time playing. We got the crazy idea to try to smoke like the grown-ups. Having no cigarettes, we used corn silk.

One last cousin story: It was decided by our families that the children would not attend Uncle Dubois's funeral. Aunt Hattie had parked her Ford in the tree lawn out front. I came up with the great idea to play in the car. All the cousins loaded into the car with me behind the steering wheel. I pushed the starter and across the tree lawn we went. I stopped when we came to the driveway, went into reverse, and back up the lawn we went. I did this several more times until the car wouldn't move. We had worn down the battery. Luckily for us, the engine gave out just where she had parked the car. We all ran inside and busied ourselves, swearing secrecy to what we had done. With the funeral and meal over, Hattie jumped in her car to take off. The engine wouldn't start, so out came the men to give her a push and off she went, none the wiser to our antics. There were fun times and great memories in Grafton, West Virginia.

The letter ended with "The Whistle!!" a sign to immediately assemble for the march. This got me off the hook from writing to my mother's mom, Cricky, or my dad's dad, Granddaddy.

Granddaddy, Charles Lewis Stitt, lived in Bridgeport, Ohio. He was the railroad Yardmaster for the B&O Railroad. He owned his house, the next house down, and two additional lots. He rented the lots. Between 1933 and 1938, my family lived with Granddaddy. Mush was a frequent meal during this time. My brother and I laugh that the last time we ate mush was the last day staying in Bridgeport.

The depression of the 1930s left many people without jobs and a means to provide food. Granddaddy had a generous nature. So, if someone came by, he would give them mush, toast, and a cup of coffee. Working near the rail lines, transient people would mark an "X" on the sidewalk outside Granddaddy's house, indicating food could be gotten here.

The empty lots were rented by a Romani family. They had a little girl about my age. She told me that if I gave her some of my popcorn, I could do what I wanted to. I didn't mind sharing the popcorn but was clueless about the rest.

Granddaddy eventually came to live with us when he started having paranoid thoughts that the FBI was bugging him. He dragged his chair outside and set it on fire. As the ashes came down, he was sure they were bugs. Granddaddy was sure the reason the FBI wanted him was for firing the drunk Irishman who had fallen asleep under a shed. Granddaddy never wanted to fire the man, but someone higher up forced him. He was a kind man with a good heart. Hopefully I made good on my promise to write to him later.

The letterhead I wrote on contains my father's initials, most likely his work stationary. I can only assume my mother sent it to me so I'd keep writing.

Letter #18: postmarked June 28, 1943

Dear Family,
Well! The restricted kid is writing again.

Yesterday I was restricted for having a used bar of soap for inspection but I got the best of the bargain. We had to clean guns. I cleaned mine and helped several other boys put theirs together and a Lt. happened to be watching me. He (Lt) told me to form the detail and wait for him. When he came back I had the detail form and he dismissed me. I had the rest of the day off, but today I have to clean a tank.

Here is a strange coincidence. The last day of basic training is July 24 (birthday remember?) After then we are eligible for ratings and furloughs.

Next week we go on a four-day bivouac so I can't write for a while.

I have seen the Forte boy Dick mentioned, he is in the Infantry. I saw H. Bremson about a week ago.

So Long
Walter Jr.
P.S. Thanks for writing so often I am always glad to get a letter.

Everyone in training was supposed to know when inspection time came, they should hide any used soap and put out a fresh bar of soap. Oh brother! It was the Army's way of keeping you from getting a pass off base.

With the phrase "helped several other boys," my parents must have enjoyed this letter from the former Star Boy Scout. The context to this story is I didn't like just standing around with nothing to do. Helping others was a good trait and kept me from mischief. Of course, I think cleaning a tank might have been a bit more cumbersome and wouldn't allow for time off.

I was looking forward to new ratings. What I probably really wanted was to be made an officer, a general, but what I was in line for was Private First Class. The last day of training was my birthday. It was my first birthday away from my family. At home on your birthday, mom let you pick the meal for the family. My choice was always potato soup. This elicited lots of groans from my siblings. Who wanted hot potato soup in July?

Bivouac was additional training and got you off base in one of two ways. The first was a truck that would load you up and dump you somewhere with your half a tent and buddy for the other half. There would be training exercises, a firing range, fighting with other units, etc. The other way was taking the tanks. Then the exercises became maneuvering the tanks and setting the sights on targets. No showers, limited food (unless you snuck along gum, cookies, and candy), chance of rain-soaked tents, and mosquitoes. Preparing the troops for war was the purpose. Complaining about the conditions often was the outcome, making a return to base welcomed.

Dick and I went to school with lots of Fortes. This particular Forte enlisted the same time as me in the 8th Armored Division. He went infantry and I was in tanks. We passed each other but didn't find time to get in trouble. I was trying my best to show I was worthy of time off base and a furlough home.

My mom must have known how homesick I was. I missed my family, my freedom to roam, and my own bed. My letters had been mentioning furloughs for a while. Ever the optimist, I was hoping one would be given to me soon.

CHAPTER 2

Maneuvers

Camp Polk, Louisiana, July 1943–January 1944

Bonus Letter: postmarked July 4, 1943[1]

Dear Aunt Hattie,

Boy! Does Louisiana taste wonderful. I crawled ½ mile on my stomach today and ate a mouth[ful] every other foot. I was in charge of a detail to engage the enemy before the main party arrived. We only lost about 3 men out of 20 some.

I got your candy. It was really swell. Thanks a lot. It took it out in the field and had a snack at night.

Lately I have been working extra hard. Slow but sure I am reaching the top. I hope to get a rating before I go home, if I can.

Well! It's time for lights to go out. You can tell how fast I am writing by my writing.

Love

Walter Jr.

P.S. Hope Uncle Huck is well.

P.S. II May be home in 2 months.

---

[1] This letter wasn't numbered as it was sent to my Aunt Hattie.

You'll notice in the right-hand corner of the envelope my aunt telling my mom to save the letter because she is just "too tired" to write. It sounds like something I would have written. The side note on the letter to my mother Ruth reads, "Dear Ruth, when I said Walter could 'Take it on the chin, shin, and tummy,' this is what made me say as much. Hattie." She seemed to be reassuring my mom that I would be fine. I'm sure my mom worried about me, especially with all my complaining about being so tired, full of mosquito bites, and turned ankles. Hattie, as the older sister, was helping mom cope with the situation by reassuring her that her nephew was still the smart aleck he always was, eating Louisiana mud!

I wrote the letter while on field exercise. We all had to train to do what infantry did. The Army's idea was to hose down an obstacle course with water, turning it into a mud pit. Then a sergeant picked someone to be in charge. Lucky me, I was chosen. I led about 25 men through the Louisiana mud. Losing three wasn't bad. They most likely stood up, threw up, or gave up—three things I'm sure crossed everyone's mind. When we finished, the hose for watering the course was turned on us.

A little aside: I did sneak candy out for a late-night snack. I loved candy and cookies and my family all knew it. As a two-year-old, my dad was supposed to take me upstairs for a nap. He fell asleep and I crawled out the window to run along the roof. The neighbor alerted my mom. My mom, not wanting to startle me, said, "Walter Jr., I've got a cookie for you." I jumped right in the window and gobbled it up. My father was no longer in charge of nap time. To this day, I keep myself well stocked with cookies and candy.

During this time in the service, I tried to be an example to those in charge of giving ranks. I hoped they would notice how well I was performing. Again, the homesickness arose in the desire for a rating increase before I came home.

Another relative mentioned in the letter was Uncle Huck. He was a dentist in a previous life, which ended when he married my Aunt Hattie. He lost his practice due to alcoholism. However, this didn't keep Hattie from bragging about her husband, *Doctor* Heinlein.

Home in two months was wishful thinking.

Letter #19: postmarked Friday night in July

Dear Family,
Well! We really had a big week. We crammed two weeks' studies and works into one week.
We went into the field Sunday afternoon and fired the 30-cal. machine gun for three days. For two days I had complete charge of the pit detail. Lt. McCune said I did very well. On Wednesday we came back to camp and left again Thursday morning. Thur. and Fr. we

had weapons instructions all day. While we were having instructions some officers for the 3rd Army Corp. came around to give test on what we have learned during basic training. I was selected by several lieutenants to represent the company. There were about 10 of us picked. Our company commander gave us the results and our battalion ranked first in the regiment and our company was rated excellent.

Monday I was made a squad leader or acting sergeant.

Rudy Rife is supposed to be my cousin, by some underground method she got my address and wrote me a letter. (Does that answer your que[stion]?)

You may notice some flaw in my writing but I am so tired and cramped from sleeping on the hard ground, it is an effort to move.

Thanks a lot for the cookies they were really swell. And keep sending newspaper clippings I enjoy them all.

Will you do me a favor and write a letter to Aunt Hattie and thank her for the packages she sent me tell her I will write soon.

I am going to send some money home this week. I will send a money order.

H. Bromsen is going home on the 15th. I am sending some things home with him (the films are among them).

Well! That's all for now as I need some sleep and tomorrow, we have an inspection (have to clean barracks, shine shoes, etc.).

Love

Walter Jr.

P.S. Cookies are extra good. (Hint, hint, hint)

Oh, how my parents must have loved this letter! Nothing but good news with the usual appeal for more cookies. And money going home! Oh, happy day!

I was really working on impressing the higher ups. I was in charge of the pit detail, selected for a weapons test (scoring "Excellent"), and a squad leader. I guess I learned a thing or two while in the Army.

In addition, I had a good relationship with my fellow trainees. There were times I was appointed to take the company, about 200 men, on a short march. Again, I was working on getting a new rank. I wanted to show the officers they could trust me.

I knew I could sleep anywhere, but while in the field, I had to sleep on the ground. No tent, no sleeping bag, only a blanket to either be a pillow or a mattress. Anyone who has ever slept on the ground knows it's hard to find a level of soft space.

This letter broke the money record by sending it home rather than asking for it. Every payday, $10 of my pay was sent home. During my time at Camp Polk, I probably asked for all of it to be sent back.

Henry Bromsen bringing the film home is good to know. Getting my pictures developed does explain where some of my money was going. I must have kept the camera and pictures well hidden, because it was still against company rules.

Letter #20: postmarked July 19, 1943

Dear Family,

Well! Here I am again.

Remember in my last letter I said I needed some sleep? I slept in 5 min. too late the next morning and was on detail Sat. The whole division was restricted till 5 o'clock Sat. and all day today. This morning I went to church but we are cleaning guns this afternoon.

So far, I haven't been over to the photographers. It takes a pass and about 8 spare hours which I haven't got, but I will get them soon.

Enclosed is our Easter service program. I found it on the bottom of my locker. (I had forgotten it.)

Hope Pop's Victory Garden turns out alright. One of the funniest things I saw was when I came down here in the winter and the flowers were in bloom.

Well! I have to go back to work. Give my love to everybody.

Love

Walter Jr.

P.S. Hope Sara has a good time at Scout camp.

They wouldn't cut me some slack for taking an extra five minutes of sleep. I was on the lower level, but it does make one wonder how I managed to sleep while the entire barracks, approximately 30 men, were up and moving. Stuck with detail meant cleaning the grounds, picking up cigarette butts, and whatever else the man in charge could think of to keep me busy.

Promising to enclose the Easter service bulletin didn't happen. However, I went to church, which probably was a good excuse to get me out of more detailed assignments. Again, practice with the guns made sure we could be infantry men if needed.

I'm sure my parents wanted a picture of me in my uniform. Lake Charles was about four hours, round trip. It seems it might have been easier to just have someone take my picture with my own camera. However, a professional photograph was more impressive, even though it would take a pass off base, ticket for the bus, money to the photographer, and a return ticket to base. Not to mention money for refreshments and food. A lot of things had to work for me to accomplish this feat.

The Victory Garden—the government encouraged families to plant a vegetable garden to feed their families and prevent a food shortage for the troops. The government was sending food overseas, a lot packaged as C-rations or K-rations. There's a story that goes with the Victory Garden. My dad liked to brag about his tomatoes. One day my parents were sitting on the back porch swing when one of my dad's friends rounded the corner of the house, looked at dad, and said he came to see the "tomatoes as big as grapefruit." Of course, it was my mother who told the story with laughter in her eyes.

Letter #21: Friday night

Dear Family,

Excuse my not writing sooner but we were out in the field four days.

Life is getting a little easier now. We have been firing the big guns and that is about all.

The furloughs are a problem. You hear a different rumor every 5 minutes. One thing I do know, 40 men from out battalion went overseas, and the "old man" won't say anything about them (furloughs)

Thanks a million for presents and cards for my birthday. I think this is my first birthday which I haven't spent with the family.

In case you didn't read about it, they shipped 500 German prisoners into the camp where the W.A.C.s used to be. Don't let anybody kid you. The German army is well fed and they are really men. I was talking to a guard and he said some of his prisoners were 16 and had been in the army four years.

Next Sat. is payday and I am planning on going to Shreveport, Louisiana, it is about the second largest city in Louisiana and has a reputation for one of the best U.S.O. in the south.

Well! I am running out of words so I will sign off now. Promise to write very soon.

Love

Walter Jr.

P.S. I have been pretty lucky lately, especially on that telephone call. Everybody was home.

P.S. II—Pardon writing I just came off K.P. It is 11:30 p.m.

Recurring themes: furlough, a sign of homesickness, K.P. again. I had now been away for six months. My first birthday away from my family. I went to the P.X. and stood in line for the only phone to make my call. It was money well spent, as I talked to the whole family. I'm not sure if hearing from everyone helped or encouraged my homesickness.

Life was getting easier because we were in tanks and didn't have long marches or hikes. Shooting the big guns meant we were shooting the tank cannons.

"The Old Man" was the company commander. I'm sure behind his back we all probably called him names and "The Old Man" was the nicest one. He wouldn't let us know where the 40 men from our battalion were sent, the Pacific or European Theater. In addition, he wouldn't even give us a time within this year for a furlough.

The German P.O.W.s were brought over and put to work doing nominal jobs. The few times I saw them, they were doing maintenance on the ditches, clearing rubbish, removing branches, etc., anything that would have blocked the ditches from having water flow through them.

Sixteen years old and having been in the German army for four years is hard to believe. Hitler started the Hitler Youth program for boys aged ten-to-eighteen. The goal was to prepare them for war. As Hitler attempted to gain more territory, he needed more soldiers, thus sending the Hitler Youth to war at a young age. The Germans remained at Camp Polk for the rest of the war. We saw them but had no other contact with them.

P.O.W.s in the United States

As the war progressed, Britain had problems housing prisoners of war and so, after the United States entered the fighting, the two countries reached agreement to send P.O.W.s across the Atlantic on Liberty ships for incarceration. At the peak this amounted to around 30,000 a month, and by war's end some 425,000 German, Italian, and Japanese P.O.W.s were housed in over 500 camps in 46 states. Supervised by the Office of the Provost Marshal General, most of these camps were reused U.S. Army facilities although some were specially created.

The P.O.W.s maintained military discipline and were treated well—strictly following the terms of the 1929 Geneva Convention. Most wanted to work—by April 1945 91 percent were working—and did so in the fields, with livestock, in factories, and some even helped stem the rising Red River in summer 1944 with sandbags.

Although public feelings were roused when the concentration camps were discovered in Europe, in general relations between P.O.W.s and captors were good and the prisoners often became friendly with the local population they encountered, although it was illegal for a P.O.W. to marry in the United States. Some P.O.W.s spent over three years in captivity and many thousands of the half million Germans who emigrated to America between 1946 and 1960 had spent time there as prisoners.

Camp Polk was used to house a large contingent of P.O.W.s who started to arrive at Leesville by rail in 1943—mainly members of the Africa Korps who had been captured in the fighting or were part of the surrender of over 250,000 Axis troops at the end of the Tunisian campaign. There was a large compound where Honor Field, Fort Polk's parade ground, is today.

The P.O.W. camp at Fort Polk held German prisoners until 1946. (WikiCommons/NARA)

While Shreveport had the best U.S.O., it was too far away for a weekend pass. If I had gone, I would have been there merely a couple of hours before having to come back. It would have been a waste of time.

That final postscript stumps me. Why in the world would I just be coming off K.P. at 11:30 at night from a 6:00 p.m. supper shift? I must have been the slowest floor scrubber or dishwasher. Why again, I wonder, was I on K.P.?

Letter #22: postmarked August 7, 1943[2]

Dear Family,
I am really having a good time. Our battalion had from Sat. afternoon until Tues. morning off. I came to Lake Charles with Smith (a fellow from Missouri), and we have done about everything there is to do. We rented a motor boat for an hour and really had a time riding all over the lake. We went swimming as well, and have really had a glorious weekend. We had a hotel room with a bath, it is the first time I was in a bathtub in almost 5 months. The room also had a big fan and an innerspring mattress, what more could you ask for in Louisiana (pronounced Lousy-an).

How is everyone at home? I hope you have been having as much fun on trips as I have. I guess I told you about my new job, Smith drives Maj. Britton the battalion C.O.

I'm at the U.S.O. now (as you can tell from the stationery) with some boys from our camp. They are playing ping pong and pool and I finally talked Smith into writing home (he hasn't written in a month). Smith's mother died when he was born and his father died soon after. He lives with his aunt on a farm.

Well!! I am going to take on the winner in a ping pong game so I will sign off for now.
Love
Walter Jr.
P.S. The first bunch on furlough left Thurs.
P.S. II They have started giving P.F.C. ratings.
P.S. III I always appreciate cookies.
P.S. IV Send pictures as soon as you can.
P.S. IV Try to buy me a single edge safety razor. I lost mine and I need one for inspections. A plastic one is O.K. Get black if possible but any kind will work.
P.S. VI I am using one of those damn post office pens. I hope you can read this letter.

"A glorious weekend"! A motor boat ride (my first), swimming, a bathtub, an innerspring mattress! And a bonus! I learned that playing ping pong was not a talent one got with one's genes at birth, although I did get better as time went on. After so much time in the field, this break was really welcomed.

My family taking trips meant going to visit family in Grafton, West Virginia, most likely. It could also be taking Sara to Girl Scout camp. From this letter, I doubt they were having as much fun as me. I loved the freedom of a pass off base.

---

[2] Somehow letter 22 became letter 23, and there are two letters numbered 23 but no letter 24.

The new job was jeep driver for the company commander. I didn't request it; the commander just asked if I would be interested in driving a jeep. I guess my resume of being a potato chip truck driver was known to the higher ups. Smith and I had the same position, but we reported to different commanders. I was at the beck and call of the company commander. He didn't go much, but when he did, I had to get the jeep from the motor pool, which was a walk about a block and a half away. This wasn't bad unless it was raining. Then it was a quick sprint with hopes the sides and top were already up.

This letter contained several postscripts. These show I was feeling very hopeful that I'd be getting my furlough and a new rank. The tables had turned. I wanted them to send pictures. The cookies again!

I wonder how you lose a razor that is much needed daily. I also wonder why I didn't take some of my pay and go to the P.X. and buy a black razor. Oh, that's right. I was spending my hard-earned money on fun times in Lake Charles.

How in the world could anyone tell the difference between a regular pen and the "damn" post office pen? The pen wouldn't produce ink and I had to push hard sometimes to get it to write. Funny thing, I wrote four pages with that damn pen.

Letter #23: postmarked August 17, 1943

Dear Family,

I meant to write sooner but I have been pretty busy and haven't felt like writing.

I am one of the medics' best customers. They are treating me for heat rash, which I have very bad all over my back, and ringworm, which is a very common thing down here. I have slept on my stomach all week now and really suffer when I get in the sun.

Well! Here's the news you have waiting for!!!!! My furlough starts November 4. Well, Dick, I will be home on your birthday. They changed my assignment number again and I am now classified as a peep driver. This isn't such a bad job. I drive the Co. commander and his last driver went to Fort Knox to maintenance school.

I hate to ask (notice the touching start) but I need about 5 dollars and about 10 for pictures. I agree with you, I am more bother than I am worth.

Well! They are kicking me out of the day room because it is so late so I will sign off and try to sleep and I do mean try. My chest is about caved in from sleeping on it.

Love Walter Jr.

P.S. We were given test for the last 2 weeks by the 3rd Army. Our regt. was 1st in the division, our battalion was also first, and our company ran a tie for first. We were congratulated by Gen. And Col.

Heat rash is the blocking of the pores, not allowing adequate perspiration, thus causing red lumpy bumps. Heat rash, you would think, might have been brought on by boating and swimming at Lake Charles. It just as easily could have been daily life at camp in the Louisiana heat in August, which averaged a temperature in the 90s all day. My back was covered. At times it would itch, which had me searching for a way to rub my back and ending up looking like a cow on a fence post. The medical treatment for heat rash was to stay cool, take cool showers, or use calamine lotion. No air conditioning, no time for extra cool showers, and putting lotion on your own back doesn't work. I paid the price for a heat rash by sleeping on my stomach, a position I never used. Poor me!

I was familiar with ringworm. I had it once before from using the community wading pool at the local playground back home in Elm Grove. Both cases got a purple paint job. The medical term would be gentian violet, an antiseptic, which leaves the person purple. There were a lot of purple painted bodies every summer.

Furlough on November 4th! My brother's birthday is November 6th. Any time to go home would have been great for me.

Peeps or Jeeps?

One of the great success stories of World War II—Eisenhower included it in his top list of war-winning contributions by U.S. industry—what we today call the Jeep was built in large numbers. Its story started in July 1940 when the U.S. War Department approached 135 car manufacturers with a requirement for a light utility reconnaissance vehicle. The specification proposed reduced the number of potential entrants immediately and the timetable—an 11-day deadline for the proposal, 49 days for a prototype, and 75 days for production-ready test vehicles—saw only three responses, from Bantam, Ford, and Willys-Overland. Bantam's design was chosen as it hit the deadline and was the best. It went to prototype but soon it became obvious that Bantam was too small a company to produce the numbers required so the War Department gave Bantam's blueprints to Ford and Willys. They finalized their versions and by November 1940 the Willys Quad and the Ford Pygmy were ready. Of the three designs, the Bantam was lightest at 980kg, the Quad the most powerful with 2.2-litre inline-four 60hp engine, and Ford's the best designed and built. The 60hp engine saw the contract awarded to Willys who ended up building around 360,000 of the vehicles. Ford built 278,000 and Bantam built jeep trailers.

How did it get its name? Well, there's no single answer. The military—as can be seen from Walter's letters—called it a "peep" because it was primarily a reconnaissance (peeping) car. The word "jeep" was originally (since World War I) associated with new recruits or vehicles. In the end, whether it stems from Ford GP or Popeye's "Eugene the Jeep" character, that was the name that stuck.

I was a peep driver. Army jargon for jeep drivers.

The pay didn't increase with the new job, and again, I needed money for what else? Pictures! After all the times I'd written for money so I could get pictures, you'd think I had an album full of pictures, but now I can only find a few.

The day room was a common area with tables for writing, couches for lounging, a place to hang out and drink soda and just relax.

The final postscript shows how well the battalion was doing. We all wanted a new rank and were working hard to prove we deserved it.

Letter #25: postmarked August 30, 1943

Dear Family,

Well! I really did it today. I hit a tank with my peep. I had a major and a captain with me. The major had just finished telling me I was a good driver. I was passing the tank and couldn't see it for the dust. The tank did a column left, and I hit it broadside. The major and captain were both thrown clear. I dislocated my shoulder but I put it back myself, a lieutenant saw me trying to lift my arm and sent me to the medics. I have my arm in a sling and they said I would probably have to keep it that way for some time.

Gas Rationing has done something for our family. Reunion back home.

Hope everyone back home is well.

My arm is beginning to hurt so I will quit for now. But I have plenty of time to write now.

Love

Walter

P.S. Can you get those Kodak films printed again? The fellows whose pictures I took will pay for them!!

P.S. II the Major signed my accident report and said I was not to blame.

I really liked the role of "peep" (jeep) driver. As indicated in my letter home, I was even complimented on the quality of my driving. My account of the accident speaks for itself. Dust in my eyes caused me to shut them, then *Bam!* right into the tank. I was embarrassed at having a wreck and so thankful the only person hurt was me. Standing on the road after the accident, I realized my left shoulder was out of joint. Gripping my left wrist with my right hand, I lifted my left arm, which put the shoulder back in place. However, this was not the way the medics would have done it.

There are some stories that go with my jeep driving that need to be told.

Approaching the motor pool with the captain as passenger, there was a small dip in the road before the guard house. I, with deft use of the gas pedal, slipped from third into second without depressing the clutch. The captain observed this maneuver and made a comment to the effect that "it would not happen again." Technically, you would push in the clutch every time you shift gears.

The same captain, company commander, was a passenger out of camp to another area. As the end of the paved road approached and a dirt road lay ahead, I went into neutral, switched in the front-wheel drive and went back to third gear. The captain knew more about the vehicle than I thought he did and asked, "Isn't the S.O.P. [Standard Operating Procedure] to stop and put in front-wheel drive?" Caught again. Lectured again.

An early evening call from Henry Bromsen at the Red Cross was for me to get the jeep and drive a soldier into Leesville to catch a bus home on compassionate leave. Compassionate leave meant someone at home was dying or had died. I was changing my clothes to something more appropriate for going off base when I was approached by a fellow trainee about purchasing a quarter-pint of Kentucky's finest when in town. I was brought up to be kind to one's neighbor. No problem. The M.P.s at the gate only wanted to see your pass. When this happened a second time, the request for refreshments was tripled. The jeep had a convenient storage area, which ordinarily was for chains but held whiskey quite conveniently.

Everything that the military needed for the war effort was rationed and this included gas. My dad was an insurance salesman and needed gas tickets for work. My brother had a car and good friends who worked with the coal company, essential work. Dick's buddies willingly shared some gas rationing tickets with him. This allowed the family to motor along to visit family in Bridgeport and Grafton, and Dick got to haul good friends around. It paid to have friends in essential work.

Having to end the letter because my left arm hurt must have left my family confused. I write with my right hand. The sling lasted maybe a couple of days. It would have allowed me time to write letters. However, after a couple of days, the pain became minimal and the desire to get back behind the wheel got the sling tossed away. The next letter doesn't get written for another week.

Pictures again! This time someone else would pay for them.

Letter #26: postmarked September 6, 1943

Dear Family,
This week I am going to make an honest effort to write every day. I should be ashamed that I don't write home oftener but you know how I am about putting things off till tomorrow.

I really had an experience today. I drove the company commander and his girlfriend around. He got special permission for her to ride in a government vehicle. The whole company is calling me lucky.

My arm is O.K. now and I am back to work. My heat rash is almost cleared up but the ring worm is still there. My ring worm is on my right side almost on my hip, it is not painful but I wish it was gone.

I am on K.P. this weekend because I did not report back from sick call (I came back and went to sleep). I was supposed to be on for 5 meals but I got out of two.

This week Jim Gilleland was transferred to our company. Dick and daddy probably remember him. He played football for Linsly and was acting corporal when we left for Fort Hayes. He is going to be sent to West Point sometime in the future. He has a subscription to the morning paper (Intel?) and, boy is it nice to see a paper from home.

Friday, I drove Major Britton (who was in the accident). When I reported in the morning when I reported he said "Stitt, if you turn me over again......!!!!!!" I said "Sir, I learned my lesson!!" He laughed and the rest of the day he was nice as pie to me. He even bought me a Coke.

Well! I have to get up early for K.P. so I will sign off now.

Love

Walter Jr.

P.S. I hope you like the picture leaflet I sent.

In Samuel Taylor Coleridge's *The Rime of the Ancient Mariner*, the speaker refers to sleep as a "gentle thing, / Beloved from pole to pole!" However, it was not my best friend. Time and again, it did me in. After going to the medics, I was to report back in for duty. Instead, I went back to bed. Most likely the company clerk spotted me and arbitrarily came up with K.P. as punishment. K.P. was an all-day assignment: breakfast, lunch, and dinner. I can see myself after the first full day putting my sling back on and reporting for K.P. I'm sure the person in charge thought I would be worthless with a bad arm and sent me on my way.

The *Wheeling Intelligencer* was the morning newspaper. Jimmy and I were in the same barracks for a brief time before he left for Fort Benning in Georgia. He'd read the paper and give it to me. A newspaper was valued like the Internet would be for soldiers today. I read articles about people back in Wheeling, saw pictures of places and people I knew. It also gave information about the war effort and rationing back home. It was a great gift to have the newspaper. Unfortunately, Jimmy didn't stay long, but I did enjoy it while it was available.

I was back to work driving the jeep. Driving the company commander and girlfriend around, I was surprised I didn't end up with a nickname of "Lucky."

The postscript more writing about pictures. This time a leaflet. Since it wasn't in the box of letters, one can assume my family wasn't that impressed.

Letter #27: postmarked September 7, 1943

Dear Family,

I am writing this letter sitting in my tent. There is a breeze blowing straight through my tent and for once I am comfortable.

I got up this morning at (01:15) 1:15 and had driven 20 miles before the rest of the company got up.

We are firing the 81mm mortar, which dad can explain to you. We have had so many dry runs in the past that our scores are exceptional. (We even killed a cow or two!!)

I guess I told you I was on K.P. yesterday but I didn't have it so hard. Most of the company had passes.

I am going to try this week and catch up on my writing. I will try and write home every day this week and make up for missing a week.

It seems funny to hear that school has started and I don't have to go. But I will guarantee (spelling!!!) you I am working harder and having more fun than any 10 fellows in school. (Noon)

I had to quit my writing at noon and do some driving. Since then, it has begun to rain and I am now floating around inside my tent.

The chow truck is going in soon so I will quit and send this letter in.

Love

Walter Jr.

P.S. I think you can get the negatives made of the big pictures I sent home. (Mr. Rogers, Alice's dad, can do it.) Did you give away all those big pictures??

"Having fun" during Army training was probably not in the manual. However, everything new or different in my experience turned out to be just that—with one exception. I never stopped complaining about the water that leaked into my tent. I commented on numerous occasions that I could dig a ditch a foot deep around this tent and water would still get in! However, the fact that I mentioned a cool breeze blowing through the tent does seem to indicate that the tent wasn't well sealed against the elements. No wonder the tent was floating in the afternoon rain.

Driving the jeep at 0115 most likely was due to someone needing to return to camp. The company commander would have had to give the okay for me to drive. I wonder if he accompanied me or just sent me on my own with the person in need. I did say I liked jeep driving, but the loss of my favorite thing to do, sleep, might have started to change my mind about this job.

Dad would have explained a mortar round to the family. The 81mm was just a bigger gun than the tank had. Now, my father could tell a story (I guess it is an inherited trait), so I'm sure it went something like this.

Picture this: First you find your target, measure the distance you're going to shoot, and set the aiming device. A large metal tube is on the ground, the mortar round is dropped into the pipe. The round ignites and explodes out of the tube, making a large looping arch and *Bang!* it hits the target. I'm sure there might have been some confusion when it came to the part about our training exercise for mortar practice being exceptional, and we killed a cow or two.

I think maybe I got carried away with telling the story. No order came to make the cows a target. One can hardly believe the Army firing range would have cows running loose. Even farmers in Louisiana would keep the cows at home if mortars were flying.

The Germans were very accurate with their mortars. Thus, we had training exercises to see if we could perform as well.

I seemed to have not learned about K.P. being the end result for goof-ups. It wasn't fun, but "not having it so hard" has to border on another "not too bad" experience. I'm sure the company clerk saw me without the sling and figured I could finish my five days.

School was back in session and I didn't have to go! I was a student who liked hands-on learning. The Army was giving me this and challenging me to learn new things. I'm sure the fellows back home were just happy not to have K.P. and camp detail.

Yes, the chow truck did more than just bring food. They brought out mail and, in my case, took mail back with them to base. A yell would go out, "Mail call!" and the company would gather around waiting to see if their name would be called. As you can imagine, if you got a package, maybe full of cookies, it was hard to hide. Hoarding the cookies didn't work, and they were quickly eaten by all who were nearby with a request for me to write home for more.

Promising to write more and getting pictures seems to be the common thread through all my stories thus far. Mr. Rogers, Alice's dad, making prints of the big picture negatives. Who and why? The big picture in question is visible to the right.

Mark it down: This letter did not ask for money!

Letter #28: postmarked September 10, 1943

Dear Family,

I am really writing this letter in a hurry. I just finished chow and at 1:00 I am going on bivouac with Majors Britton & Conley.

There is not much new down here. Just the same old drag.

I meant to tell you (if I didn't) my arm is a little sore but it is almost well. My heat rash doesn't bother me anymore and my ring worm is almost gone. I had a big lump on my back where a boil was starting but that is gone now too.

There haven't been any changes in the furlough list as yet. I am still scheduled for November 4 to 18 inclusive. (15 days & 1 day of grace.)

The other night in bivouac one of the fellows took sick. It was the worst case of chills I ever saw. It was raining and plenty muddy but I still have the record for making the best time coming in from our area. The medics at the dispensary said he had busted his appendix. When he got to the hospital the interns claimed he had heat exhaustion but they finally ended up with pneumonia.

The whistle just blew and that means I have 15 minutes to get ready.

Love

Walter

P.S. It is about time Dick or Sarah wrote. Or dad.

In the last letter, I bragged about how good things were, but not a week later, I complained how everything was the same old drag. My medical issues were bugging me and, in addition to all I mentioned in the past, I had a boil, but it was gone. I'm sure reading between the complaints told my family how much I wanted to go home. The furlough was still on for November 4th through the 18th, but that was still two months away. I missed my mom's cooking and care for me. I missed my dad's stories. I missed hanging out with my siblings and other relatives. I missed walking the streets of my hometown and seeing friends. At this point, November seemed far away.

But there was nothing like a little excitement to get my mind off my woes. The company commander came to get me to take a very sick soldier back to base. The company commander did not accompany me, and I understood the urgency and drove accordingly. I was going as fast as the jeep and conditions would allow. The jeep bounced through puddles, splashing mud all over as we left the field. This produced a fair amount of jarring for the passenger. Then we hit the paved roads and I really cranked it up, flying through turns. This had the sick passenger sliding side to side. When we reached the dispensary, the poor guy was nauseated after our ride, which probably made the medics think appendicitis. Thinking he'd need surgery; off he went to the base hospital. The doctors determined he must have had heat exhaustion since he was nauseated, dizzy, and sweating. I'm sure my driving saved his life and wasn't the cause of the confusion with the Army medics and doctors.

When the company got back from bivouac, we found out the final diagnosis was pneumonia. Interesting.

Left out of this letter was my failure to learn from my first mistake on Army Axiom #1: Never volunteer. I eagerly raised my hand when asked for those who knew the "Manual of Arms with a Rifle." A Retreat Parade in the Louisiana sun and standing rigidly at Parade Rest with a Springfield '03 rifle more firmly embedded this lesson in my brain. The heat rash was a good reminder, as well.

Three things stand out with my postscript. First, there was no request for money or pictures to be sent. I think this was a first, for sure. Second, the spelling of my sister's name kept changing. Her birth certificate said Sara, and somewhere along the line, we started adding an "h" at the end. Third, asking my dad to write a letter brings a laugh even today. He was not a letter writer. I guess my brother inherited this trait.

Letter #29: postmarked September 20, 1943

> Dear Family,
> Well! I have some news for a change. This morning we had a forced march of 4 ½ miles in 50 minutes. The whole division had to do it. One sergeant from our Battalion [2/80th] and one each from 4[9]th [A.I.R.] and 36th A.R. dropped dead!![3]
>
> Tomorrow tells the tale. If everything goes right we will be a separate tank battalion soon!!
>
> I got my pictures taken over again Sat. I saw the proofs today and the pictures will be done on the 15th so expect them on the 18th. I will send four home (I got six) and I want to send two to some friends of mine (naturally women).
>
> The package you sent me was in good condition. I got the razor and tag chain.
>
> I have to turn in now so
>
> Love
>
> Walter
>
> P.S. I now have more ring worm and a million mosquito bites.

I'm glad my mom opened and read the mail first. I can just imagine my little sister seeing this and getting upset.

The whole division would have been over 10,000 strong—so there were a lot of men running. The average temperature this time of year in Louisiana was in the high 80s. It was possible people passed out, but died?

Soldiers were subject to lots of rumors. Hardly a day went by when someone didn't come up with an "I heard…" My knowledge of what happened in the battalion may have some accuracy. However, these battalions were so far removed from my unit that it leads one to wonder if the rumors were true.

---

[3] Walt's letter mistakenly said 40th Infantry instead of 49th Armored Infantry.

Even 70 years later, I think I would remember seeing people drop dead on a four-and-a-half-mile hike. A forced march so strenuous that three young men dropped dead along the way seems unlikely. It could be true, but one wonders! The barracks was a good place to pass along the "I heard…" Each passing on was inclined to change the "facts." It was best to take everything with a grain of salt.

On these hikes, our first sergeant stayed with us until the end of the company street and then took off for the P.X. There, he'd relax and have some coffee. As soon as we hit the street, there he would be again to take us back to the barracks. No one said anything because he outranked us. Besides, who wanted more K.P. or camp detail?

There were plans to reorganize the division. I hoped nothing would change. I liked the group I was with. I was familiar with our officers and their idiosyncrasies. A change in any of this would have meant learning all over again what you can and can't get away with. By this time, I'd had enough of the K.P.

Now, I was sending pictures to women. I hope Lenore, my girlfriend back home, was one of them. I also hope my mom didn't mention to Lenore I was sending a picture home since she might not have been the recipient. Remember, I had met a beauty queen!

I got a package! Once again, I was popular with my barrack mates. No mention of sending money, but there were the same complaints of ringworm and mosquitoes.

Letter #30: postmarked September 22, 1943

Dear Family,

Well! The shakedown finally came. I am now in the 80th Armored Tank Battalion. We are getting a new Company Commander too. He (new C.O.) is about 20, he got his bars through R.O.T.C. and as a company commander he isn't worth a damn. He is sissified he looks like a good day's work would kill him. They are going to increase our company by another 150 men. Where they are going to sleep or eat is a mystery.

Today we are going in the gas chamber. We will stand in a room while they turn on Chlorine. If I don't write soon, my gas mask didn't work.

They just blew the whistle so bye for now.

Love

Walter

P.S. I need 10 dollars to get my pictures. They are done and waiting.

Armored Division Reorganization

When constituted, U.S. Army armored divisions had two tank regiments (8th Armored's were the 36th and 80th) and one armored infantry regiment (49th), all with three battalions, and three artillery battalions (398th, 399th, 405th).

Analysis of battlefield events showed that more flexible arrangements were required, so from 1943 the regiments disappeared and the division was remodeled. Two combat commands (C.C.A. and C.C.B.) along with a C.C.R. (reserve) provided subheadquarters to which the divisional commander could allocate units to suit the required missions.

From this point on the divisions comprised three battalions of tanks (8th Armored's were 18th, 36th, 80th), three of armored infantry (7th, 49th and 58th), and three of artillery (398th, 399th, 405th).

As an example of how this worked in combat, in 1944–45 8th Armored had the following formations:

Combat Command A: 7th Armored Infantry Battalion, 18th Tank Battalion, 398th Armored Field Artillery Battalion

Combat Command B: 49th Armored Infantry Battalion, 36th Tank Battalion, 399th Armored Field Artillery Battalion

Combat Command R: 58th Armored Infantry Battalion, 80th Tank Battalion, 405th Armored Field Artillery Battalion

Service battalions (attached by companies to combat commands): 53rd Armored Engineer Battalion, 78th Armored Medical Battalion, 88th Armored Reconnaissance Battalion, 130th Armored Ordnance Battalion, 148th Armored Signal Company, 508th CIC Detachment, Division Trains, Division Artillery, American Red Cross, Military Police Platoon

Temporarily attached units: 473rd AAA AW (SP) Battalion, 809th Tank Destroyer Battalion

I was spoiled by having a commanding officer who was older and looked the part of an Army officer; this led me to labeling a newly graduated "90-day wonder" as looking "sissified." However, there would be a new commanding officer; he would give the orders, and whether you liked it or not, you were going to do it. To think someone two years older than me, fresh out of R.O.T.C., was going to lead a bunch of men was what I found difficult.

In addition to the new commander came another 150 men. Jammed together already in our barracks, it was hard to imagine where we would put all these extra men. The barracks were made of wood. When you entered the building, on the left-hand side was a private room for the sergeant. Lined up on both sides were metal cots. My barracks didn't have bunk beds like some of the other barracks did. At the far end on one side were four toilets. The other side had half a dozen wash basins, and along the back were the showers. No privacy. The barracks did have windows, which could be opened for fresh air. As you can imagine, the open position was often needed.

Something important to know is the Army had us do this exercise because during World War I, the Germans used gas. The "gas chamber" at Camp Polk was a room that would hold 20 or so men. The doors were closed. Everyone listened to instructions then put on their gas masks. The chlorine was started, and a signal was given to take off the mask, followed by what seemed an hour holding your breath as you waited until a whistle blew. Then there was a mad dash out of the door for fresh air. Tears in the eyes were the worst result. Not being able to hold your breath until the whistle sounded gave everyone a good whiff of what you hoped you never got again. The exercise was to demonstrate how quickly you needed to put on your mask if you heard the cry, "Gas!" Did my mother share this letter with Sara with the caveat "Your brother is joking about the gas chamber"?

By this point in my letter writing, I had almost made it a month without requesting money from home. And what did I need money for? Pictures!

Letter #31: postmarked October 22, 1943

Dear Family,
Today I am the barracks orderly (B.O.), so don't be surprised if I write a couple of letters.

They took my peep and gave it to some other outfit (I don't know who) and I am getting a new one. I am still going to miss my old peep (Kite), it was the best one in the motor park except the Colonel's.

They transferred over 40 fellows from our company to the infantry. I sure hated to see them go, I have made a lot of friends here and I hated to see them go as much as they hated to go.

Our new company commander's name is Griffen (1st Lt.) he got his bars through R.O.T.C. and is strictly a book man. The new battalion commander is Lt. Col. Bacon, he is old but is really a soldier.

Sara! I hear you like school this year. Do you have the same teachers Dick had?

Dick: What is Jimmy Mull doing now? I heard he quit the A&P.

Dad: Parts of this army are rotten. One fellow whose father owns a fleet of trucks was keeping the motor Sarg's car going on T stamps. The fellow is now at Fort Knox mechanics school on the motor Sarg's recommendation.

Mom: The cookies and candy arrived in excellent condition and the cookie I had tasted very good. So far, I got everything you sent me from home. I can't remember all I got but everything you asked me about I received.

I am running out of words now so I will write later when I think of something more.
Love
Walter Jr.
P.S. I now have my long underwear on and the heaters are going. But about eleven o'clock I will have to them off and start sweating.
P.S. II Short on cash. Couldn't stretch it far enough. Don't get paid till week from Sat.

The barracks orderly's job was to sit around and write letters home, according to me. However, the assignment was to see to the cleanliness and order of the "Rec Room." Once an officer caught me sleeping on a sofa. A slap on my feet had me coming up in a fighting stance ready to work vengeance on the culprit, only to quickly smile when I saw it was an officer. I don't remember getting K.P. and there's no mention in the letter, so I must have had a winning smile and a very clean Rec Room.

I named the peep (jeep) "Kite" because it would fly like the wind when I was behind the wheel without any officers on board. Or because it held steady in the wind as we traversed down the road with the company commander.

They transferred 40 men from our company. Infantry wasn't an easy assignment. They did lots of walking with a rifle as their weapon. They were easy targets in war. Sometimes if they were lucky, they could ride on the tank or walk behind it helping to avoid stepping on landmines. However, in war, infantry was a tough job. I admired those who performed it and honored those who gave their all.

I'm sure First Lieutenant Griffin's youth and inexperience led to my negative attitude about him. He tended to be standoffish with the soldiers. In my opinion, this meant he wasn't confident in himself and his new position. If you act like you know more than those who do, it tends to turn me off.

Now Lieutenant Colonel Forsyth Bacon was older and more amicable. He had served his time in the military. He understood what we were going through because he had been in the same place at our age. He took time to talk to you, shared stories, and offered respect which, in turn, earned mine.

Right in the middle of the letter I wrote a specific question to both of my siblings. My goal is easy to see: write me a letter!

I told dad how rotten the Army was, but I was learning a life lesson. The man whose father owned a fleet of trucks had T-stamps (rationing tickets for gas) and kept the sergeant's car running was privileged. Thus, he received a new assignment: mechanics training school, no war assignment. This was all due to what his father could provide him. The lesson? Sometimes life isn't fair, so recognize it and move on.

But the funniest part of this letter is me telling mom everything arrived in excellent condition. And the *cookie* (one cookie!)—tasted very good. I've told you cookies in the barracks go fast.

I had on long underwear and the heaters were going. I was going to sweat to death if I didn't take them off soon. Here is a sign that I really didn't know what to write, but this issue was on my mind. I think this is called stream-of-consciousness writing.

I really needed my family to understand the last part of this letter. I changed the writing utensil from pencil to pen to state "Short on cash." Let's see. Free food, clothes, and transportation. Left to be purchased were beer, cigarettes, candy bars, and 25 cents to have fatigues washed.

Letter #32: postmarked October 4, 1943

Dear Family,

Boy! I really got changed around this time. I got back in tanks again but not medium this time. I am in a light tank. When they told me I was going to be transferred I remembered that old saying about "First impression is a lasting impression," so I really tried to start out right. I washed, shaved, got a haircut and put on my Sunday-go-to-meeting-clothes. I think I stand a pretty good chance in this company with the experience I have had. I hated to move at first but I have met some new fellows and they are pretty swell. There is one boy here from Bluefield, West Virginia.

I received the money order and it came just in time. I needed 40 cents for a haircut. (If you see any loose hair on this paper, it is because I just got a G.I. (half-inch) haircut and I haven't got rid of all the loose hairs yet.)

Moving from one company to another has changed my furlough status but I don't think I will get it any later than Nov. 10th (Knock on wood).

This is all I have time for now will write later.

Love
Walter
P.S. I drove a tank today (first day) but I am going to be a gunner, I think.

Unfortunately, or maybe fortunately, I was no longer a jeep driver. Twice when the captain returned from his meetings, I was asleep and should have occupied myself doing something to stay awake. Now it was back to being a tank gunner. Of course, it might have been my excellent score as a gunner that got me this job.

Making a good first impression was important since I had no idea who I was going to report to first. As fast as my hair grew in my younger days, I probably could have had a haircut weekly and a shave twice a day.

Though I sent home $10 from every paycheck, it appears I asked for it back almost every time. My intentions were good, at least.

Tank Companies

Tank battalions were divided into an HQ and six companies—HQ company, service company and four tank companies, A, B, C, and D. On paper there were 80 tanks in each battalion. The four tank companies had 17 tanks each. Companies A, B, and C each had three platoons, each with 5 × M4A3s, a M4A3 (105mm), and a M4A3 for the company commander.

Company D had three platoons, each with 5 × M5A1 Stuarts, and a section of two M4A1s including the company commander's tank. The M5A1s were changed to M24 Chaffees when the division reached Europe, after Walter had left.

The service company had tank recovery vehicles to enable them to retrieve damaged or broken down tanks. It also had tanks equipped with anti-mine devices, and medical units etc.

Walter had started training on M4 mediums (Shermans) but moved onto M5 light tanks (Stuarts). These were only armed with 37mm guns (rather than the 76mm or 105mm guns of the Shermans) and their role in combat by this stage of the war was limited because of their lack of armor protection and firepower. They were often simply used to augment the reconnaissance battalion.

I got moved to D Company, 2nd Battalion, which was light tanks. They moved about a dozen of us, some of whom I knew. I wasn't really close to any of them.

There were many differences between light and medium tanks, the most obvious being the size and weight. In addition, the light tank had an automatic shift. My previous experience in the medium tank was a manual shift. The steering levers in the light tank were overhead and pulled down to brake; whereas, the medium had bars that came up from the floor. The light tank could go much faster and was more maneuverable. This tank had a selection of automatic gear shifts: drive-drive, drive-low, or low-low. It would not be a guess which one this young man with a lead foot would pick.

I got to drive a light tank down to the wash rack, which was a concrete platform with a hose for washing. In turn, I then got to wash the tank. This was the extent of my driving.

The fun part of tank training was you had to learn every job. On occasion, I was tank commander for training purposes. However, my M.O.S. (Military

---

Military Occupation Specialty (M.O.S.)

Putting people into the right position to make best use of their skills, identifying skill sets and training, ensuring the right replacements for casualties with specific skillsets: all these things require definition of soldiers' abilities. The U.S. Army classified soldiers by specification serial numbers (S.S.N.s) based on their training, experience, and abilities. They then matched soldiers with suitable S.S.N.s to certain duties. Walter was given the 616 number meaning gunner. In July 1944 the U.S. Army technical manual *TM12-47 Military Occupational Classification of Enlisted Personnel* provided an updated method of classifying military occupation specialists. The 616 S.S.N. was given a range of military occupational specialty (M.O.S.) numbers to identify Army jobs, the two pertaining to Walter being 1736 Light Tank Crewman and 2736 Medium Tank Crewman.

Occupation Specialty) code was still 616, which indicated I was still listed as a gunner.

The furlough was sorted like the rumors; the facts weren't always there.

Letter #33: Thursday

Dear Family,
I had been out in the field six days in less than 2 weeks and haven't had time to write.

I am feeling swell and the weather is getting warm again. (It was cold for a while.)

I hate to tell you this and I don't know how to say it, but I am now a Private (buck) again. I was supposed to stand guard over the tank to 10 o'clock and then go to bed but I didn't have a watch and what I though was 10 was only 9:30. My tank commander a Lt. came back and found me sleeping, (he is from some small-town Grantsville or something outside of Clarksburg), he warned me in the morning that it better hadn't happen again. Another Lt. (Walker) found out about it somehow and told the C.O. He called it inefficiency and so I am a buck private again. The C.O. said I could earn it back again if I tried (They say every dog has his day and if I ever get half a chance Lt. Walker better look out, I'll never forget or forgive him and I guarantee you he will never come back from combat.)

I received a package from you today it was very good and in good condition.

Please forgive me for not writing sooner but I was just too tired and mad when I came in from the field.

Love
Walter Jr.

M5 Light Tank

Walter trained on the M4 medium and M5 light tanks. While identified as a gunner, he would have trained to be able to perform any of the duties of a tank crewman. For the light tank these were:

"Drives the vehicle to secure maximum fire effect without undue exposure to enemy fire. Operates radio to maintain communication with other elements. Fires the weapons of the vehicle, including cannon and machine guns, to destroy enemy personnel, lines of communication, vehicles, pill boxes, and other targets, and to protect the vehicle against attack. Inspects and checks engines, oil levels, inner phone headset communication, radio, vehicle operating equipment, turret mechanism, tracks, bogie wheels, ammunition, and weapons. Cleans and services .30- and .50-caliber machine guns and cannon, and bore sights cannon.

At supervisory level. Is responsible for control, coordination, and tactical employment of tank and crew members.

The M5 light was developed from the M3 light tank—this M3 seen at Fort Banning, GA. It shows the crew positions of commander (standing, head out); the gunner to his right (legs visible behind driver); driver (at left of photo); assistant driver (at right). These positions were the same for the M5. (NARA)

Must have sufficient knowledge of the tactical employment of light armored vehicles to be able to anticipate commands, take advantage of cover, and maneuver to obtain targets and secure good observation positions in reconnaissance. Must be skilled in entering and leaving vehicle under combat conditions and capable of fighting with hand weapons when dismounted. Must be familiar with the principles of armed reconnaissance. Must be able to employ the gunnery techniques of direct and indirect fire on moving and stationary targets."[4]

The M5's crew of four were:

- Tank commander (loader or assistant gunner and tends voice radio) —usually a lieutenant or sergeant, positioned in the turret, standing on the floor or sitting or standing on the seat on the right of the 37mm gun.
- Gunner—seated in the turret at the left of the 37mm gun with his left hand on the power traverse control handle, his right hand on the elevating handwheel, and his head against the headrest of the periscope.
- Bow gunner (assistant driver and radio operator)—seated in the bow gunner's seat at front right in hull.
- Driver—seated in the driver's seat, front left in hull.

M5A1 light of 33rd Armored Regiment. Note the different glacis plate and driver/assistant driver hatches to those of the M3 and the lack of sponson M.G.s. (NARA)

---

[4] FM 17-68 Crew Drill, Light Tank M5 series.

P.S. Also received money from bicycle. Thanks a million.

P.S. Jr. (VERY IMPORTANT) I have some money ($20 or so) but it cost 38 dollars to come home and I get my furlough sometime in Nov.

P.S. III—There is really a swell bunch of fellows in this company. They call Sgt. by their first names.

P.S. IV—Am now in good physical condition and my present weight is 152 lbs. My waist has increased 1 inch and I grew almost an inch so far.

P.S. V—I have a G.I. haircut.

Guilty as charged! Long day. Cool evening. Nearby steel box that had been sitting all day in the sun and was still warm. Long day, cool night, warm in the tank, sleep!

Then that rude awakening with the shout, "Who's on guard here?!"

Quick thinking, I came up with the answer, "But I thought it was ten o'clock." This was not the right answer. There was a severe warning that this kind of conduct in war time could be the reason for a fatal ending. This episode must have been shared with other officers who felt a warning was not sufficient punishment for the crime. So, now I was back to "buck private." I lost my P.F.C. (private first class) rank, and I was at the lowest rank.

The face-saving action for this embarrassment was a rant about what could happen to a certain person in combat. It's easy to write bold things in a letter home, but trust me, I didn't ever say anything like this to an officer.

My brother Dick found a buyer for my unused bike and sold it for the lofty price of $10. It's interesting that with this $10, I came up with the amount I had on hand as "20 or so." Very loose accounting.

The first sergeant in my new company was a fan of Notre Dame's quarterback Lujack. In touch football games, he was the quarterback. He had a lot of "Lujack fades back to pass." This led on occasions to me yelling, "Lujack missed again!"

The Army was turning a 132-pound eighteen-year-old into a 152-pound nineteen-year-old. The five-miles-in-fifty-minutes was showing good results. Plus, there was the food and P.X. beer with an occasional candy bar. I could do the 5 miles in 50 minutes without a lot of strain. The workout was to march for 3 minutes, double time 3 minutes, back to march and double time for 50 minutes.

The light tanks were newer and faster. I was officially the gunner.

This letter had to be good for a family discussion. It would remain to be seen about the furlough in November.

Letter #34: postmarked November 10, 1943

Hi! Dick,

Boy! It's been a long time since I have heard from you, I was glad to get your letter.

You must have really used a super sales talk on that McFarland kid to get 10 dollars out of my bike. If you can find anything else of mine to sell like that just go right ahead.

You'll probably end up buying a car like I did!!

Mother said you were passing up some school dances. Take it from me you're crazy if you do.

It is raining cats & dogs and the lights are starting to flicker so I will quit now.

Walter

P.S.-Have been on maneuver problem since Tuesday. Go out again Mon. and stay till Thur, then go out Fri & Sat. We are going to spend 23 out of next 25 days in the field.

P.S. II This does not affect furlough.

P.S. III Tell Bette Davis I said [shorthand notation] and to write.

What a joy that money would have been! My brother now had permission to sell anything of mine. I imagine my parents suggested sending the camera home; the picture developing was costing a fortune.

I had a car, a 1937 Pontiac. When I enlisted in the Army, I sold the car. I'm sure I spent the money.

In the field there was no place to spend $10. I would have made up for that when I got back to camp.

At this time, we were getting lots of field exercises, simulating war scenarios, improving our skills in the tanks, and learning how to work as a team and stay safe. My favorite part of field exercises was getting away from the boring activities like marching. I also really liked it when I got to be the gunner and actually fire the gun. This didn't happen very often. It goes without saying my least favorite part was the pup tent when it rained. Trying to sleep while soaked and floating around was no fun.

Steps in Gunnery Training

FM 17-12 Armored Force Field Manual Tank Gunnery (April 22, 1943) says that gunnery training should be divided into 17 steps: "Insist on a satisfactory standard for each step. Give simple tests to determine proficiency in each step.

a. Basic training period (first fifteen weeks).

(1) Operation and handling of equipment.

(2) Care and maintenance.

(3) Crew drill.

(4) Simulated firing, direct laying.

(5) Range and speed estimation.
(6) Ammunition.
(7) Subcaliber firing, direct laying.
(8) Proficiency test.
(9) Basic firing, direct laying.
b. Unit training period (second twelve weeks).
(1) Platoon drill, direct laying.
(2) Platoon firing, direct laying.
(3) Drill, indirect laying, single tank.
(4) Firing, indirect laying, single tank.
(5) Drill, indirect laying, two or more tanks.
(6) Firing, indirect laying, two or more tanks.
(7) Combat firing of small units.
(8) Combat firing of large units."

It goes on to identify the main problems the instructor should be aware of:
"Gunner.—Accuracy is the principal quality to develop in a gunner. Look for and eliminate the following common faults:
(1) Failure to lay precisely on the target.
(2) Failure to verify the laying for direction and elevation for each round after the breech is closed.
(3) In indirect laying, failure to lay always on the same part of the aiming point or aiming stake.
(4) Failure to take up the lost motion in the traversing and elevating gears when firing at a stationary target.
(5) Failure to bring pointers into exact alignment with index marks when using graduated handwheel or azimuth indicator.
(6) Failure to level bubbles exactly.

Loader (assistant gunner).—The loader wipes off the ammunition with a rag or waste before loading it. Teach him to insert the round smoothly into the breech recess and push the round home with sufficient impetus to seat it in the chamber. Timid loading, caused by fear of getting fingers caught in the breechblock, results in the breech not closing, and may cause a jammed round. A fuzed round must not strike against any portion of the materiel. Hold a round to. be loaded well out of the path of recoil. Loaders always wear gloves to handle the hot cases ejected from the gun."

Hot and dusty, a tank crew stands in front of their M4 medium. This photograph was taken at Fort Knox, KY in June 1942 by Alfred T. Palmer. (Farm Security Administration–Office of War Information photograph collection, Library of Congress)

Gunnery training: on the ranges in M5A1 light tanks. (NARA)

My mom must have thought I could convince Dick to go to school dances. I'm sure her letter to me went something like "Dick doesn't want to go to school dances. I know you liked them. Tell Dick how much fun they are." My response was likely "You're crazy if you don't go." I wonder how helpful this advice was. What I should have said was that dancing isn't always about dancing, which was something I didn't do, and when I did, it wasn't impressive. However, in the summers at Wheeling Park, they put on dances. The dance floor was in the middle and there was a concrete path all around it. You got a couple of buddies and cruised the outside of the dance floor, giving you time to check out the pretty girls. If you got really lucky, some would even spend some time just talking with you.

Dick had a job. Buying a car would surely be on the list. Even as a little boy, he loved cars. Mom told the story how when Dick was just about three years old, he got a picture of a car and buried it. When asked why, he replied, "I'm going to grow myself a car."

Bette Davis (not the actress) was a friend of Dick's from Elm Grove. She was very attractive and really nice. And shorthand? I never took shorthand and what I wrote isn't in any shorthand guides. I'm sure it stands for something nice like "You are very pretty!"

Letter #35: postmarked November 20, 1943

Dear Family,
Forgive me for not writing sooner, but, (to be truthful) I don't feel like writing when I do have time.

Keep your fingers crossed beautiful. I saw my furlough papers today and my furlough is supposed to start on the 26th, which means I will be home (I hope) on the 27th or 28th.

Boy! I'm king for a day!! The company is out in the field and I had to stay back to work on my tank. There is no one to give me any orders and I am living the life of Riley.

I heard someone say there was a couple of inches of snow in Pittsburgh, so I guess it must be the same in Wheeling. It gets plenty cold down here in the morning but about 10 o'clock it gets warm enough to go swimming.

Well! I have some clothes to wash so I will sign off now.
Love
Walter Jr.
P.S. I have just enough money to make it home and that is about all.
P.S. II Will send wine from St. Louis or Columbus.

Keep your fingers crossed, beautiful? Who in my family was I addressing? I wonder if I started the letter to Lenore and then decided to send it to my family instead. I had been away from home for eight months. Furlough sounded really good. To get this opportunity meant I'd spend a whole day getting home by train. It would be a more than 30-hour trip. There were no assigned seats, so if the train was full, I stood. At the next train stop, I watched who was getting off and took their seat before anyone else. The train wouldn't go to Wheeling, West Virginia, more like Columbus, Ohio. From there, I took the B&O rail. Even with all this before me, I really wanted the furlough.

As I wrote this letter home, I told them I was living "the life of Riley," which meant I was having an easy and carefree life with everyone else out in field exercises getting mosquito bites and eating mud. Instead, I stayed back to work on the tank at my leisure. "Taking the gun out of the battery" was what I was doing. To do this, the bolts were released and the cannon pulled inside the tank. Then I put the cannon back together and sighted the barrel. This meant what the gun was aimed at was what you were supposed to target.

Now about the weather commentary in this letter. Yes, Pittsburgh was really close to Wheeling, and I'm sure there could have been November snow. However, the average temperature in Louisiana in November was usually a high of 69 degrees Fahrenheit. Unless there was a heated pool, and there wasn't, this was the only way I'd be swimming.

I stated I was going to work on my tank. Instead, I wrote letters home, dreamed of furlough, and did some laundry.

I think the letter gave a warning to my mom that I'd be needing money once I got home. One wonders how the last postscript was translated at home. My dad was a beer drinker. My mom wasn't a drinker at all. My sister was too young. My brother and I might have shared this bottle if it ever made it home. Remember, 30 hours on a train.

Letter #36: no date

Dear Family,
It doesn't seem like Thanksgiving but Pres. Roosevelt says it is so I'll take his word for it.

I will try and copy the menu for today, boy, it is really a 20-course meal. The stuff they fixed just for today is enough to feed us for a week. I started starving myself last night so I could eat enough today.

I fired the 37 mm yesterday (pardon me, the day before yesterday) and got 6 hits out of 8 shots. Ask dad, that is pretty good!!

I got my furlough canceled again. If I don't leave by the 10th it is going to be too late. I think I will get it for sure on the 5th or 9th of Dec.

There is a buck sergeant in the company is from Barton O., his name is Ballint. I always give him the Sunday paper when I am done.

J. Gilleland is not in my company now. I thought I told you once, but I see him about once a week.

I can't think of a whole lot more to say so I will close now.
Love
Walter Jr.
P.S. I saw my furlough papers made out for the 26th. I guess they tore them up so some reason.

I, the future gunner, got six out of eight! This was done in a light tank which had a 37mm gun. This was cause to strut around the barracks when back from the field.

The turkey dinner left nothing to be desired. The meal came on a plate with everything. An order of gravy on your meal meant even your dessert got gravy. Not exactly appetizing.

The canceled furlough got its fair share of complaining from the group of us who didn't get to go home. I really wanted to be home for Christmas and if the paperwork didn't come through by the 10th, I wasn't going home. It was an arbitrary cancellation of the furlough. Even though I saw the paperwork for my leave, again, I didn't get to go.

It is safe to say I never visited Sergeant Ballint in his hometown of Barton, Ohio. Barton was beyond Bridgeport, where I had lived for three years. Barton was a small mining community at the end of the streetcar line.

Unfortunately for me, not seeing Jimmy meant I didn't get the newspaper from back home. Jimmy Gilleland's story needs to be told. Jimmy—an athlete, a leader, an academic, and one of the most likable persons you would ever want to meet—didn't stay long after basic training. With his natural talent and his background from a military high school, he was quickly offered the opportunity for Officer Candidate School (O.C.S.). Jimmy accepted the offer on the condition it be an infantry O.C.S. and not tanks at Fort Knox. He was off to Fort Benning, Georgia. Later we received word from home that he was killed on his first day in combat in the South Pacific. A true loss. You could bet he would have been somewhere in the lead.

Letter #37: postmarked December 4, 1943

Dear Family,

I, by some strange reason, was picked to stay in camp and work on a tank. The rest of the company (all but 4 men) are on a division problem and will be out in the field till Sunday morning. I am getting that bad habit again of sleeping. It is almost an unknown word in the army.

I have been trying to find some Christmas presents in Leesville but so far I have only gotten one for Mother and Sara. I think I know what I will get for Dick and Daddy. Leesville seems to think the only things soldiers want is junk jewelry and it is hard to find anything else, and when you do it cost twice as much as it should. Down here everything is "new and improved" so they charge 100% more than it is worth.

The furlough question is a thing of the past until Jan. The whole division moves out Dec. 11 for Jasper, Texas and there are to be no passes, furloughs, or leaves until we come back to camp 21 days later. As you can see this includes Christmas!!!

I got a letter from Uncle Howard the other day and I damn near dropped dead. He said Sara made him sit down and write so, thanks Sara for thinking of me.

It's almost time for lights out now so I'll sign off.

Merry Easter

Walter Jr.

P.S. I will probably send the presents before Christmas (around 10th) so do not open until Christmas.

Interesting that I mentioned I'd been sleeping again and strangely I was staying back working on a tank. The two items could have been connected; perhaps I was caught sleeping when I should have been working and now, I was working on a tank. Or maybe the Army thought I was so good at resolving division problems they wanted me back at camp showing those who were left how to work on a tank. I'm picking the latter.

United Services Organization (U.S.O.)

On February 4, 1941, the U.S.O. was incorporated, bringing together six civilian organizations to help military personnel and their families with a range of services including travel information, mobile canteens, and entertainment—the latter being made more exciting after U.S.O. Camp Shows, Inc. was established on October 30, 1941. The first camp show took place at March Field, California with entertainers Bob Hope, Frances Langford, and Jerry Colona. The first on mainland Europe was in July 1944, only a few weeks after the invasion.

With the government building suitable establishments near domestic military camps, the U.S.O. was tasked to raise private funds to pay for itself. The first national campaign chairman, future presidential candidate Thomas Dewey, raised $16 million in the first year. The number of U.S.O. clubs and lounges expanded quickly and reached its peak in March 1944 with 3,035 locations. Mobile U.S.O. units were provided from January 29, 1942, to serve servicemen in training areas, on maneuvers, and in remote locations. At the U.S.O., servicemen could get free donuts and coffee, and attend dances with local young women—all strictly supervised.

The first building actually built for and exclusively used by the U.S.O. was in DeRidder, Louisiana. Constructed in 39 days it opened on November 28, 1941, a day before similar centers opened in Galveston, TX and—according to U.S.O. lore as shown on its website—Fort Bragg, in Fayetteville, NC. Whichever was indeed the first, it was the DeRidder U.S.O. that saw immediate use by personnel from Camp Polk. Shortly afterwards, another center opened in Leesville—this is the one that Walter remembers visiting. These clubs were extremely well frequented. In a July 1943 survey, 82 percent of those questioned visited a U.S.O. club between once and three times a week; 59 percent of them had a club they could visit with 10 miles of their base; and 70 percent were within an hour's travel of a club. As well as the U.S.O., the majority of whose facilities were in the United States, the Red Cross ran clubs in all theaters of war and "Clubmobiles" closer to the front.

The U.S.O. did more than arrange dances. Waiting for trains at the Pennsylvania railroad station—the information booths and servicemen's lounges made a big difference to wartime travel. (Farm Security Administration—Office of War Information photograph collection, Library of Congress)

Leesville had a U.S.O. Always crowded. Not a place to spend a lot of time. Leesville's attractions, as far as soldiers were concerned, were bars, tattoo shops, and stores selling what I identified as "junk jewelry." There were military trucks with the appropriate unit marks to haul back to camp those who hit one too many bars. I can't imagine, with the options that I presented, what Dick and dad's gift might be. Maybe alcohol?

Once more, the furlough went out the window. It was good news that it was not a case of punishment but someone's arbitrary change of plans. I had now missed Easter, my birthday, and would soon miss Christmas at home. This was a big disappointment, and I wasn't the only person who felt this way.

One of the members of my unit got overcome with homesickness and took off. Ironically, he was from West Virginia, too. Word was wired ahead that he was coming and the authorities were waiting for him at the bus station. His plight must have struck a chord with the police because they let him go home and spend the night before putting him back on the bus the next day. Since he came back voluntarily, he was given "company punishment," which meant scrubbing pots and pans for a week.

Uncle Howard writing a letter was hard to believe! He was my father's next youngest brother. A few minutes with Howard left little doubt that the wires were crossed. My mother explained this as Howard having been in an automobile accident where he sustained a head injury.

Howard had been drafted and went into the Army. He was quickly classified as an officer's orderly. In that capacity, he cleaned the officer's quarters and ran general errands. Howard told the story of how he was told to find wood for the fireplace in the Officers' Club. He provided wood by chopping up the "duck boards" (wooden flooring in the showers). He soon received Honorable Discharge for the convenience of the Army. On coming home, he got a job at a defense plant, cleaning the men's restrooms.

Sending home presents on December 10. I can only hope this happened, unlike the promises I made to send my brother a shirt for months on end.

Unnumbered Letter: December 4, 1943 (same as Letter #37)

Dear Dick,

It has been a long time since I have heard from you. I know you're not dead or I could get an emergency furlough.

How is your work going? You don't have Tom Jarrett's job of carrying feed sacks out to cars do you? I thought I was rid of that kind of work but when it came my turn to be K.P. I had to carry 100 lb. flour sacks.

Mother tells me your head mathematician of the neighborhood!! Tell Guy P. that 4 years of math has been very helpful to me, I never use it. I have learned another formula since I have been here, it is called the mil formula. There are 6400 mils in a circle. The formula is: A mil is an angle which subtends a line of one unit at 1000 units. By units they usually mean yards. If you are sighting a gun, if you move it one degree it makes too much of a difference at long ranges so they use mils. (Enough of that B.S.)

Every time I get a letter from mother, she tells me you are in a different car. I hope you are taking in all the dances.

I can't think of any more to say so I will sign off.

Buck private,

Walter

P.S. How is the wrist watch situation????

Interesting that my mother didn't give this a number. I wonder if my brother took it to our room to read and mother found it while cleaning. My brother and I were close. Unlike me, Dick was a good student and he loved cars (still does). I'm sure he was into getting a car, fixing it, and selling it for more than he paid. I'm also sure my explanation of the military formula for indicating distance for firing a cannon was to impress my brother with my newfound knowledge. Mentioned in the letter was Guy P., whose last name was Rollins, the Dean of Boys at Triadelphia High School. Trust me, I never called him Guy P. to his face. He was the math teacher in addition to being Dean.

The director of music, Stephano Ceo, had asked me in study hall if I would like to learn a musical instrument and play in the band. Since I wasn't using study hall for lots of studying, I said yes. I asked for drums. He said he had plenty of those already. He asked me if I would like to play a French horn. I had no idea what a French horn was, but I said yes. Arrangements were made for my instruction on the French horn with the Wheeling Symphony Orchestra French horn player. He came once a week for instruction. Along with a classmate whose last name was Winters, we went to the music room for an hour several times a week to practice the scales. This got boring, so a friendly wrestling match ensued, during which a music stand was knocked over. The noise brought Guy P. from the next room. This marked our last days as French horn students.

Going to school every day was boring. Making some money driving the Royal Crown truck was a better deal, in my opinion. Upon my return to school, I was required to present a written excuse from my father for my absence to Guy P. He would compare the written excuse from home with one he had on file. They matched. Unbeknownst to him or my parents, I had previously written a dozen with my father's signature. My mother found my unused supply in a sock drawer after I left for the service.

Asking about the wrist watch might have been my way of finding out if Dick needed a watch. Leesville had jewelry stores and a watch might have been a good gift. However, upon recently asking my brother, he doesn't remember receiving anything from me, including the promised sweater, shirt, or wrist watch.

Letter #38: postmarked December 24, 1943

Dear Family,

Boy! Am I having a wonderful time. Wish Dad was here (instead of me). It has been below freezing for 2 days now. In the morning the water in your canteen is frozen, so you can imagine what it feels like to get up. We haven't had a fire since 6 o'clock Wed. night. It snowed for about 30 seconds Tue. afternoon, there were flakes as big as quarters.

We leave Texas on the 29th and I expect to get a furlough as soon as we hit camp.

This company is going to the dogs, we have one fellow who has been AWOL since Dec. 9 (now up for desertion and can be sentenced to death), one who came back to camp a day late, and one who is under arrest for knocking an M.P. through a plate glass door.

I got your package from home Wed. Boy! I was never happier to get Christmas presents. I have on one pair of new socks, am using new handkerchiefs, I have a mouth full of chewing gum, I am stuffed full of candy and cake, we had a marshmallow toast, and I hid the cigarettes for future reference.

My hands are about frozen so I will sign off now. Thanks a million for the presents.

Love

Walter Jr.

PS. Last night I walked guard from 12 to 3 and then spent 10 minutes trying to get the lid off my canteen.

My first Christmas away from home. I was in Jasper, Texas, on field exercise. This was about an hour away from Camp Polk and sat on the border of Texas and Louisiana. The letter described a weather event, snow, not really typical of this area. However, low temperatures in the 30s with a brisk breeze was typical, thus leading to frozen canteens.

Obviously, there were those who couldn't wait for a furlough. Again, the Army rumors around camp included someone who could be sentenced to death and a soldier in military prison. I didn't witness or know either individual, but it sure did make for an exciting letter. I'm sure my mother skipped this part when sharing the letter with the family.

The Christmas package did not last long. One should note there was no mention of having help with the consumption of the contents. I imagine lots of us were getting packages, so I was able to hide my cigarettes in a musette bag, the only hiding place for something small while out in the field.

It was on this maneuver in Texas that I had my first cup of coffee. I told my crew if I couldn't drink it, I would put it in my helmet and stick my feet in it to warm up. Ample sugar and milk with minimum coffee made it drinkable. While the Army had issued winter attire, i.e., long johns, heavy socks, wool uniform, and winter coat that stopped at the waist, it wasn't enough to keep you warm outside in freezing weather.

My postscript shows I learned an early lesson: no sleeping while on guard. Along with my canteen, I was frozen.

Letter #39: postmarked December 25, 1943

Dear Family,

Talk about changeable weather!!!! Today you couldn't ask for anything better, it is nice and warm, no breeze, and for a while nothing to do!

Yesterday we had a break. We wash fatigue clothes, cleaned the tank and guns, and got a few hours sleep. I went in town for about 2 hours and had to walk 5 miles to get there.

Gen. Grimes (Div. C.O.) said we must leave Texas by the 29th to make room for some other division. Everyone has his fingers crossed hoping we go back to camp.

In case I haven't told you before: I am a gunner now! My tank commander is Sgt. Prussia from Neb., he volunteered for air corps and is waiting for the C.O. to sign his papers. The driver is Corp. Simpson, he is from Boston and his family had money, he thinks we should all wait on him. The assistant driver (McKinney) is from Kansas City his dad is a reporter for the *Kansas City Star*, he and I get along swell.

I am hoping for the best but it looks like rain again.

Well! I'm run down again so Merry Christmas and Happy New Year.

Love

Walter

Oh, the difference a day can make. The weather was now nice and warm. The Army gave us a break. Mark this down because it didn't happen very often. Of course, the break included washing your fatigues and cleaning a tank. The nice part was I could even sleep a little. This was probably why I felt energetic enough to walk five miles into Jasper and hang out for a couple of hours. It was like any little town, five and dime stores to buy essentials, like a candy bar for the trip back to the field.

With General Grimes, the division commander, talk of leaving Jasper, Texas, by the 29th came with some interpretation. Did he mean we were going on maneuvers somewhere else? Or was it that we would be leaving the States to enter the war? All of us, myself included, hoped for a return to Camp Polk.

By this time, I'd only told the family I was a gunner about a dozen times. What is interesting is my listing of the people in my tank. Every tank I was in had a loader, but there was no mention of a loader. So how would I have practiced using the gun if there was no loader? In addition, I added a new position of assistant driver. McKinney was a bow gunner but was called upon to drive, as well. It goes without saying that I didn't come from money and wasn't impressed with those who felt the need to tell you they did and then expected me to wait on them. Didn't happen with me.

I learned a lesson on this exercise. Weather could change from beautiful to soggy, making earlier decisions dangerous. Don't sleep under a tank when it rains! Tanks are heavy, the ground gets soft, tanks sink down, rolling over reveals that you best get out while you can. Get in the tank and close the hatch. No rain.

Letter #40: postmarked January 10, 1944

Dear Family,

No! I'm not dead yet but they are trying awful hard to work me to death. We have been fixing guns every day. This morning, we got up at 4 o'clock and went out to fire the 37 mm. My average so far is 80. On the first exercise I got 60 and on the next one I got 100 so I'm not doing bad so far.

I was really lucky getting seats on the trains. As strange as it may seem I had a seat all the way back. I got in camp at 8 o'clock Tue. night.

We are going on maneuvers the first of the month and boy! There are a million things to do. We have to send all personal belongings home so you can expect a package anytime.

There's not very much excitement around here now and I can't think of much to say. I would have written sooner but I spent 2 nights in the field and was too busy the other nights.

I have to quit now mostly because I'm out of words but they are turning out the lights besides.
Love
Walter Jr.
P.S. I got the package Thursday. Thanks a million.

The furlough happened! A bus took me from camp to Leesville. There, I hopped the train. Riding the train home was sometimes a test of how long you could stand up. The ride home was 36 hours, ample excuse to complain about having less time at home. My furlough lasted 12 days. My complaint to the first sergeant was that everyone else got 14 days. His response was "Take it or leave it." An easy choice.

Furlough and Leave

In Army parlance of the time, there were three types of time off:
- A pass was an authorized leave of absence from military duties for up to three days.
- Furlough was an authorized vacation from military duty for longer than three days for an enlisted soldier.
- Leave was the same as furlough but for officers.

Understandably, young men—many spending their first extended period away from home—thought a lot about time off. As can be seen from Walter's experience, he did get a furlough home, although it was some time coming and for the first time in his life, he had to spend Christmas away from home.

Once units moved overseas, time away from a unit became more of an issue. Following the declaration of war, the length of service changed to the duration of the war plus six months. Many servicemen would spend more than a year away from home without returning; some over three.

There were many reasons why a furlough home to the United States wasn't possible: the high cost of bringing men back from overseas; there were never enough available transport aircraft; and the combat arms couldn't spare the men. Casualty figures led to shortages of front-line infantrymen and the replacement system couldn't adequately cover this, leading to the granting of even emergency leaves and furloughs being very restricted. Some individuals were allowed to return to the U.S. on temporary duty for rehabilitation, recuperation, and recovery, the criteria were very strict.

To compensate for this, centers were organized in Great Britain before the invasion—cities or other localities specifically set aside for military personnel on leave, furlough, or pass. Additionally, recreational areas were established. Both were handled by the Red Cross. In Great Britain, they included 42,555 bed spaces, mainly in London. Because of the imminent invasion, authority to grant leaves and furloughs in excess of 24 hours was cancelled in April 1944 and this edict remained in force till August 17, although even then troops on the Continent weren't allowed to return to Britain. From September 4 the army commanders of 12th (U.S.) Army Group were authorized to place cities and towns on limits for 48-hour passes. Paris was the first large leave center opened and was used by those with passes from October 22, 1944. The first proper leaves and furloughs for combat troops on the Continent—of seven days' duration plus travel—were only granted from January 1945.

However, unit rest areas were set up for use by troops rotated out of the front line for rest and relaxation. The unit commanders selected who would go and preference was given to those who had been in combat the longest, or those whose physical and nervous condition made rest desirable. Duration was usually 72 hours. Facilities of the larger rest areas included billets in requisitioned hotels, mess halls with waitresses and music, theaters for films or stage shows, Red Cross clubs, postal facilities, P.X., clothing exchanges, ordnance shops for weapon reconditioning, financial offices, chaplains, and recreation halls for dances with locals. Smaller rest areas might only have clothing exchanges, hot baths, and warm meals.

I spent 10 days with a few friends who were not in the service. I visited the Megahans, the parents of my best friend Bill, who was in the Marines. I took advantage of sleeping past 5:30 a.m. I let my mom do my wash. She prepared and cooked me three meals a day. There were cookies I only had to share with my family and not 50 other men. I hung out with my brother and borrowed his car for trips to local hang outs. My dad took me to one of the hang outs and bragged about my service record as a gunner. I joined my mom and siblings for Sunday service at St. Mark Lutheran Church, surviving the four-minute walk up the street in winter weather. St. Mark's gave me a pocket-size notebook I carried throughout my time in the service. This break was what I needed.

I asked my siblings recently what they remembered of my furlough. My brother said he didn't remember anything about it. My sister's comment was that I went out with friends a lot. Beer-drinking buddies, I'm sure.

"Working me to death"—I just came back from a life of leisure and doing whatever I wanted to do. I had to adjust to a set get-up time and lots of orders. I spent time in the field and was too busy other days to write. Too busy? Probably the P.X. and a beer was how I was keeping myself occupied.

Sending home all personal belongings was in preparation for going overseas, although this was not communicated to the troops. All we were left with was Army-issued items. You know, those fine olive drab clothes.

My mother saved and numbered the letters I sent home during my time in the service. She put them all into this box. I didn't see them until my daughter discovered them. I had to laugh. No 18-year-old writes home and tells his family what he is really doing.

These pictures were taken outside my barracks at Camp Polk. While relaxing on the steps, I think I might be out of uniform with the rings on my fingers. I wonder if I was allowed to wear them on duty. The middle picture shows what looks like a shirt hanging out of a window. I'm not sure this would have passed inspection. The picture on the right shows what I would have worn for going off base or in parades.

Ruth Crickenberger Stitt, my mom.

My dad, my mom, and my dad's siblings. Left to right: Dad, Mom, Herbert, Mildred, Edward, and Howard.

My mom's sisters. Birth order: Hattie, Marie (not pictured), Helen, Mom, Virginia, Margaret.

Mama Cricky, Ida Payne Crickenberger, my mother's mom. She was loved by everyone. She was considered the sweetest woman ever.

My paternal grandfather, Charles Lewis Stitt. We lived with Granddaddy in Bridgeport, Ohio. He was a generous man who gave mush and coffee to anyone who knocked on the door for food.

Me (left), my sister Sara (center), and my brother Dick (right).

The bracelet I sent my sister from England in 1945. I promised to get her a bracelet in one of my letters home dated April 1943.

Bill Megahan, my best friend, and me in front of his house. Bill joined the Marines and was sent to the Pacific Theater. While serving in Saipan, Bill was point man for the day, which meant he was in the lead. He was shot by a Japanese sniper. His fellow soldiers told the family he died instantly.

These pictures were taken in Leesville when I was part of the 8th Armored Division. I thought my mom had given these away.

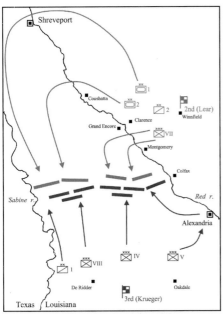

This is an example of the maneuvers in the Sabine Forest. I signed the letter sent around this time as "Blue Stitt Army." (Citino, 2017)

Advance to Contact: Louisiana Maneuvers, 15-16 Sep 1941

The KP badge that let me wander all over the *Queen Elizabeth*.

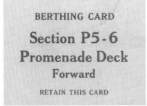

BERTHING CARD

Section P5-6
Promenade Deck
Forward

RETAIN THIS CARD

MESSING CARD

MESS A HALL

1 SECTION

FIRST MEAL 6.30 a.m.
SECOND MEAL 3.30 p.m.

MESSING CARD

MESS A HALL

2 SECTION

FIRST MEAL 8.00 a.m.
SECOND MEAL 5.00 p.m.

Berthing and Messing cards for the *Queen Elizabeth*.

My Aunt Hattie felt I would be protected with this Saint Christopher medal, the patron saint of travel. It must have helped; I made it home, though I was wounded twice.

This was German money during World War II. I gave one like this to a fellow wanting a souvenir, and in return, he gave me a carton of cigarettes. I made out on this deal. The wheelbarrow full of this money didn't amount to much.

This was in England in 1945, shortly before I came home. Behind us are men sitting around outside our Quonset huts (living quarters).

This is a picture of the enlisted men's beer hall manager. Having a G.I. cut was no longer necessary. The wheelbarrow was used to bring the kegs from the train up to the beer hall. I faithfully tested all kegs before serving them to the men.

This picture was taken in the backyard at my house in 1945. I was finally home from the war.

Here, I am posing with my brother, Dick. He was stationed at Camp Atterbury in Indiana. After the war, they shut down the camp. Dick and his fellow soldiers were responsible for moving equipment to Fort Indiantown Gap.

These pictures show the bricks and 95th Bomb Group memorial statue at Wright Patterson Air Force Base.

I received the French Legion Honor medal for my service to France.

Walt today.

CHAPTER 3

Honing Skills

Camp Polk to England, January 1944–May 1944

Letter #41: postmarked January 24, 1944[1]

Dear Family,

I am really busy but I will try to write a few lines.

We are moving out of the barracks tomorrow but we won't go out in the field 'til the 1st or 2nd.

Did you get the notice of my address change? It is the maneuver address.

I decided not to buy a sleeping bag. If I change my mind later I will send the money home.

Do you remember the wart I had on my left forearm? I went to the hospital and had it burned out with an electric needle. They gave me a shot in the arm first and it killed most of the pain. When he touched me with the needle and made contact I jumped about 2 foot in the air, mostly from being scared!! They used a needle shaped like this fine wire, plastic handle, and cord and made a cut something like this arm, wart, cut. In civilian life it would probably cost 5 dollars to turn on the machine. They gave the shot, cut and bandaged my arm in less than 5 minutes!!

I am going to send my camera home as soon as possible!!

I am running down now…

Love

Walter Jr.

P.S. (1) Received the package in good condition.

(2) Got seat(s) on train(s).

(3) Tell whoever you are supposed to on the Triadelphian staff that my address was changed.

My address for this letter changed. The envelope contained the same address for the first 40 letters: Pvt. Walter Stitt, Co. D. 80th TK. BN., ASN (my service number), North Camp Polk, Louisiana. If my family didn't get the new address, I'd be out on maneuvers and too busy to get it. It might have been better if I had just gone ahead and gave it to the family. The third postscript relates to the fact that Triadelphia High School attempted to keep track of former students in the service.

---

[1] The letter states I wrote it on January 30, 1944. Either I forgot the date with all the time in the field or my mother put it in the wrong envelope.

I'd just sent everything home. I didn't have a sleeping bag and decided I didn't need one. Sleeping was done inside the tank while sitting up or occasionally in a pup tent using our Army-issued olive drab blankets outside on the ground. Though I sent everything but Army-issued items home, that didn't include the camera, which certainly wasn't issued by the Army. I still had it. It wouldn't have fit in my musette bag. I guess the Army inspection didn't cover my foot locker. I really wonder if I ever sent home the camera. Knowing my desire for money, I might have thought about selling it.

Getting the wart removed made for a good story home. I even included drawings so everyone would have a good idea of the experience. Having the Army pay to cover medical needs was a bonus. I sort of think this whole section could have started with "I Can't Think of Things to Write."

The Louisiana Maneuvers

Between December 1943 and April 1944 Walter spent much of his time training in the field. There were two specific periods: the "D" Series of exercises in December followed by the Louisiana Maneuvers proper that lasted from February 7 to April 3.

This was the final iteration of the maneuvers of which the first two—those of 1940 and particularly 1941—are the best known. The 1940 Maneuvers took place in spring and fall 1940 and provided a stark message: the U.S. Army needed to train more for motorized warfare. In particular, its command procedures weren't effective, and overall, U.S. armored forces were inadequate. The autumn maneuvers highlighted the poor training of the National Guard troops and the desperate need for modern equipment.

There were maneuvers in Louisiana in June, August, and September 1941—the latter involving Second and Third Army saw half a million soldiers in nearly 20 divisions test a range of tactics and concepts from the use of tank destroyers to the new C-ration. Most important to the future U.S. Army's performance in combat, the maneuvers also tested leaders. Of the 42 field commanders in the 1941 maneuvers, U.S. Army Chief of Staff General George C. Marshall sidelined as many as 31 to make way for a swathe of younger men including Omar Bradley, Joseph Stilwell, Mark Clark, and the brightest successes in 1941—George Patton and Lesley McNair. There were three further maneuvers in 1942 involving the divisions of VIII, IV, and IX Corps. During 1942, and to a considerable extent thereafter, McNair gave priority to the training of divisions, which were seen as the ideal team.

1943 saw Third Army exercising five times before the 1944 Louisiana Maneuvers (in which Walter took part) involved the divisions of Fourth Army. They were the last of the maneuvers. After them 8th Armored spent nearly a month more in the field for maintenance and learning lessons from the maneuvers before finally returning to Camp Polk.

"Blue" tanks, supported by cavalry, advance in downpour of rain during Third Army maneuvers in Louisiana, 1942. (NARA)

While the troops maneuvered, the Army had to sort out the logistics. Important lessons were learnt. This is Third Army in 1942. (Library of Congress)

The Second Letter #42: postmarked February 1, 1944[2]

Dear Family,

Well, this is my last day in garrison after tomorrow noon I am a field soldier.

Boy! We have done nothing for 2 days but scrub and mop. The place really shines.

The next division to move in here is going to be the 9th Armored. That is the one H. Winters, and that Yarling boy are in. So far, I haven't had a chance to see either one of them.

The weather down here has been swell since I came back. It has rained several days but most of the time it is nice and warm. The nights get a little cool though.

I was just sorting out some old letters I have and I came across one from Vince Ream and Mae Kidd. See if you can get their addresses for me and I will try to find time to write them.

The 1st sgt. just came through and found some more work for me so I will quit trying to write for now.

Love

Walter Jr.

P.S. My watch stopped again?!!!!

"Last day in the garrison" meant leaving Camp Polk for some remote desolate area in Louisiana to get more practice with the tanks. The nearest major city was Shreveport, where our mail would be delivered. The envelope listed my new address: Pvt. Walter Stitt, Co. D., 80th TK BN, APO 258 Postmaster, Shreveport, LA.[3]

I had to answer a roll call with my number. The man in charge would say "Stitt" and my reply would be my service number.

A funny thing, years later while filling out paperwork for the U.S. Department of Veterans Affairs, I couldn't remember that number. I had to call my sister, who knew the number by heart. She had memorized it when I enlisted. Over 70 years later, she still knew my Army number.

Riding in the tank, we headed to the Sabine National Forest.

A field soldier was still in the tank. I was still the gunner in a light tank with five crew members. The tank was cozy or, you could say, cramped. For this exercise, no live ammunition was used.

H. Winters was Howard. Three years older than me, but a friend of years standing. As civilians, Howard drove a route for Coca-Cola and I did the same for Royal Crown. When we met on rare occasions, we loved comparing notes on customers we shared. Bill Yarling and Vince Ream were high school classmates. Even if mother was able to get addresses for these friends, the chances of me writing them a letter was slim at best.

---

[2] This letter was received before the next letter, also numbered 42.

[3] An explanation of this address is as follows: PVT = Private and my name; The number is my Army issued number.; Co.—Company; D.—was the unit number; 80th—Regiment; TK BN—Tank Battalion; APO—Army Post Office; 258—8th Armored Division.

Mac Kidd lived down the street from Lee Winters, and we ran around in high school. Mac joined the Air Corps. Our paths crossed towards the end of war when I was working in the P.X. while serving in England.

The first sergeant came through. My watch stopped working. Sitting around writing letters must have made it appear as though I needed something more productive to do for the Army. Or was it that I was given a break of 20 minutes? My watch stopped and I had no idea I had taken a 30-minute break. I imagine my mother was telling the family, "We need to get Walter Jr. a watch."

The First Letter #42: postmarked January 30, 1944

This is the bulletin I promised to send home to my family in May 1943. I had (have) a tendency to save things, intending to send them home. When we were ordered to send home all civilian items, this came from the bottom of

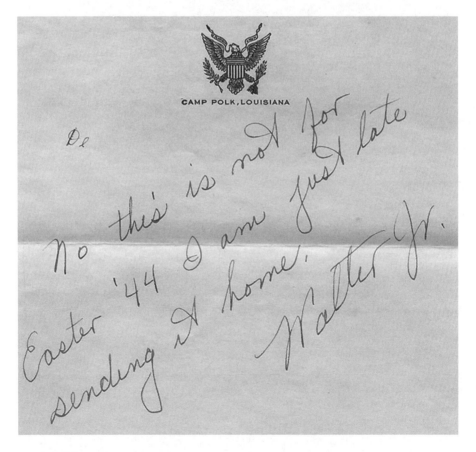

Easter

SUNDAY, APRIL 25, 1943

8th Armored Division, North Camp Polk, La.
Major General William M. Grimes, Commanding

Easter Field Service

8th ARMORED DIVISION

Division Bowl

April 25, 1943

Catholic Easter Services

Church Parade—0830—36th and 80th Armored Regt. Bands

Solemn Easter Mass 0915

Celebrant _____ Chaplain Edmund P. Kielty
Deacon _____ Chaplain Martin J. Diamond
Subdeacon _____ Chaplain Clement J. White
Master of Ceremonies _____ Chaplain Ladislaus A. Polewski
Sermon by — Chaplain Ladislaus A. Polewski
"Missa de Angelis" sung by the Schola Cantorum of the
11th Armored Division

Protestant Easter Service

Church Parade—1000—36th and 80th Armored Regt. Bands

Service 1045

Organ Prelude "Christus Resurrexit" Ravanello—
Sgt. Paul McKnight
Doxology
Praise God from whom all blessings flow;
Praise Him, all creatures here below;
Praise Him above, ye heavenly host;
Praise Father, Son, and Holy Ghost.   Amen.
Invocation _____ Chaplain Fredric Witmer

Hymn "All Hail the Power of Jesus' Name"

All hail the power of Jesus' name!
Let angels prostrate fall;
Bring forth the royal diadem,
And crown Him Lord of all,
Bring forth the royal diadem,
And crown Him Lord of all.

Let every kindred, every tribe,
On this terrestrial ball,
To Him all majesty ascribe,
And crown Him Lord of all,
To Him all majesty ascribe,
And crown Him Lord of all.

O that with yonder sacred throng,
We at His feet may fall;
We'll join the everlasting song,
And crown Him Lord of all,
We'll join the everlasting song,
And crown Him Lord of all.

Morning Prayer _____ Chaplain Wilbur K. Anderson

Responsive Reading _____ Chaplain Milton A. May

O sing unto the Lord a new song;
For He hath done marvelous things.
**His right hand, and his holy arm
hath gotten Him the victory**
The Lord hath made known His salvation;
**His righteousness hath He openly
showed in sight of the heathen.**
He hath remembered His mercy and His
truth toward the house of Israel.
**All the ends of the earth have
seen the salvation of our God.**
Make a joyful noise unto the Lord, all the earth:
Make a loud noise, and rejoice, and sing praise.
Let the sea roar, and the fullness thereof:
The world, and they that dwell therein.
Let the floods clap their hands, let the
hills be joyful together before the Lord.
For He cometh to judge the earth.
With righteousness shall He judge the world.
And the people with equity.

Vocal Solo — ..The Heavenly Resound" — Beethoven —
Pvt. Harry Clarke

Easter Gospel _____ Chaplain Willis H. Kimzey

Confession of Faith (in unison) ____ Chaplain Gerald Ramaker

I believe in God the Father Almighty, Maker of heaven
and earth: and in Jesus Christ His only Son, our Lord; Who
was conceived by the Holy Ghost; born of the Virgin Mary,
suffered under Pontius Pilate, was crucified, dead, and buried
He descended into hell; the third day He rose again from the
dead; He ascended into heaven and sitteth upon the right hand
of God the Father Almighty; from thence He shall come to
judge the quick and the dead. I believe in the Holy Ghost; the
holy catholic church; the communion of saints; the forgiveness
of sins; the resurrection of the body; and the life everlasting.
Amen.

Anthem "Christ the Lord is Risen Today" Traditional Chorale
8th Armored Division Choir—T/5 Robert F. Olson, Dir.

Sermon "The Resurrection Morn" Chap. Vaughn H. MacArthur

Closing Prayer _____ Chaplain John E. Batterson

Hymn "Fairest Lord Jesus"

Fairest Lord Jesus,
Ruler of all nature,
O Thou of God and man the Son;
Thee will I cherish,
Thee will I honor,
Thou, my soul's glory, joy,
  and crown.

Fair are the meadows,
Fairer still the woodlands,
Robed in the blooming garb of
  spring;
Jesus is fairer,
Jesus is purer,
Who makes the woeful heart
  to sing.

Fair is the sunshine,
Fairer still the moonlight,
And all the twinkling, starry host;
Jesus shines brighter,
Jesus shines purer
Than all the angels heaven can boast.
Amen.

Benediction _____ Chaplain Thomas K. Spande

Recessional—"Onward Christian Soldiers."

SERVICES HELD REGULARLY IN DIVISION CHAPELS

Protestant

Headquarters and Artillery Chapel

Chaplains Kimzey and May _____	Morning Worship	10:00 A.M.
Chaplain Kimzey _____	Fellowship Service	7:30 P.M.

36th Armored Regiment Chapel

Chaplain Anderson _____	Morning Worship	10:00—11:00 A.M.
Chaplain Anderson _____	Fellowship Service	6:30 P.M.

80th Armored Regiment Chapel

Chaplain Witmer _____	Morning Worship	9:00—11:00 A.M.

49th Armored Infantry Regiment Chapel

Chaplain Spande _____	Morning Worship	10:00 A.M.
Chaplain Spande _____	Fellowship Service	6:30 P.M.

Engineers and Reconnaissance Chapel

Chaplain Batterson _____	Morning Worship	9:00—11:00 A.M.
Chaplain Batterson _____	Fellowship Service	7:00 P.M.

Division Trains Chapel

Chaplain Ramaker _____	Morning Worship	10:00 A.M.
Chaplain Ramaker _____	Fellowship Service	7:00 P.M.

Catholic

Hq. and Artillery Chapel	49th Arm'd Inf. Reg't Chapel
Chaplain Polewski 9:00 A.M.	Chaplain Kielty 8:00—11:00 A.M.
36th Arm'd Reg't Chapel	Engineers and Rcn. Chapel
Chaplain White 8:00— 9:00 A.M.	Chaplain Polewski 8:00—10:00 A.M.
80th Arm'd Reg't Chapel	Division Trains Chapel
Chaplain Diamond 8:00—10:00 A.M.	Chaplain White 11:00 A.M.

Jewish

Every Tuesday evening   Headquarters and Artillery Chapel   7:30 P.M.

the foot locker. My mother, a Lutheran minister's daughter, would have been happy to know I attended Easter services even though I didn't send it home until almost a year later.

As you can tell from the bulletin, I attended the Protestant service. The Army provided a Catholic service, a Protestant service, and a Jewish service. While there were people of different faiths, the Army saw fit to provide religious services for what they perceived most soldiers to be.

Looking over the bulletin, you'll see that for Protestants, there were many opportunities to worship, fewer for the Catholics, and one for those of Jewish faith. An example of the enlisted men's thinking regarding religion is the story of the commander of the 3rd Armored Division (the one I was assigned to during the war). General Rose was raised Jewish. Yet on his paperwork for the Army, he listed Protestant. The speculation was that listing this popular religion might help him increase his rank within the Army.

General Rose was riding in a jeep on March 30, 1944, in Paderborn, Germany, when he and his driver encountered Germans. Told to put their hands up, Rose thought he was told to drop his gun. When he went to his holster the Germans shot and killed him. His driver and a rider escaped to report the general's death. Rose was buried in a military cemetery; a Christian cross was placed on his grave site. When his family found out, they ordered a Jewish Star of David to mark his grave. The Army and the family had quite a battle over his grave marker, which to this day, remains a Christian cross.

I was familiar with all the hymns listed in the bulletin, but it is safe to assume I didn't join the choir.

Letter #43: postmarked February 6, 1944

Dear Family,
Well: Here is my first letter from the field!

Last night we had a real rain but for some strange reason my tent didn't leak.

We haven't done much of anything for the last 2 days and we have had time to wash clothes and sleep.

They are offering of prize of more than $25 and a furlough to the tank crew which does the best maintenance on maneuvers. Our crew is trying hard and keeping our fingers crossed.

We just had a softball game the team I was on lost in the last inning.

We have a new company commander now, Lt. Oles. He is from West Virginia (Grantsville I think). He is a lot easier on us than Capt. Burr was, and everybody likes him. He is like Capt. Rosser he plays ball with us and sits around the fire and talks. Capt. Burr still sneaks around once in a while though, and when I say sneak, I mean just that.

Well: I have to go to a lecture on malarial control so…. Please pardon the pen.

Love
Walter Jr.

P.S. See if you can get a knife from Mr. Johnston, I will pay for it.

My tent didn't leak. I finally mastered putting together a tent and avoiding touching the sides. How nice it was to sleep while the rain stayed out. I found it interesting that every time there was downtime in the Army, something must get washed. In this letter, it is my clothes. Another time, a tank. And of course, downtime wasn't complete without the all-important time to sleep.

I don't believe the Army was going to randomly give $25 away, much less a furlough to a crew. I suspect this was said for motivation purposes and not at all possible. Not to mention, how would they measure this prize? Our tanks were always ready and cleaned when starting out on a maneuver. However, if there was any chance it was true, I'm sure my crew wanted it.

As for Captain Burr, he thought he was a detective. He was in constant search to find soldiers doing things they shouldn't be doing. The rest of the group and I found him to be annoying, while the opposite was true of Lieutenant Oles. I'm sure part of it was his upbringing in good old West Virginia. He was raised in Grantsville, a small town where everyone most likely knew everyone. It would have been considered good manners to be friendly, even if the soldiers were under his supervision. Putting on airs of being better than someone else would have been frowned upon by his town folk.

The malarial control lecture was in case the group got sent to the South Pacific. This lecture wasn't as nearly interesting as the movie and subsequent lecture on syphilis.

Why Mister Johnson, a retired mine electrician, would have a knife will remain a mystery.

Letter #44: postmarked February 8, 1944

Dear Family,
Well: Three minutes from now maneuvers start. We will go for ten days on what they call flag maneuvers. After that we will fight other divisions. There are 3 divisions maneuvering in La now at one time. They are 8th (Armored) [44]th (Infantry) and [92nd] (Colored Div.)[4] We will maneuver against one another.

My time is up now. The "situation is tactical" we have to wear gas mask, helmets, and carry tommy guns at all times (except when sleeping).

Boy! The weather so far has been swell!!! You couldn't ask for any better. It rained for about a half hour last night but this afternoon it was really warm as a matter of fact I am getting a suntan.

Our new C.O. is really swell. Yesterday and today he was playing softball with us. He takes off all bars and raises Cain the same as the rest. Capt. Burr came around looking for him (C.O.) and when he saw him on first base the Capt. looked about half mad. It may seem strange but since we changed C.O.s we are getting more work done.

[4] Walt's original letter mistakenly identified the 95th Infantry and 44th Infantry Divisions.

I can't write for too long because I have too much to do so I will sign off now.
Love
Walter Jr.
P.S. I boiled my clothes (underwear) in Lux and rinsed them in cold water but they didn't get too clean. Does borax or something like that make them cleaner????
P.S. II Please pardon pencil!!

I referred to the 92th Division as "colored", a reflection of norms at the time. At that point, there was segregation in the Army. Thankfully, things changed after World War II, with the army desegregated in 1948. My language has evolved alongside the armed forces, and the country as a whole.

I was going to be inside a tank simulating combat. I would be wearing ear phones so I could hear my tank commander. The rest of the gear would only be worn outside the tank. There was no real ammo in the tommy guns. How dramatic the letter makes it sound!

The important part of this exercise was to execute your assignment at your highest level. There were observers recording what you did and how well you performed. I'm sure the Army officers then used this information to decide what needed practice when we returned to camp.

It seems that the company commander knew how to get the best out of his company. Treat people with respect and earn respect in turn. The attitude that we are all in this together proved to be very motivating for our company.

My parents must have been thrilled to know my underwear didn't get cleaned. When the Army didn't have anything for you to do, cleaning your clothes seemed to be the assigned task.

This letterhead contained the "WBS," meaning my mom sent me more of my dad's business stationery. The P.S. could also read as "Please send me a pen."

Letter #45: postmarked February 18, 1944

Dear Family,
I received your package today. WE (meaning about 50 other guys) enjoy the cookies. I am hoarding the candy and gum. Cpl. Simpson (John for short) got some candy from his aunt (not ant) so we are well supplied, for a couple days.

We have just finished what is called flag maneuvers and are on a break. On the 19th the two-sided maneuvers really start, and there are going to be plenty of bloody battles. I've got myself a pick handle for protection.

Two nights ago, I went through the most miserable night I ever spent in the army. We pulled into an area about 9 o'clock, just after dark and it was badly raining. After staying around for about an hour, just long enough to dig slit trenches and camouflage the tank, the order came to move out. We only moved 20 yards before we were stuck and were only stuck 2 times after that. By this time, I was fairly wet. When we finally reach some solid ground, we drive for about an hour at 4 miles an hour. Finally, they decided to stop and have supper it was 12 o'clock then. At one o'clock the order came that we could go to bed. It had stopped raining but was plenty cold. I was so tired I threw my blankets on the tarp and went to sleep. About 2:30 it started to rain and by 3:00 I was practicing my lifesaving. We weren't allowed to build fires and there was no place to change clothes. (We could use the tank for a bath tub.) Later on, that day we built fires, and I rang out my blankets and dried them. In spite of all my troubles I guess I'll live.

Well! It's time for bed now so I'll sign off.

Love

Walter Jr.

P.S. Get me Keith's address.

P.S. II Can anyone spare $5.00??!!!!

We were out in the field. I borrowed a pen and wrote this letter. We had cookies, candy, and gum. One of my tank crew also had candy! Life in the field didn't get any better than this, except for the rain.

Maneuvers would start in two days. It was going to be bloody, in a simulated manner. I didn't have a pick handle. I know this because where in the world would I have gotten one in the middle of the Sabine National Forest? I don't think the P.X. was selling pick handles for protection.

The tank getting stuck was more like it was sliding in the mud and couldn't get traction to move forward. If you were lucky, there would be another tank that the stuck one could hook a cable to and get pulled out. If this didn't work, putting something behind or in front of the tracks for it to roll over could work, too.

Time was spent digging a slit trench (a toilet to straddle, shovel wide and several feet deep) and breaking off pine branches to camouflage the tank. We moved down the road and repeated the toilet process. Being too tired to care meant I ended up swimming by morning inside a wet blanket. I didn't want to sleep in the tank because I couldn't spread out. One wonders about my logic.

Tanks used in this simulation had a tarp that could be used to cover the tank. It was located off the back. Seems like we could have used the tarp as cover for us and thus avoided the rain. I'm also sure we didn't leave the hatch open so the tank could fill up with water like a bathtub. More of my humor.

Keith Linton was another classmate and friend. Keith's dad, a World War I soldier in Europe, owned a dry-cleaning shop. Keith and I worked for his dad soliciting dry cleaning. We'd go house to house to see if anyone had anything they wanted dry cleaned.

Now Wheeling had bordellos in a four-block area. Keith's dad did their laundry. He had an older gentleman who delivered to them. The man went on vacation. Keith and I went into the shop to pick up the laundry to return to the customers. When we reached for the returns for the ladies of the night,

Keith's dad said, "Whoa. No, put that down." After he thought for a minute, he realized there was no one else to do the delivery. He reluctantly agreed we could make the delivery but there was to be no trading for services. So off we went. When we gave the laundry to the madam in charge, she was not happy with how the dress was hanging. She said it wasn't right. We disagreed. She looked at us and said I'll show you it isn't right. She took off her clothes, stood naked in front of us and proceeded to put on the dress. I can't remember if it hung straight or not. I was a teenager, and a woman was naked in front of me. I think we got our payment, and I know we got more than we expected.

I didn't get rich doing this job, but I learned a lot. It gave me skills I used later in life as a salesman.

Keith was also my ride to school in the Model A his dad bought for him for $75. If I decided to go to school and got to his house in time, I could hitch a ride. The other advantage of having a friend with a car was we had an hour for lunch. We'd hop in his car and go down to the pool hall. We'd shoot a game of pool while downing a cold beer. I have no idea why I wanted his address or if he was even back home or enlisted.

I was going to need $5 in a week? Why? Lost the cigarettes in the rain? Some questions will never be answered. Now the chances of me getting money from my dad were slim to none. My mom was a different story.

My mom had been a school teacher in El Paso, Texas. She was living with her older sister, Marie, who had tuberculosis. There was no cure and the thought was that warmer weather would help. She taught until Marie passed, then returned home and married my dad.

She never worked outside the home again; however, she did manage to open a bank account and save money. As my father would prepare to leave for work, mom would ask him for money to buy a loaf of bread and a bottle of milk, something like 83 cents. Dad wouldn't know what was needed or how much it would cost. So very reluctantly and with much vocalization, he replied, "Oh Hell, money, money, money. How much do you need?" Reaching deep in his pocket for change, he would count out the exact amount she needed then storm out the door. Mom would have asked for twice what she needed. The extra went into her bank account. If $5 was coming, my mom was providing.

Letter #46: postmarked February 27, 1944

Dear Family,
I don't know what to write about but I will make a stab at something.
Today we are in an assembly position we move out at dark and attack at dawn tomorrow. The sun is trying hard to shine but is not having much success.

The biggest problem now is cigs. The P.X. hasn't been around for 7 days and everybody is out. We are opening our rations now and taking cigs from them.

When we pulled into this area this morning (about 7 o'clock) we were the first tank to be camouflaged and have our slit trenches (small foxhole) dug. The Col. Came passed and stopped long enough to say it was a good job.

As you can probably tell I am all cramped up writing this letter. I am an air-raid sentry (plane spotter for short) if I see an enemy plane (anything but a B-26 or P-39) I give the alarm by tramping on the siren. The weather is pretty bad today and there are very few planes flying around.

It is time for chow now so I will sign off. At least I said hello!!

Love

Walter Jr.

PS. Dick owes me a letter!!!

Assembly position had all the divisions lined up ready for the simulation. In war, tanks do not like moving in the dark but sometimes they have to. For this exercise, it was determined that we would. The tank had two tiny red lights in the rear. Seeing one red light meant your distance from the tank in the lead was okay. Two red lights meant you were too close to the next tank.

We had to smoke the cigarettes provided in the rations. During World War II, mini-packs of either three or four cigarettes—Westfield, Raleigh's, and other assorted brands (along with a fold of waterproof paper matches)—were included in the rations issued to the troops. I was smoking more than the Army provided, obviously. And typically they didn't have my brand, Lucky Strikes. I'm surprised I didn't include a *hint, hint send cigarettes.*

Did the colonel say the slit trench was a good job? Could it be that I was bragging a bit about my crew's high performance? Although I mentioned slit trenches on several occasions, this was as close as I ever came to explaining their use. Perhaps I just couldn't bring myself to tell my mother that this 1-foot-wide by 1-foot-deep by 2-feet-long was what you flushed when in the barracks.

I didn't spot any enemy planes while sitting on top of the tank. However, if I had yelled down to someone in the tank to hit the siren, located down by the driver, the sound that would have emanated from it would have been like fingers on a chalkboard. It was a very poor siren.

Ah, two pages after saying, "I don't know what to write!" I wonder how my writing indicated I was cramped. One also wonders how you spot planes while looking down to write a letter home.

Letter #47: postmarked February 28, 1944

Dear Family,

I don't remember when I wrote the last letter but no doubt one is due.

Yesterday afternoon we got into our first real attack. It was really exciting! We were firing blank ammunition but the powder charges in the land mines were no fakes. It may sound fantastic or something but so far 13 men have died or rather been killed on maneuvers (this isn't so bad considering there are 60,000 men in the battles). While we were moving from our bivouac to the attack it took two days and I only missed three meals, but they made up for it today.

It has been raining off and on all day. We are on a break now, so nobody minds very much.

The first bunch left this morning on furlough. They have 14 days. There were only 7 or 8 that went.

Today I took my first real bath on maneuvers. In between showers (rain) I took a bath in a stream, it was plenty cold, but I feel a hundred times better.

I am going to ask another favor, please put a bar of lava soap in the next package you send. That is about the only kind I can't get.

Well, I'm run down now so I'll be seeing you.

Love

Walter Jr.

PS. Can you get me a cheap pen (35 cent)??

I'd now been in the field for almost the whole month. Moving at night and fighting in the day meant little sleep. "I'm sure I owe you a letter" seems a little strange since the last letter was dated the previous day. Of course, I wrote letters and then had to find someone to mail them.

Thank goodness my mom was the censor of the letters home. I can imagine my little sister reading this and becoming quite upset. Thirteen men killed in a simulation. They weren't literally dead, just out of combat due to a mistake they made.

The land mines were done using dynamite. A hole was dug, and dynamite placed in it. As the tanks rolled along, an order came to blast the mine. Even if

Death During Training

During wartime there are many non-battle casualties. The war—and the preparation for it—took precedence over any idea of safety. Young, inexperienced operatives of large vehicles and firearms in a variety of weather and terrain conditions was bound to lead to problems. Today Walter's attitude might seem cold-blooded, but in wartime it simply seems realistic. On Memorial Day 1944 (May 29) 8th Armored Division assembled on the North Camp Polk parade ground and honored the memory of 32 men from the division who had died in training since March 4, 1943. Captain Charles R. Leach recorded the event and the names of the men concerned in his excellent history of the division, *In Tornado's Wake*. It was rare for a month to go by without a death, many of them in traffic accidents—a drawback of the jeep was its lack of rollbars, seatbelts or the sort of safety features commonly seen today.

the tank had been sitting right on top of the mine it wouldn't have damaged the tank. It would have covered it in dirt.

Bivouac is where we spent the night. There was no pup tent for this activity. We slept in or outside the tank. Missing three meals meant the kitchen truck didn't keep up. Or maybe this was more simulation of the war experience. There wasn't always going to be food readily available.

I took a bath in a stream to show how brave I was. As a little kid, I went swimming in a creek and I came home with leeches. My poor mother must have been panicked as I came in screaming, "Get these things off of me!" I wonder how deep the stream was since I didn't float and soaping up your body while treading water would have been difficult. A little time in the water must have felt good, either way. I made no mention of anyone joining me, so I must have enjoyed a little time alone.

I requested Lava soap. It had a smell or, some say, odor to it. If I washed with it, everyone would know I was clean because the smell lingered.

The final request was for a cheap pen. One, I'd already asked for a pen and obviously lost it. I didn't want the family to send a good pen. I wrote this letter in pencil and borrowed a pen to meticulously go over every letter.

Letter #48: postmarked March 6, 1944

Dear Family,
Well! Only one more month of Louisiana/maneuvers. I guess I'll live that long.

I got the money order but had a little trouble cashing it. It sure came in handy. I guess we will get paid sometime this week.

I just pulled a tick off my chest!

I'm really having a hard time writing this letter. I can't think of anything new.

Just got another tick!!

I want to call home sometime soon. But when I do get some time off, I have to take a bath in cold water, dress, ride 30 miles in the back of a truck and wait 3 or 4 hours on the telephone. But I'll get inspired someday.

When you said you were sending a German knife from the last war you got the whole crew excited. They want to see it as much as I do.

Did I tell you a buddy of mine, Al Volleger, returned all the way to Leesville from Pitts. On emergency furlough and found out his mother died the night he left. He didn't bother to go back he said it was easier this way. She had been slowly dying all the time he was home.

Before I forget, Haskell Yadlooker, the Jewish boy I told you about, said to tell you "Haskell likes 'em," meaning your cookies. He only ate about half of the last box.

Got to go now.
Love
Walter Jr.

We spent the months of February and March in the field. Cashing a money order would have taken some doing. I wonder if another soldier took my money order and gave me the cash for it. Or was it the kitchen or supply truck willing to take a money order? Either way, I had money. Now the more important question: Why did I need money while sitting on maneuvers in a forest?

Sleeping on the ground provided the ticks ripe eating along with mosquitoes and any other parasitic insect crawling across my body.

I'm not sure why I needed a bath to call home. However, getting dressed and riding in the back of an Army truck, bouncing along the road to get to a telephone line where the line of people would have stretched for miles, didn't seem like something I wanted to try. Besides, the conversation on the phone would have cost me money. The typical phone call was three minutes before the rate started going up.

My tank commander finally decided we had to fire at something to make it look real on maneuvers. When you fired the cannon, it meant that you later had to use a long brush with soap and water to clean the barrel. We finally found a target and fired. The referee climbed aboard and sat in the gunner's seat to observe the target we identified. Unfortunately, the turret would not turn far enough to the right to aim at this target. No hit. Clean the barrel.

On a field trip, Haskell's tank commander, a lieutenant, was asked his position. He replied, "Directly behind the unit in front of me!" This provided laughter for both officers and enlisted men. On the next drive, the company commander, with a hint of mirth in his voice, asked the same question. Up popped Haskell with a map. He put his finger on the coordinates, which the lieutenant promptly read. No more laughs.

The company supply sergeant, also Jewish, was a frequent target of Haskell's orneriness. When the sergeant walked through the barracks, Haskell came up with a phrase sounding like "Alta sockem and shoa." Haskell always smiled as the sergeant glowered. Haskell said it was a phrase in Yiddish which meant "old clothes and shoes" and was what men pushing a cart down an alley would say.

The message about Al Volleger translates to "He got back to Leesville only to find out his mother died the night he left, and he turned down going back home on another emergency leave for the funeral."

Letter #49: postmarked March 8, 1944

Dear Family,

This may be the last letter for several days as we start another problem tomorrow.

We got paid yesterday so I am pretty well supplied now.

I also received your package yesterday. The knife is swell, it is just what I wanted. The cookies were in excellent condition and tasted very good.

General Geo. Marshall (Chief of Staff) visited the 8th Div. today. The 1st Sgt. was the only one in the company who saw him.

The supply Sgt. as usual is right "on the ball," we were issued overshoes (Arctics) yesterday and it hasn't rained (hard) for almost a week. I guess the rainy season is about over.

We went to a demonstration today by 7 men from intelligence. They gave a play on how they process and get information from prisoners. All seven of them could speak perfect German and they all talked with an accent. The officer in charge has been at the front processing prisoners.

My turn for using the pen is about done so…

Love

Walter Jr.

P.S. Thank (for me) the man who gave me the knife.

General George Marshall, Chief of Staff, would not have been anywhere near where my crew was performing. Instead, he and the first sergeant would have been at the command post (C.P.) discussing how the commanders and soldiers were performing. At this point in the war effort, replacements were needed. I'm sure part of the discussion was *How soon can we get these men to war?*

Thank you, supply sergeant, for getting our boots after the rain had stopped. Having no need for them now, the tank became a storage unit for our overshoes. Hidden behind the radio, we also used them to hide things like candy, gum, and cigarettes.

Cold Injury

Walter's mention of Arctics—rubber overshoes—being delivered *after* the rainy season is symptomatic of wider Army supply problems. Surgeon General Major General Silas B. Hays said, "It is a lamentable but nonetheless incontrovertible fact that most of the serious losses which occurred from cold injury among United States Army troops in World War II should not have occurred."[5] This candid admission shows just how little the Army had learnt from the problems of trench foot in World War I. Trench foot was already a serious problem in the summer of 1943 during the battles in the Aleutians. Of the 2,900 casualties during the Attu operation, about 40 percent of the total casualties were not directly attributable to enemy action but to exposure—chiefly, trench foot. In Italy that winter, over the six-month period ending on April 30, 1944, there were more than 5,700 casualties from this cause in the Fifth U. S. Army.

The solution was either Arctics—rubber overshoes—or Shoepacs, although in both cases frequent changes of socks, and proper training and discipline, were also

[5] Foreword to *Cold Injury, Ground Type*, part of the U.S. Army Medical Department's survey of World War II.

required to keep trench foot to a minimum. The trouble was that stocks of the new model of Shoepacs did not reach the theater until January 1945. This was because the Army took a gamble, as General Bradley said: "When the rains first came in November with a blast of wintry cold, our troops were ill-prepared for winter-time campaigning. This was traceable in part to the September crisis in supply for, during our race to the Rhine, I had deliberately by-passed shipments of winter clothing in favor of ammunition and gasoline. As a consequence, we now found ourselves caught short, particularly in bad-weather footgear. We had gambled in our choice and now were paying for the bad guess."[6]

It's not just infantrymen who suffer from cold injury when the weather worsens and foot care is impossible. Dry socks, preferably woolen, are essential. Note at left the Arctic overboots into which the standard boot (on right) fits. (Nara via Battlefield Historian)

---

[6] Bradley, Omar N.: *A Soldier's Story*; Henry Holt, 1951.

Between October 10 and November 28, 1944, 11,348 trench foot casualties were admitted to six general hospitals in the Paris area from the First, Third, Seventh, and Ninth U. S. Armies. Between October 1944 and April 1945, 46,107 cases of cold injuries of all types required hospitalization. This loss of manpower amounted to more than three combat divisions. While most of these were infantrymen, many were from armored regiments too.

It wasn't helpful that the winter of 1944–45 was particularly severe but that this was both foreseeable and preventable as shown by the comparison in between the American and British troops in Fifth (U.S.) Army under General Mark Clark. While U.S. troops suffered 4,560 cold injuries in the winter of 1943–44, the British suffered only 102. The reasons were identified as: excellent boots; heavy wool socks in contrast to the lighter socks provided for American troops; the daily sock exchange; the fact that the British rotated troops to keep them in the line for shorter periods of time than the Americans; and the strict foot discipline enforced on British troops.

Shoepacs—laced waterproofed boots. (NARA)

The demonstration was to help us understand what to do if we were captured. The rule was to give your name, rank, and serial number. The most important rule: Don't get captured!

We were starting a problem the next day, which meant a new simulation, not that I was causing a problem and would be unable to write for a while.

The knife was a gift from one of my father's friends and not Mister Johnson, the mine electrician. My dad's friend had taken it from a German prisoner during World War I. The knife made me the envy of many men.

Letter #50: postmarked March 17, 1944

Dear Family,
The first thing I will do is answer a few questions.
　1. Received knife (box in good shape)
　2. " " pen (" ")
　3. " " money order (Thanks)
Now that that's done, I will try to think of something interesting to say.

Our maneuvers will be over in ten days! Then we move by train to Camp Bowie, Texas. That is supposed to be two hours' ride from Houston. What we will do there no one seems to know.

Enclosed is 20 dollars I have been wanting to send some money home but couldn't buy a money order. I finally decided to send it anyway. Buy a war bond and give whoever furnished the last donation ($5) the rest.

I am using the pen you sent me. You said it was grandaddy's so I wrote him a letter and thanked him.

Do me a favor, please. Call up Lenore and tell her if she doesn't write soon you won't give her any more eggnogs. In case she didn't tell you, the eggnog you gave her contained her first drink of "fire water," she said she was afraid she'd get drunk.

Yesterday I found a wallet a fellow had lost in 1942. The C.O. took all the papers to mail to him.

In about four days we are going to do something which should furnish some excitement! We are going to cross the Sabine R. on a pontoon bridge.

Thanks for addresses, as soon as I get some V-mail stationery I am going to write them. (They tell me it is quicker that way.)

Well! I guess I'm run down now so.
Love
Walter Jr.
P.S. Will try to write Dick a letter tomorrow.

Along with the knife came a sheath which was attached to my belt. It was small enough that I could wear it all the time, even in the tank.

Moving to Bowie, Texas, would have been a train for the soldiers. The tanks might have been loaded onto a flatbed. There was no riding or hiding inside a tank for the train ride.

I can't believe I sent money home! I might have felt guilty about owing someone $5. With much patriotism, I told my family to buy a war bond with the rest: "A war bond is a debt security issued by a government to finance military operations during times of war or conflict. Because war bonds offered a rate of return below the market rate, investment was achieved by making emotional appeals to patriotic citizens to lend the government money."[7]

The value of war bonds didn't really offer much until 10 to 20 years later. If my mother bought a war bond, I'm not sure I ever saw it. And if I did, I probably cashed it after coming home from the war.

Lenore, my heartthrob at the time, was one of an Irish family of four girls. A non-drinker! I'm not sure telling her she wouldn't get any more eggnog would have inspired her to write.

We had to cross the Sabine River on a pontoon bridge. Driving the tank onto the bridge caused some nervousness. Buoyed on the water, the tank would roll across the bridge with a slight bounciness until it rolled off to the ground on the other side where we all took a big sigh of relief. Tanks don't float.

Wandering around outside the tank, I found a wallet. This soldier must have been like me, short on cash, because the wallet was empty of money. It had all his identification so turning it in was the right thing to do. I imagine my integrity was appreciated by my superiors and the wallet's original owner.

V-mail—Victory Mail

Mail is a vital part of a soldier's wellbeing, and absence of mail increases stress and combat fatigue. The U.S. Army set up military postal services through numbered post offices (A.P.O.s)—these helped keep units' locations secret. Some of the A.P.O.s were linked to unit numbers (eg. A.P.O. 1 went to 1st Infantry Division); others were geographic (eg. 950–966 assigned to Hawaii). Originally postal rates were applied.

There were a lot of personnel involved in postal work (an officer and 11 soldiers served 75,000–10,000 troops) and the amount of mail sent was huge: by 1945 2.5 billion pieces of mail went through A.P.O.s and 8 million through Naval Post Offices.

To save space, American planners looked at the British Aerograph system of microphotography and then developed the Army Micro Photographic Mail Service using Kodak Recordak equipment at three main centers: New York, San Francisco, and Chicago. Here the outbound letters were opened, censored, and filmed.

V-mail was introduced on March 27, 1942. It used standardized stationery combining letter and envelope into one piece of paper that could be reproduced on

---

[7] Ancheta, 2022, para. 1.

microfilm and then printed by the recipient at about 25 percent of original size. This was its only drawback: magnifying glasses were often necessary to read the reduced-size writing. As many as 1,600 of these letters would fit onto a 100ft reel of 16mm microfilm, at 40 a minute. The space savings were immense—one bag of V-mail fitted what 37 ordinary mailbags would carry. The transportation of the letters was handled by the military—by air, so it was quicker than normal post—to V-mail stations overseas where the letters were printed out. The form was specially designed by the Government Printing Office and was provided free at the rate of two sheets per person per day. Civilian senders from the United States paid a small charge. It was free to use by servicemen.

Between June 1942 and November 1945 over one billion items were sent like this and the service continued until 1947. Walter remembers "I eventually started using V-Mail on occasion. The first letter I sent was in June of 1944. V-mail cost the sender three cents. If my mom sent me stationery and pens as needed, I could send a letter home for free. A penny saved is a penny more toward beer at the P.X."

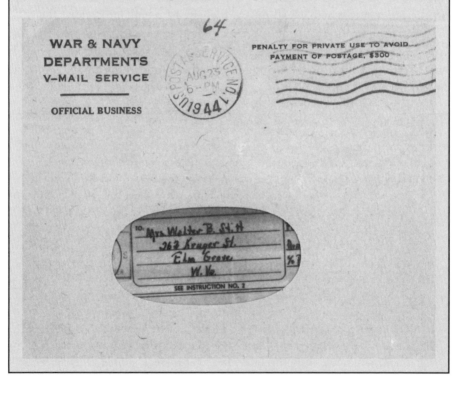

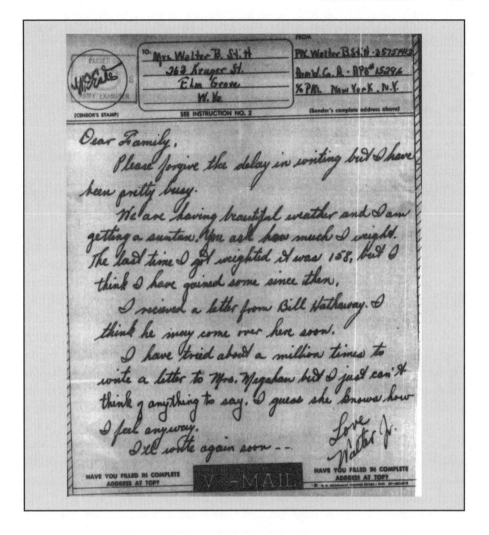

The letter pictured reads:

Dear Family,

Please forgive the delay in writing but I have been pretty busy.

We are having beautiful weather and I am getting a suntan. You ask how much I weigh. The last time I got weighted it was 158, but I think I have gained some since then.

I recieved a letter from Bill Hathaway. I think he may come over here soon.

I have tried about a million times to write a letter to Mrs. Megahan but I just can't think of anything to say. I guess she knows how I feel anyway.

I'll write again soon - -

Love
Walter Jr.

Letter #51: postmarked March 25, 1944

Dear Dick

Mother said you wanted to write but couldn't think of anything to say, so I'll write and ask a few questions for you to start with.

I am going to ask a favor of you. Ask Mrs. Lister (if she is still chemistry teacher) if I can buy a used or slightly worn chemistry book. If she will, I'll send you the money and you can get it for me.

You seem to be going to a few dances lately. More power to you, you won't regret it after you are in the Army a while.

Mother said something about you wanting to get into the Air Cadets. I know for a fact it is easier to get into the cadets after you have been in the Army awhile. There is a fellow in

Hdq. Co. who tried 4 times and finally made it on the fourth try. The Air Corp has priority on all other branches of the Army. They tell me it has been changed lately??!!!

Yesterday a fellow killed a 6-foot water moccasin, it was a good 2 inches in diameter. The bugs, snakes, ticks, and so forth are really starting to come out now.

I thought I had more to talk about, but I can't think of any more so

"Blue" Army

Stitt

P.S. If you still want to take that trip when school's out let me know.

Not having anything to write about was in most of my letters. I see my brother picked the same excuse for not writing to me.

This letter to my brother, Dick, holds yet more mysteries! Why the chemistry book? I have no recollection of needing or getting a chemistry book. I did like chemistry and the excitement of the labs.

What was "that trip?" Maybe Dick wanted to check out colleges. I know I was beginning to think that, after my service, I wanted to get more education. My dad and his brothers, Hebert and Edward, all went to Marietta College in Ohio. My mother had gone to Normal School to become a teacher. I had two aunts who had master's degrees. Going to college was expected of us.

A little aside here: Dick, Sally, Betty (my sister's roommate and my future wife), and I all attended Marietta College. My brother and I joined the Alpha Sigma Phi fraternity, Delta chapter, and my sister and Betty were Alpha Zs. Three of the four us were Marietta graduates. Instead, I met with the Dean to find out they felt I was wasting their time and my money. In truth, I had no idea what I wanted to pursue as a career and just took courses to see if I had any interest. At the age of 35, I returned to college at Wittenberg University, graduated with a Bachelor of Arts in Sociology and went on to graduate school to obtain a Master of Divinity from the Hamma School of Theology.

I must have made an impression on my brother about the advantage of attending dances but not dancing. I'm sure my mom was pleased to see my brother taking such an interest in social events. I also wonder if "dances" was a hidden way of saying "drinking" between us. Dick did not make the Air Cadets. He headed to Texas to be a cryptographer and ended up a sergeant at Camp Atterbury, Indiana.

I was still in Sabine National Forest when I wrote this letter and still slept outside. Critters were making their appearance more often now. I can assure you I didn't go bathing in the stream without first making sure there were no 6-foot water moccasins. The letter was signed "Blue" Army Stitt—clearly, I was on the blue team in our simulation. While I don't recall the outcome, I'm sure we were victorious.

Letter #52: postmarked March 26, 1944

Dear Family,

I guess I'm just not in the mood for writing. I have tried to write 3 times but tore them all up.

I have some questions to ask now. Did you get the $20?

Well! We are now in Texas! We moved 90 miles yesterday and are 4 miles from Jasper. We have 1 more short problem and then we start moving. We clean our tanks and are going to give them to another division on the 1st. We move into Camp Bowie on the 6th. Camp Bowie is just a firing range, so we probably won't be there more than six weeks.

I am being rushed for time so I will sign off now.

Love

Walter Jr.

P.S. I am writing this letter in a hurry and by fire-light so I hope you can read it.

Forgo the train; we were now moving in our tanks and outside Jasper, Texas. It's funny to me that the simulation was over and, rather than moving northwest, we headed southwest. It seems an odd way to get to Camp Bowie.

Camp Bowie was a military training center during World War II. Camp Bowie seemed to be a goal that was being arrived at very slowly. Six weeks at a firing range? The camp was a military training center and, like Camp Polk, had German prisoners. After just spending two months doing military simulation, it seemed odd our division needed more military training, especially at a firing range.

It is obvious that I didn't always know what the next move was in the Army. This was typical of most Army assignments, since the decisions were made by the men in charge, not a lowly private. As I wrapped up this letter, we were still sleeping outside the tank. We'd been allowed to build a small fire, which provided little light and hopefully kept the critters away.

Letter #53: postmarked March 30, 1944

Dear Family

Well! We're still in Texas, but for how long nobody seems to know. We were supposed to leave today but it doesn't look as though we will.

There hasn't been much happening that I can write about. It's just the same old grind day after day. Yesterday I was laying by the tank, stripped to the waist, sunning myself when the mail came. It sure seemed funny when you talked about how cold it was and how deep the snow was getting.

I guess you misunderstood me when I said I had to destroy my letters. I only have to destroy the envelope. If we are captured they can search all our personal belongings and if any important documents or anything that gives any information is found they can assess losses or at least make it hot for you.

Well! I'm run down again but at least you know I'm alive and kicking!

Love

Walter Jr.

P.S. Will be in Camp Bowie by 6th.

Camp Bowie was only six more days away and I was still "alive and kicking." In the meantime, there was nothing to do so the Army came up with something to keep us busy. Eat three meals a day, clean the tank, remove the cannon and put it back together, march in formation, hike, just about anything they could think of to keep us busy for another six days.

Part of the Army's instruction was if you are captured and have personal mail on you, the Germans could threaten whomever the letter was from. Somehow this information got scrambled in transmission to my family. The rule was destroying all envelopes with any identifying information. I listened to the advice about how to take care of envelopes when in the combat area. I destroyed all my envelopes and letters from home. Just what my parents thought.

Letter #54: postmarked April 4, 1944

Dear Folks,
Don't have time to write. Just 2 important changes to make.
(Change) P.F.C. Walter B Stitt
CoD. (L) 80th Tank BN.
APO #258
(Change) Camp Polk LA

The company sergeant had the troops gather. He announced that several men had earned a new rank. He called out my last name, "Stitt," and handed me a stripe. I was a private first class. Now I had to sew that stripe on! I'm sure there was a place to get the needle and thread for such a procedure. I just don't remember what it was.

What happened to Bowie? At this point, the only thing I'd been told was we were returning to Camp Polk. Hallelujah! Back to the barracks and off the ground. Closer to the P.X. and a nice cold beer. I figured I might even be able to make a phone call home.

Two things to notice about the address: I list myself as Walter B. Stitt but I never put the junior on my address. However, I sign every letter Walter Jr. I'm not entirely sure why I included an "L" surrounded by parentheses.

Letter #55: postmarked April 10, 1944

Dear Family,
I hope you'll excuse the delay in writing, but for the last week we have really been busy.
We are now bivouacked about 5 miles from Camp Polk. We have everything arranged like it was in camp and it saves a lot of trouble. We will be here at least 11 days and probably move. It is nice to be able to pitch your tent and leave it in one place. We finished cleaning

the tank this morning so now I can wash my dirty clothes and get cleaned up. It is a lot better than being in barracks because you don't have to shine shoes, make beds, clean floors, and stuff like that.

I haven't seen H. Bremson since I came back. He lives and travels with Division Staff and is usually 5 or 10 miles behind us.

Jim Gilleland and I have had quite a few talks since he came back. He is now a Corp. and will probably make Sgt. in time.

By the time you get this letter, Henry Moore will be back in camp but will you ask his mother and find out his address. I can get off at least 6 nights a week so I can go see him a couple times.

There have been quite a few rumors going around about where we are going next but no one seems to know for sure. We couldn't go to Bowie because the 13th Div. was still there. We are probably waiting now for them to move out.

The weather down here is getting better all the time but pretty soon I will probably be complaining about it being too hot.

I have been wanting to thank Sara for a long time but keep forgetting. I enjoy reading those little jokes and always pass them on.

I guess I'm about done for now, so I'll sign off.

Love

Walter Jr.

We'd been busy getting back to Camp Polk. We never went back to Bowie. Back at Camp Polk, we were still in the field. Still had to clean our clothes and the tank but not polish the shoes.

There was no sharing of the newspaper, but Jim Gilleland probably shared current events from back home.

At the time of this letter, I was in south camp. My friend, Henry Moore, was in the north camp. This was why I needed his address so I could find where he was located. I either walked or took a bus over to the south camp with free time after chow to meet up with him, take in a movie, locate a beer.

I'm sure my 12-year-old sister's jokes were to make you groan. Something like, "Why couldn't the pony sing a lullaby? He was a little horse." Ugh!

This letter, postmarked April 10, bore the constant rumor: *We were going somewhere.* Inferred was Europe or the Far East. I'd been in the Army for a year now and trained as a tanker. I knew without saying in the letter that my time at Camp Polk and in the United States was coming to an end.

A quick change of topic in the letter to the weather was a way of putting the uncertainty out of my mind.

Letter #56: postmarked April 19, 1944

Dear Family,

Boy! We've had some really busy days lately. We are doing everything the same as if we were in garrison. Monday, we started training again and are going through a series of firing test.

Here is something which should really surprise you! I met H. Moore and B. Yarling. I looked up Henry in South Camp and we went to Leesville. The first place we went into we met Bill Yarling! The 3 of us spent the evening together and really had a good time. Bill said you can put one of the pictures in the paper. It doesn't look as though Henry and I will see much of each other. His outfit is ready to move.

I don't remember when I wrote the last letter so I will thank you now for the Easter package. It was swell!

Last week we got our booster shots for typhus, tetanus, and a vaccination. Both of my arms were so sore I could hardly lift them. The typhus shot made me sick. My temperature went over a hundred and I was having chills at the same time. We are supposed to get these shots every 6 months and every 3 years you get the series (8 of them) all over again! Some fun!!

I wish I could write 2 or 3 more pages but I can't seem to think of anything interesting, so I'll sign off!

Love

Walter Jr.

P.S. Tonight I am on guard and it is raining! Hard!!

Keeping the troops busy was the Army's motto. We didn't make it to Camp Bowie for firing range practice, so we practiced at our home base. I'm sure busy days included tank cleaning and assembly. Marching with no particular place to go. Just keep moving and wear them out before their free time.

My mom sent me the address for Henry. I found Henry and shared a half case of beer while regaling with stories of our antics back home and in basic training.

The next time we got together, we found Bill Yarling. Off we went and "the first place we went into" tells a lot of this evening together. This "first place" was the trademark of Leesville: bars. Three nineteen-year-olds from back home would have had a good time. It was great seeing friends from home and hearing their stories and antics during their enlistment. In addition, I wanted to hear what they could share about people and things back home. Bill told me we could put pictures of us in the *Wheeling Intelligencer* newspaper. I still had the camera. Maybe I had someone take our picture. I wonder if it was a picture of three guys from home sitting at a bar drinking or three drunks in the street?

The shots were with a needle that everyone swore was dull. Getting the "shots" had its interesting moments when someone's anxieties caused a fainting spell. The medics were kind and gave the dose while the soldier was out. I did not have this problem.

Hard rain and guard duty left me with the choice of wearing my helmet, raincoat, and my rain boots (if they could be found), all while walking outside. The other option was standing inside the tank with my head outside the hatch, wearing my helmet. You can guess what I chose. So could the rest of the crew who stayed inside the tank as the moisture came inside.

Letter #57: postmarked May 1, 1944

Dear Family,

I've finally caught up on my work so I'll try to think of something to write.

I was on K.P. today (by turn). It wasn't so bad and I had plenty to eat.

The night before last I was on guard. The guard ended at 6 p.m. but the O.D. made us stay in the guard house till 11:30 so I got plenty of sleep. Last night Henry Moore and I went to the show. I don't know whether I told you or not, Henry M. and I are only 3 or 4 blocks away. He and I have been out about 4 nights now.

There has been a lot of talk about Pvts & Pfc. being transferred to other outfits but I don't know how much truth there is in it.

We have it pretty nice here in S. Camp. We are pretty close to everything but the swimming pool.

Last week I qualified as an expert tank gunner.

I could go ramblings on for another page or two I guess but I am pretty tired, so I'll sign off now.

Love

Walter Jr

P.S. If I am transferred it will be by Thur. so I'll write then and let you know.

The Army is full of acronyms: O.D.—Officer of the Day; Pvts.—Privates; P.F.C.—Private First Class; K.P.—Kitchen Patrol. I was on it because it was my turn, not for anything else. The purpose was to help out with the kitchen, anything from serving food to cleaning up. I don't think the purpose was to ensure I was well fed.

Why the O.D. had the men stay on guard duty is unknown. However, I took full advantage of the extra duty by doing the usual—sleeping. I probably needed it after hanging out with Henry Moore, seeing shows and drinking beer.

I qualified as an expert tank gunner by scoring a 100 on the paper test and just as good on the firing of the gun in the tank. I had sealed my fate. I would be a gunner wherever the Army chose to send me.

Again, the rumors flew. Soon, I would be moving. In the letter I wrote, "I don't know how much truth there is in it." I had finally caught on that rumors were rampant and not often to be believed.

Time would tell if this rumor was true. I had no idea where I would be sent. It could have been the Pacific Theater or European Theater. At this point in my training, it didn't matter where I went. I was now an expert gunner and was prepared for anything—or so I thought.

Personnel Shortages

It's not surprising that there were rumors about personnel movement. The U.S. Army underwent serious personnel shortages in 1943–44 because it didn't make suitable provision for battlefield attrition—particularly felt by the infantry—and the expanding commitment of ground troops following the invasion of Sicily. The immediate solution was to strip units in training to supplement those coming from replacement training facilities. Already in May 1943 replacement centers were short 20,000 men; that figure increased by 57,000 in June, and 26,710 in August. The 63rd Division was activated in June 1943 and only had about half its tabled strength in mid-September. On September 21, 1943, newly activated units were short a total of 75,000 men.

Matters were made worse by deferments. This applied to those classified as unfit for military service (usually for physical or mental reasons) but it also covered occupational deferments—industry and agriculture. By far the largest category of deferred men was fathers—because only single men were drafted—not employed in agriculture. Politics intervened when the Army tried to include fathers and the draft was expanded to 18-year-olds before fathers. Nevertheless, by 1945 a million fathers had been called up.

Another area was the loss of men to the Army Specialized Training Program and the Air Forces. By February 1944 the shortage had reached 87,000. But most disruptive of all was the repeated stripping of units to provide men for overseas replacements. In the latter part of 1943, 14 infantry divisions lost an aggregate of 24,541 men to overseas replacement depots. In the late spring and early summer, 17 divisions lost 64,411 men; and a final draft in July and August 1944 took away 12,057 more. It wasn't just enlisted men. There were heavy losses in officers: in June 1944, 94th Division had no second lieutenants who had been on divisional maneuvers seven months earlier.

While primarily an infantry crisis, all combat branches felt the strain, which would lead to Walter's move from the division with whom he had trained—8th Armored—to the division with whom he fought, 3rd Armored.

The shortages had another effect. Training areas closed because heavy drafts for overseas operations left an insufficiency of service units for support of divisions in the field. The California-Arizona Maneuver Area was closed in April 1944, Tennessee saw its last maneuvers in March, and Louisiana in April.

Letter #58: postmarked May 9, 1944

Dear Family,
In between inspections and so forth I'll try to write.
There is nothing definite about moving yet except that we are going.

I am sending home a bunch of stuff I have had laying around some of it is valuable and some of it you can throw away. Any personal or rather all of our personal equipment must total 5 pounds. I have been trying to think of a system so you will know where I am. If I think of a good one I'll send it.

I am afraid I will need some money. I will send a telegram and let you know where to send it. I'm sorry this letter is so short, but I am pretty rushed for time.

Love
Walter Jr.

It was true! We were shipping out. All the privates and privates first class, plus, what I did not know beforehand, all the second lieutenants.

On my final day in camp, I was assigned K.P. Reporting for K.P., I told the mess sergeant to give me something easy to do, as I was exhausted. The man must have hated me for some unknown reason. Cleaning the grease traps was the assignment. I was the last person to leave the kitchen that night and probably the maddest.

For some of the people in the camp, not knowing exactly where we were going caused some anxiety. I, on the other hand, liked some uncertainty in life. I saw it as a chance to have new experiences and go places I'd never been before.

I never did come up with a secret word to indicate where I was. I wanted my parents to know where I was, but I didn't know for sure where I would end up. I guess I could have sent a message like, "This bloody rain is soaking me clear through." Or, "We're having rice for all three meals." Of course, the soon-to-be mail censor would have not approved.

Leaving it up to my parents to decide what to throw away in my package home left them a lot of room. I saved everything. It might have been wiser to pitch what I didn't need since my mom was a saver too. I'm sure upon my return, everything I sent home was still in the box in my room. I wonder if the camera made it home.

"Please send money" was back in style.

Postcard #3: May 9, 1944

Dear Mom,
I don't know where I'm liable to be on Mother's Day but wherever it is, I'll be thinking of you.
Love
Walter Jr.

I was currently in the 8th Armored Division. I was heading to who knows where and unsure whether I would be able to write. Mom and I had a really good relationship. I knew I could count on her to be there for me. My brother

This was a postcard given to soldiers to write home to their mothers for Mother's Day.

used to say, "Mom likes you best." Of course, as the oldest, mom probably expected more from me, thus giving me more attention.

After the war and college, I got a job in construction. I made good money. My mom was wise to my spending ways and started having me pay some rent to live at home. This way she made sure I had extra money if I ever needed it.

In 1977, my father died. Mom moved to an apartment and lived alone for several years. She had taken to medicating all her pains with aspirin. This led to a very upset stomach, then not feeling well and not wanting to eat. I left South Bend, Indiana, and went to Wheeling, West Virginia, to see mom and take her to the doctor. He advised, "Mrs. Stitt, we are going to have an aspirin break." Mom's younger sister, Virginia, came to help her. I told mom goodbye and headed for the car. Virginia came running out to get me. Mom was crying and saying she would never see me again. I went back in to reassure her she would get better, and she wasn't dying.

Through her tears she looked at me and said, "Walter Jr., you never did give me any trouble."

My response, "Now I know you've lost your mind!" Her laughter stopped the crying.

My mom went on to live to the ripe old age of 95.

Letter #59: postmarked May 10, 1944

Dear Family,
I hope you can read my writing as I am writing in a hurry. By the time you receive this letter I should be on my way.

There are all sorts of rumors where we are going but no one knows for sure. Everybody hopes it will be England.

We are restricted tonight, and they told us to get all the rest we could because we will be needing it.

I don't know what to write because our letters are liable to be censored, but wish me luck.
Love
Walter Jr.

I was about to be on my way to some unknown location. The rumors from the soldiers who had been in the Pacific Theater described conditions as horrific. The Japanese hid in caves and attacked at night. The Japanese were relentless fighters who easily gave their life for their country, killing themselves while killing you.

Now the Army was telling us to get some sleep! I bet I did not sleep as well as I could have. I did not know where I was going, and I was going to need money for sure. How would my parents ever get it to me if they did not have my address? Besides, our letters were due to be read and censored if information was shared of our whereabouts.

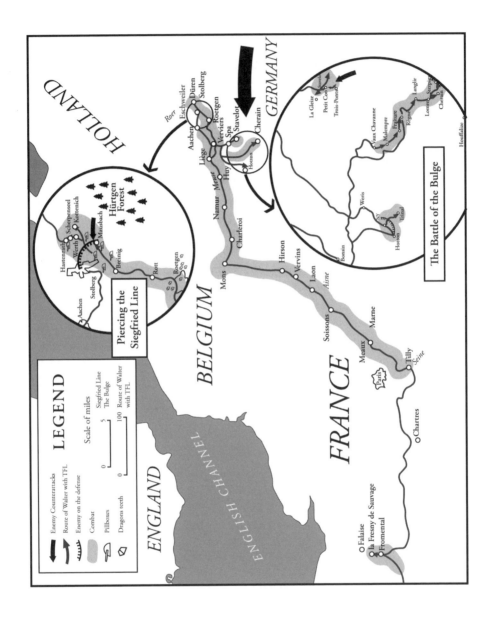

CHAPTER 4

In Combat—European Theater

Postcard #4: postmarked May 20, 1944[1]

From Fort George Meade

Dear Family,

Just a line to let you know I am O.K.

I received the money O.K. and I really needed it.

I write as soon as possible.

Love

Walter Jr.

Oh good, my parents found a way to get me money and I was okay.

This was the last letter I sent while still in the States. Although it was from Fort George Mead, Maryland, I later went to Camp Kilmer before leaving the United States. Camp Kilmer was the port of embarkation, meaning this was where they loaded up the soldiers for the next journey.

My mom had come to New York to see me before I left. She had bought two tickets to New York City and brought Lenore. We visited together for one night and they went back on the B&O railroad to West Virginia. I would not see my family again for another 15 months.

I began the journey to the European Theater on May 30, 1944. The sergeant called, "Stitt," and my reply was my first name and Army number, and along with over 10,000 other men, I boarded the *Queen Elizabeth*. I was assigned a berth on D Deck. This deck, I determined, was on the water line of the ship, which gave me some anxiety. My "bed" on the trip was a bunk I could not sit up in. Bunks were three high, and I had to roll in and roll out. While the restroom was on D Deck, it was one person at a time. There were facilities to wash your face and brush your teeth but there was no place to bathe.

---

[1] This postcard was enclosed inside Letter #59.

Troopships

During December 1941 and August 1945, the Transportation Corps embarked over 7 million passengers and 125 million tons of cargo through all ports, with by far the largest proportion through the New York Port of Embarkation. The two major embarkation camps were at Camp Kilmer in New Jersey, and Camp Shanks in Orangeburg—"Last Stop USA."

Walter left the United States from Camp Kilmer, which was well situated near New Brunswick, a transport node for road and rail. The unit Stitt ended up joining, 3rd Armored, was one of 20 divisions that left through Fort Kilmer, named after poet Joyce Kilmer who was killed in France during World War I. The camp was constructed between January and June 1943, covered 1,500 acres, and had recreation, entertainment, and living facilities that saw it become the main receiving center for soldiers returning from both Europe and the Pacific at the end of the war.

The Battle of the Atlantic had seen the loss of many Allied ships, and although early 1943 saw the fight swing against the U-boats, sending soldiers across the ocean was fraught with dangers. The most famous troopships were the great passenger liners which were noted not only for their carrying capacity—both *Queen Mary* and *Queen Elizabeth* could carry well over 15,000 troops—but for their great speed of over 30 knots that left most escorts—and, thankfully, U-boats—for dead.

Queen Elizabeth and *Queen Mary* in dock at Southampton, September 27, 1946. (State Library of New South Wales collection/WikiCommons)

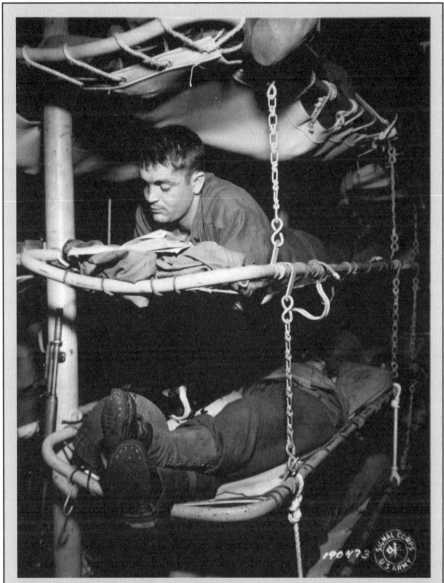

Transatlantic travel for troops on the big liners was not as comfortable as it may have sounded. (NARA)

The trip started with a drill on what to do if the ship was hit. The captain began his ranting and raving about where to find the life preservers and lifeboats and who was to go where, when, and how. A major standing next to me leaned over and said, "Give a man a little power," and shook his head.

I liked to spend my time looking into the horizon off the deck; however, there was a problem. Some of the soldiers had seasickness. I would be standing by the rail enjoying the fresh air when suddenly a soldier, unable to withstand the waves, would gag and pitch vomit over the side (if I was lucky).

The British served only two meals a day. The second day out to sea I was put on K.P. At the end of day, I convinced my co-worker to not put our badges in the basket but instead hide them in our pocket. Having a K.P. badge entitled you to wander the entire ship. Soldiers were confined to specific sections and our movements were controlled by M.P.s. The next day with our K.P. badges, our wandering led to discovering a bathtub in the officers' bathroom. Figuring a bath would be great, I told my buddy to stand watch while I filled the tub. Excited for my first bath, I got in only to discover the water was salt water. This bath just left me sticky and my buddy laughing.

On D-Day, June 6, 1944, we dropped anchor in the Firth of Clyde, located on the west coast of Scotland. Around 10 o'clock at night, I decided I wanted one last smoke. I walked out through the blackout curtains only to discover broad daylight with the sun shining on the red-roofed houses. I asked another G.I. what time it was. His reply was "22 hundred hours," or 10 o'clock at night. It hit me that it was summer and we were farther north and the sun didn't set until much later. The next day they got us off the boat.

A train ride took me to Wells in the county of Somerset, in southwest England. It was here that I spent the next three weeks.

I don't really remember when I was told that the invasion was underway, I think it might have been when we were on the ship, but it might have been after we landed in England.

Announcing D-Day

Early morning June 6 German news agencies began to report attacks on the French coast. Some American news outlets—CBS, NBC, and others—reported this but were unsure of its veracity. "Frankly," said CBS's Bob Trout, "we don't know at this time whether those German news agency reports that the invasion has begun are true or not." Confirmation came at 3:32 a.m. ET (then called Eastern War Time) when General Dwight David Eisenhower's Order of the Day was broadcast over American radio.

An Associated Press newsflash was released just after 09:30. It was headlined: "Eisenhower's Headquarters Announces Allies Land In France." Aside from confirming that Normandy was the general area of the assault, Supreme Headquarters of the Allied Expeditionary Force was silent concerning the location.

Prime Minister Churchill was able to tell parliament "I have also to announce to the House that during the night and the early hours of this morning the first of the series of landings in force upon the European Continent has taken place. In this case the liberating assault fell upon the coast of France. ... So far the Commanders who are engaged report that everything is proceeding according to plan." King George VI spoke to the people of the United Kingdom on June 6 about winning the "fight against evil."

In the United States, President Franklin Roosevelt talked on the radio and offered a prayer for the success of the invasion:

"My fellow Americans: Last night, when I spoke with you about the fall of Rome, I knew at that moment that troops of the United States and our Allies were crossing the Channel in another and greater operation. It has come to pass with success thus far.

And so, in this poignant hour, I ask you to join with me in prayer:

Almighty God: Our sons, pride of our Nation, this day have set upon a mighty endeavor, a struggle to preserve our Republic, our religion, and our civilization, and to set free a suffering humanity. ..."

Letter #60: postmarked June 9, 1944

Dear Mom,

I've tried a half dozen times to write a letter but I can't think of enough to say.

I can tell you I am somewhere in England. It is really beautiful country here.

There are a few things I could use now some of them are:

1. Cigs. (Lucky Strike)
2. Matches (if you can send them)
3. Razor blades
4. And candy or cookies plus gum

I decided not to write V-Mail, for a while anyway. Send me Tom Jarret's address there is some chance that I may see him. If there is anyone else that I know in England send me their address too.

And about the trip to N.Y. thanks for everything Mom.

Got to go now.

Love

Walter Jr.

So now the family knew I was in England. This was probably not comforting, as I was just that much closer to the war.

What wasn't really explained to the new arrivals—or the family back home—was that I was a replacement. This meant I was taking the place of a soldier who had been killed. During training, I held every position in a tank. Even though I was listed as a gunner, it was not out of the question that

I could have been a loader, driver, or assistant driver. When I got to France I knew I was going in as a replacement. I joined a crew who had lost their loader, I didn't ask and they didn't volunteer what happened to him. I knew I was the replacement.

Tom Jarret was a school buddy. His grandmother was the landlady for my family. Tom's job in the service was to raise homing pigeons, these were used during the war to transport messages.[2]

But I was still the same old guy. I needed cigarettes, and not just the ones in the rations. I wanted Lucky Strikes! Matches, really? I can't imagine sending matches overseas. Somehow the thought of something that if struck could start a fire doesn't seem like something the mail service would view kindly.

Request for candy and gum, no surprise. What, no money request?

In spite of "no V-mail," the very next letter was a V-Mail. I imagine I was complaining about not having enough cigarettes. I'm sure a buddy of mine told me the letter would take forever to get home with the advice to send a V-Mail. So, within a day I sent it with the same requests for cigs and candy!

Letter #61: postmarked June 26, 1944

Dear Family,
I've already written a letter but I imagine this one will get there first, so I'll tell you what you are waiting to hear.
I am somewhere in England. It is a beautiful country, but too damp for me.
I don't know how much you are allowed to send, but I would like some candy, gum, and cigs.
If I stay here 6 months more I may learn this English money.
Love
Walter Jr.

I had been in England for five days. I took morning two-mile marches to keep in shape. One day, we were taken to a firing range where I fired several rounds at a target on a hillside. We stayed overnight in an old British Army barracks where the bed consisted of three planks which were about 7 feet long, 10 inches wide, and 1 inch thick; they were supported off the floor with three 4-inch saw horses. I had a wool blanket, which likely wasn't very helpful in the summer. I managed to sleep, just not well. I was very thankful it was only one night.

I was trying to learn the difference between a *tuppence* and *thruppence* so I could purchase items at the P.X. I was otherwise confined to the area of the

[2] "War pigeon," 2022, para. 2.

quarters, about three acres surrounded by a low stone fence. The one exit was guarded by the military police.

Letter #62: postmarked June 26, 1944

Dear Family,

This letter writing is getting to be a problem. I can't think of anything really interesting to say.

I hate to start talking about myself but that at least will take up some space. I am feeling swell. I have gained some weight (I think) and I am in pretty fair condition. I have just about everything I need but I am afraid I will run short on cigs. I think I told you they (cigs.) are rationed.

Since I have been here I have gone to two dances. They have some very good-looking women and most of them are swell dancers. I have also been to several shows. In these English theaters you are allowed to smoke. It seems funny to me.

I will write Lenore a letter later but tell her I said hello! and don't work too hard.

It's getting too dark to write. (I am in my tent), so I'll say good-bye for now.

Love

Walter

Life took a new turn! We got passes to town, along with a lecture from the higher ups on behavior. "Don't piss outside on the pub wall. It drains across the walk and into the street. The town's people do not approve. Don't ask the dart players if you can get in the game. Don't use the word 'bloody'; it's a cuss word to the British. Be polite."

It was to some, as the old saying goes, "In one ear and out the other." After a couple of English beers with higher alcohol content than American beers, you heard, "What's the chances of getting in the game?" And urine did run across the sidewalk into the gutter.

However, there was other excitement for me. Room-temperature beer with hops floating in it. Smoking in the movie theater. Dances at which even a poor dancer could perform the Palais Glide and Schottische. Learning where the phrase "Who pulled your chain?" originated from (English toilets had the water stored in a cistern above the toilet and were flushed by pulling a chain).

Back at our camp, another soldier and I were given the task of emptying the "honey buckets," which were full of excrement. The person responsible for cleaning the honey buckets pulled it out from its hole, carried it down (trying to avoid getting any splashed on themselves), emptied it, rinsed it, and returned it to the latrine. There were 12 buckets. This task was despised by most, but my friend and I devised a system for making fast work of the job. We took a tent pole and put the four buckets on it. No splashing on you, dumped, cleaned, and returned. Twenty minutes tops for this job twice a day, leaving the rest of the day free. Imagine the surprise on the other soldiers' faces when we volunteered for "honey buckets" duty a second time.

Another exciting day for me was the one-day hike to Glastonbury from Wells (approximately 6 miles one way). A lieutenant familiar with the history of the area had the troop hike to the Abbey ruins associated with King Arthur. Of course, not all soldiers were impressed. As one put it, "We walked all this way to see a bunch of old stones!"

V-Mail Letter #63: postmarked August 3, 1944

Dear Family,
You'll have to excuse my not writing sooner but my new address is "Somewhere in France."
    As you can tell by the address it is my birthday. I really don't feel any older.
    I sprained my ankle again and I would have used that rubber bandage, but I got it taped up and it is all right now.
    I can't think of much tonight. Please give me love to everybody.
Love
Walter Jr.

The letter was written on my birthday and I had just turned 20. I sprained my ankle again. What was it this time? Partying, trying out new dance moves, or jumping off the tank on uneven ground?

My stay in England had lasted about one month: three weeks in Wells and a week in Portsmouth. My trip to France was on a *Liberty* ship, which arrived off Omaha Beach on July 10, 1944. The weather was bad and we rode the anchor for three days. The ship bounced up and down, causing some of the soldiers seasickness. Luckily, I didn't experience this. However, getting ashore proved to be most exciting. To board the craft, soldiers went over the side of the ship. The ship was still anchored and the waves had died only a little. As soon as the landing craft was loaded with the men, it was dropped into the water. The swells from the waves would surround the craft, looking like it might drown everyone on board. As we neared shore, the landing craft operator saw a friend and waved, moving the steering wheel straight for a concrete block. Fearing a collision, he threw the landing craft into reverse. Now the whole craft was shaking and soldiers were being tossed around. The concrete block didn't move when hit. The soldiers happily got out of the craft as the commander for the landing craft operator came screaming. The trip gave me more than a little anxiety.

This beach had been the site of a terrible battle with many soldiers losing their lives to help defend our way of life. The beach showed little signs of the tragedy that happened. On shore, we marched inland several miles and when we finally stopped, we were ordered to dig a foxhole. I thought the order was odd. That night, a German bomber flew over the area and dropped several bombs that reportedly killed 20 men. The foxhole gave some comfort.

Replacements

Every army needs to replace casualties and has a process for doing this. The problem during World War II was that as well as some 936,259 battle casualties, the U.S. Army sustained about 17,000,000 non-battle admissions to sick report. In overseas theaters about 79 percent of the admissions to sick report were for disease, 13 percent for injury, and only 8 percent for combat wounds. The replacement system had to cover these and on top of that, replace men absent because of training, furloughs, or disciplinary confinement. Added to this, modern warfare was brutal on men at the sharp end—particularly the infantry but tankers as well. There had been manpower shortages since 1943. In 1944 they became critical. One of the ways replacements were quickly pushed into the field was to take men from the divisions under training in the United States. Walter was one of these. Plucked from the division he'd trained with for many months, he and many others were taken to Europe to act as replacements for casualties anticipated in the invasion fighting.

The Army's replacement system was to fill vacancies left by casualties individually rather than as full units or smaller groups who knew each other from training. While individual replacement was an easier system logistically, it was difficult for both the replacement and for the unit receiving replacements who had to integrated them into a unit that was in combat, something that gave great concern to the combat veterans they joined. The vets looked askance at men, often with less training than Walter, who survived barely long enough for soldiers to remember their names.

Replacements arrived in Normandy and then proceeded to their units. This process changed as the Allies advanced further into France and usually took four stops: a reception depot, a stockage depot which provided the replacement the first opportunity to collect back pay since his departure from the United States, an army depot, then a forward battalion supporting a particular corps, and finally a specific unit. That process could be long, especially in the early weeks after the invasion when the replacements moved on foot to tent encampments. It was also frightening as naïve young men were told horror stories about combat and mortality by veterans.

Walter was, in many ways, lucky. When he arrived in France, he wasn't combat experienced but he had been in training for 12 months and could perform any of the duties required as tank crew. He left Fort Polk on May 9. He wasn't re-deployed to become an infantryman or left waiting long enough to get too bored or forget his training. He became part of 3rd Armored at the end of August.

Replacement troops prepare to move up to their next encampment. Omar Bradley said, "Among U.S. troops the replacement depots soon developed an infamous reputation for callousness and inefficiency." The divisions improved on this as the war went on, taking replacements into their own camp and introducing them to combat conditions and requirements. (NARA)

Every few days, the replacements moved again. Dig a new foxhole then wander around. On one of these wanderings, I heard a gunshot and went to investigate. A cook had shot a German who was attempting to hide after his crew had been pushed back by the Americans. When I walked up, everyone was standing around talking, and no one was doing anything. The German was lying still and didn't look threatening, so I walked slowly towards him. He was making his last gasps for life and then quit breathing. Getting closer, I noticed the German had a pistol, a Walther P38. I picked it up and walked back toward the cook and his friends. The one who did the shooting said, "I ought to have that gun."

My response was something like "Who went over and picked it up?" Alas, the Old West. I promptly stuck it in my belt and walked away. Later I strutted around so everyone could see it. Big time operator! Now I had a weapon!

Of course, I didn't know if the gun was loaded, and I just jammed it into my pants. Oh, youth!

V-Mail Letter #65 postmarked August 22, 1944[3]

Dear Family,

Just a line to let you know I'm O.K.

I received the birthday cards, thanks a lot. They came about a week to late so you can just about guess how long it takes to get my mail.

There's not much I can think of to say. We are still having beautiful weather and I've gotten a suntan.

I hope you'll forgive me if I don't answer all the questions you ask but I usually destroy the letters before I have chance to answer them.

If you want to send a package I could use some chewing gum and candy.

Love

Walter

Mail was delivered with the kitchen truck. The company bugler, who never used a bugle, was the mail clerk. Imagine the anticipation of getting mail from home. It would distract you from thinking of entering a combat zone. So, it was with great anticipation when my name was called to get mail.

The company had only been in France for a few days. I took my mail over to the foxhole. I sat on the ground with my feet dangling in the foxhole to read my mail from home.

It couldn't be! But it was. My best friend, Bill Megahan, from eighth grade through high school, a Marine, was dead. Killed on Saipan on June 19, 1944. Bill was the point man that day and a sniper killed him instantly. It was stunning news. My mother thought she should be the one to let me know. She sent a clipping from the paper telling of Bill and his death.

Memories flooded my mind. It was at dinner at Megahan's where I had my first shrimp cocktail. There were many happy hours at the kitchen table in the evening playing Canasta, often with Bill's father, Doctor Megahan. There were classes taken together and the antics we got into.

Survival demanded moving on. Staying focused on the present was imperative. A truck ride through the ruins of Saint-Lô told the story of what was to come, destruction everywhere. Houses and buildings were in rubble. No people were visible. The only building with a roof had a sign on it that said, "Mayor."

I didn't know it at this time, but I was close to being a combat soldier in what was to be the famous 3rd Armored Division.

---

[3] The numbering of the letters once I was overseas got a little mixed up. The V-Mail was much faster while letters took longer. While there is no letter numbered 66, I do have a letter postmarked 65.

The front was moving slowly west. Every few days, the replacement depot moved and dug new foxholes. At times, we were close enough to hear American artillery.

However, there were lighter moments, like short baseball games with truck drivers from a service company. The truck drivers were from a Black unit whose position didn't move. I went to talk with their sergeant who suggested a baseball game. They had gloves, balls, and bats. The sergeant's rule was the teams would be mixed. I agreed and rounded up enough men to play. I was playing second and the shortstop was from the truck unit. A ball hit to the shortstop was quickly fielded and thrown with such force, all I could do was duck, missing the ball. The shortstop asked, "Why didn't you catch it?"

I responded, "Did you think I was in the outfield?" The game was for fun and release of anxiety for things to come. No score was kept.

Letter #65: postmarked August 22, 1944

Dear Family,

I guess you noticed my new address on the envelope. I think that will be my address for a while. I don't think I will have enough time to write and tell everybody my address so I'll ask you to please tell them. (Lenore, Eleanor, and Aunt Hattie.)

I don't remember if I told you or not but I got a letter from Bill Hathaway about 2 weeks ago. He is going thru what I did.

A couple days ago I had some French Cognac. It didn't taste too bad, the worst part was when I saw some fellows using it in cig lighters for fuel.

I'm still feeling swell.

Love

Walter

The address was Co.E. 33rd APO 253[4] c/o P.M. N.Y.N.Y. Across the top of the envelope was written Armd. Regt, which let everyone know I was with the 33rd Armored Regiment. In late August I had been sent from the Replacement Depot to a location near Falaise, France. I was a replacement for a tank crewman. This meant someone in the crew had been killed and I took his spot. I was introduced to the tank crew, who had survived the previous battle—the division's mission at that time was to close the Falaise Gap.

At this point, I'd told my girlfriend, my younger cousin, and my aunt my new address. The reason for these three: love letters, jokes, and food! Lenore lived in town and attended the Catholic church so mom would have had to

---

[4]Company E, 33rd Armored Regiment, 3rd Armored Division—APO 253 was 3rd Armored's Army post office number.

call her to let her know. Eleanor lived in Grafton, West Virginia, and Hattie in Clarksburg. Mom probably sent them a letter with my new address.

Bill Hathaway, another classmate from home, was in the Air Force. He was assigned to the cook and baker units. He was preparing to enter the European Theater, much like I had. I'm not sure how much combat he saw. Toward the end of the Battle of the Bulge, he was taken out of the kitchen and made an infantryman.

French cognac didn't taste too bad. I left out the part about what happened after you swallowed it. Burn, baby, burn! Your whole throat would be on fire. I'm sure it could be lighter fluid. In my opinion, this was a better use of the stuff. Not mentioned in my remarks about the cognac was that the new crew were all about "three sheets to the wind." This was my only experience with what I later learned wasn't cognac—brandy from distilled white wine—but Calvados, apple brandy. There were many stories about its potency.

3rd Armored Division

Walter's new home at the end of August 1944 was a division that had only been in France for two months but had already seen considerable action—although its C.G., Brigadier General Leroy H. Watson, had been relieved of command for supposedly ineffective leadership. Whether that was true or whether he was a scapegoat for the lack of planning foresight about the difficulty of fighting through the Normandy bocage, the new commander from August 7, was Major General Maurice Rose, a more aggressive soldier who led from the front—and it was at the front of his division that he died on March 30, 1945, near Paderborn.

The invasion of Normandy had provided the Allies with a lodgment on the continent. The German reaction confined the bridgehead and both sides pumped reinforcements into the battle. Heavy fighting saw the Germans restrict the Allies but the attrition meant they were never able to launch a counterattack with sufficient strength. Instead, they had to introduce their reserves piecemeal into the battle to maintain their position. This was especially true around Caen, where the bulk of the German armor—particularly the heavies—defended against continuous British and Canadian attacks.

In the west, after slogging through the bocage hedgerow country, First (U.S.) Army finally achieved the breakout with Operation *Cobra*. The German front line was punctured and Patton's Third (U.S.) Army was unleashed through the opening to exploit the sparsely defended hinterland.

So effectively had the Allies blunted the German armored units that when they finally did counterattack at Mortain on August 6, instead of the eight Panzer divisions they wanted, they could muster less than four. Their powerful thrust was contained by the U.S. forces. This included 3rd Armored, which had entered combat on July 29, and this left the Germans in Normandy in a perilous position. The German retreat focused into a bottleneck that narrowed around Falaise. Chased by the Allied ground troops and harried from the air, the Germans managed to save a third of their men before the Allies were able to close the gap completely, but left behind their heavy weapons, 10–15,000 dead and 50,000 P.O.W.s.

It was a decisive victory. Paris was liberated by August 25, and the Allies gave chase to the retreating Germans. The Canadians cleared the Channel coast. The British reached Brussels on September 2 and Antwerp on September 4. In the east, Third (U.S.) Army reached Verdun in early September and linked up with Seventh (U.S.) Army coming up from the south.

In the north, First (U.S.) Army crossed the Seine on August 25 and advanced rapidly through France into Belgium. Leading the charge was VII Corps under General J. Lawton Collins, and leading VII was 3rd Armored Division, flanked by 1st and 9th Infantry Divisions. In spite of the early September supply problems that affected all the Allied armies, progress was spectacular and on September 12 elements of Task Force Lovelady crossed the border into Germany. Roetgen was the first town they captured and it was the first German town taken by the Allies.

3rd Armored started to cross the Seine at Tilly on the night of August 25 over an existing bridge. By the next morning the engineers had another bridge ready allowing the division to move swiftly east and northeast. (NARA)

M4A1 and M4s of 33rd Armored Regiment during the fighting around Mons, Belgium. (NARA)

An M4A1(76) of 3rd Armored Division in Chênée, a suburb of Liège, Belgium, on September 8, 1944. (NARA)

3rd Armored was a "heavy" division, with two armored regiments each of four M4 medium and two M5 light battalions along with three armored infantry battalions. This gave the division a total of 16,000 men, although attrition meant it was rarely at that level: during its 231 days in combat, it suffered 16,122 casualties. As a further example of this attrition, on September 18 as the division paused for rest and maintenance there were only 153 medium tanks operative in the whole division, and of these 30 would only run in low gear—the T.O.&E. figure was 232. The division had received 66 officers and 887 men as replacements between September 15 and 23 but was still only up to 90 percent strength.

V-Mail Letter #64: postmarked August 23, 1944

Dear Family,
Please forgive the delay in writing but I have been pretty busy.

We are having beautiful weather and I am getting a suntan. You ask much I weigh. The last time I got weighed it was 158, but I think I have gained some since then.

I received a letter from Bill Hathway. I think he may come over here soon.

I have tried about a million times to write a letter to Mrs. Megahan but I just can't think of anything to say. I guess she knows how I feel anyway.

I'll write again soon—
Love
Walter Jr.

I'm sure my mom was encouraging me to write to Mrs. Megahan after the death of Bill. What was I to write? This was often the way people dealt with bad news and I was no different. I didn't know what to say, so I just avoided it. Hopefully my mom gave me wise advice. Just acknowledging the situation and expressing my sentiments would have been enough. After the war, I did visit the Megahans, even after I had moved away. When I came home to Wheeling, I would stop down and see them. I did this until they passed away.

I was in Normandy and not yet assigned to a crew when I read the news. Thinking of what life would be like back in Elm Grove without Bill wasn't something I could even begin to process. I was reminded of the Sunday School teacher's lesson: "To lose a friend is to die a little."

V-Mail Letter #67: postmarked September 19, 1944[5]

Dear Family,
Please forgive me for not writing sooner and oftener but I just couldn't find time.

---

[5] With the V-mail arriving before letters, the numbering of the letters is off. There was no letter numbered 66.

I am in the best of health and getting older every day.

There's no doubt about the company I am in now. Lt. is the best company in the Regiment. They really are a swell bunch of fellows. There are two fellows in the Co. from West Virginia. And quite a few from Ohio.

By the way, whereabouts in France is Mrs. Johnston from?

The weather is still pretty nice although it gets chilly at times.

I guess I'm ran down for now so I'll sign off.

Love

Walter

Here was a letter home with words between the lines and an ironic postmark! "Where did Mrs. Johnson live in France?" Everyone in my immediate family knew Mrs. Johnson was from Charleroi in Belgium. The letter is headed "somewhere in Belgium." I saw a sign that said Charleroi! I wonder if my mother ran next door to tell the landlady I was near her hometown. My family could have looked at the atlas to know where I was fighting.

Between the previous letter on August 23 and the next, there was a lapse of several weeks. A lot happened!

My crew of replacements had no tank! We rode in a half-track with one other crew. A half-track is much like riding in the back of a pick-up truck. Our half-track had a 30- and 50-caliber machine gun. Sitting in the half-track a few days later in France, I was just missed by a sniper's bullet. The sniper was hiding in a nearby steeple. His shots brought the attention of an American soldier with a bazooka. The round killed the soldier. This was my first time being shot at and you can believe I prayed it would be my last.

A few days later, the half-track was parked on a rail overpass. I spotted Germans running across the rail track from forest to forest. I quickly began firing the nearby 30-caliber machine gun. I missed all three Germans.

Just as it was getting dark, someone with sharp hearing yelled, "Tanks!" It got quiet. My tank commander, a sergeant from Clarksburg, West Virginia, yelled for me to come with him. We got the bazooka from the kitchen truck (I have no idea why a kitchen truck would have a bazooka) and started down the road toward the sound.

The tank stopped but not before it was agreed we'd fire two shots then head for Paris and claim we got lost in the dark. I liked that idea but the Germans didn't continue. Our convoy of trucks and half-tracks moved out in the dark. Not a good idea either, but we did. The next morning, I was last on guard and heard tanks. Nobody missed my warning! With no guns to fight tanks, except the bazooka in the kitchen truck, we could only wait to see what was coming next. They were American tanks. Then from the opposite direction came a German column. My tank commander on the 50-caliber and I on the 30-caliber made for a quick stop and 17 prisoners. And we weren't even in combat yet.

The prisoners were rounded up. A Jewish American soldier, whose family had escaped Germany's persecution of Jews, spoke fluent German. He told the prisoners to take off their helmets, pistols, and empty their pockets. My friend went over and took a holster from one of the prisoners and gave it to me. I had a holster for my P38!

Finally, I was in a tank along with the rest of the replacements. I was assigned to be the loader. We were part of Task Force Lovelady. It was the end of August. We reached Soissons on the 28th, a day after crossing the Marne, and had to cross another major river—the Aisne—before, while fighting at Laon, we were ordered north towards Mons via Hirson and Vervins.

Task Force Lovelady

3rd Armored Division hadn't been modernized in the way that 8th Armored was, still having two tank regiments and only one of infantry. To increase the infantry levels to those dictated by the new organization, units from other divisions of VII Corps were attached—mainly from 1st or 30th Infantry. Task forces were created, comprising typically "one battalion of tanks and infantry, the latter less one company, with a platoon each of engineers and tank destroyers, with the support of an artillery battalion. Within the task force might be battle groups of an infantry company, a tank or tank destroyer platoon, a mortar squad and an engineer squad."[6]

Task Force Lovelady started off as Task Force X, commanded by Lieutenant Colonel Vincent E. Cockefaire with second in command, Lieutenant Colonel William B. Lovelady. Cockefaire was killed by artillery on August 10, 1944, and Lovelady took over.

Task Force Lovelady was part of the southern Allied pincer attempting to trap the Germans fleeing Normandy by closing the Falaise Gap. At 10:45 on August 18, 1944, they did so when Sergeant Donald Ekdahl met "the tea drinkers"—the British. 3rd Armored had played a major role in the battle, and had sustained casualties. Walter was one of the replacements, joining Company E of the 33rd Armored Regiment in Task Force Lovelady. He remained in this task force for the rest of his time in combat. The constituent elements of Task Force Lovelady changed at various stages during the fighting as will be shown in the following pages, but the nucleus was Lovelady's 2nd Battalion, 33rd Armored Regiment.

[6] Dugan, Maj Haynes: *Spearheading with the Third Armored Division* (1945) and *Spearhead in the West* (1946) via https://www.3ad.com/history/wwll/spearhead.west.index.htm.

M4 medium

The Medium Tank Crewman (M.O.S. 2736) had the same range of duties as the light tank crewman except that there was one more of them—while the light tank was crewed by four, the M4 medium had five:

- Tank commander—usually a lieutenant or sergeant positioned in the turret, standing on the floor or sitting or standing on the seat above the crew.
- Gunner—seated on the gunner's seat, on the right of the gun.
- Cannoneer (loader and assistant gunner)—standing in the turret, or seated on the cannoneer's seat at the left of the gun.
- Bow gunner—seated in the bow gunner's seat front right of hull in front of the gunner.
- Driver—seated in the driver's seat in front left of hull in front of the loader.

Walter started out as a loader. Later he'd take on the position of gunner. FM 16-67[7] informs us that: "The crew of the tank gun is the gunner, who aims and fires the piece; the cannoneer, who loads the piece; and the tank commander, who controls and adjusts fire." It goes on to detail the operation of the gun and how the gunner and cannoneer—the loader—work together to fire the gun:

- The cannoneer opens the breech.
- He inserts a round which causes the breechblock to close automatically.
- The gunner fires and releases the firing switch.
- The cannoneer reloads then signals "ready" by tapping the gunner's left leg with the foot. (This was never the practice in Walt's tank, where the crew had earphones and so the gunner could hear the breechblock close.)
- The gunner lays the gun, bringing the target into the field of the telescope by the quickest practical method, under guidance of the tank commander or by use of the periscope.
- After receiving the signal from the cannoneer, the gunner fires.

Walt remembers that the tank commander would give the order "A.P." or "H.E." and the target location. He never had gloves as a loader.

The loader was responsible for ensuring that ammunition was used in the requisite order so that ready rounds were always available for emergency use. For example, the order given in FM 17-67 for the 75mm gun was as follows: ready racks on turret floor; forward racks, right sponson; racks beneath turret floor; rear racks, right sponson. Rounds in ready clips and those in the left sponson were kept as a reserve for action where speed of loading is of utmost importance.

---

[7] FM 17-67 War Department Field Manual Crew Drill and Service of the Piece, Medium Tank M4.

M4A3(76) of 31st Tank Battalion, 7th Armored, showing four of the five crew using their hatches—commander, loader (cannoneer), driver and assistant driver. The gunner's position was in front of the commander, whose hatch he used. There were two main turret types—one for the 75mm and the other for the 76mm gun. The number and type of hatches and cupolas differed for the main types and variants of the tank. This photo is posed—crewman didn't usually wear helmets and a captain's insignia on the helmet would have made him a particular target. (NARA)

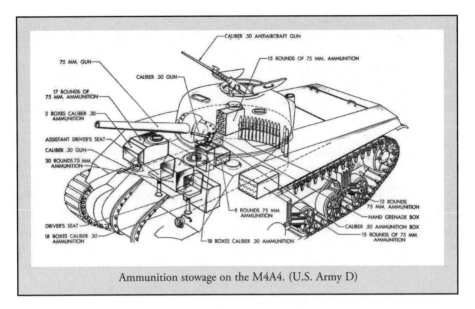

Ammunition stowage on the M4A4. (U.S. Army D)

On September 2 we crossed the border into Belgium. We drove all night and helped liberate Mons, and captured 19,000 Germans. Lack of fuel stopped the division in its tracks until September 4 when supplies reached us. We advanced again, passing through Charleroi—which gave me a chance to get one past the censor, Lieutenant Roy A. Abig.

We were outside Namur early on the 5th, waiting for bridges to be built across the Meuse. As soon as they were, we headed on to Huy where Task Force Lovelady took an undamaged bridge over the same river that twisted and turned along our advance. Next stop was Liège which we reached on September 7. On September 10 we reached Verviers, Eupen on the 11th. All these towns were in Belgium. On the 12th, the Task Force's recon company from 33rd Armored Regiment crossed the border into Germany and shortly after the task force entered Roetgen on the German side of the border. Our forces moved in and captured our first German town. The Germans fled or were taken prisoner. The infantry gathered up all the prisoners and took them back to a field for integration and processing.

Letter #68: postmarked October 8, 1944[8]

Dear Family,

Well! Here's that much awaited epistle. I have been kind of busy and couldn't find time to write. I received 2 packages of candy and a fruit cake. I never did get the first package

---

[8] The date on my next V-mail is September 23. The V-Mail had caught on with the troops and was also slowing down processing, not to mention having to go through all the censors.

you sent. There isn't anything I need real bad except a New Testament, mine was destroyed. Talk about surprises, I met Ralph Brill yesterday. I met him when I went to take a shower. We swapped stories about what we knew about some of the other fellows. I got my shower taken but he never did get his.

You asked what I wanted for Christmas… the thing I need most is socks. Will write soon.
Love
Walter Jr.

Lt. Abig had censored my last letter days before.

On the other side of Roetgen lay the Siegfried Line—the Westwall—whose defenses included wire, dragon's teeth, and pillboxes. The division first probed the area to find the most advantageous place to attack and then on September 13 thrust through the defenses towards the Stolberg corridor and, they hoped, Eschweiler and then Düren.

The trouble was that the Blitzkrieg from the Seine had taken its toll on men and machines. Additionally, the German defenses—and the attitude of the defenders—on German soil had hardened. Ammunition shortages—particularly of 105mm shells—limited the artillery as well.

The fighting in the Westwall defenses intensified. At Rott, Task Force Lovelady ran into a German strongpoint and quickly lost four tanks. However, it and the division continued the attacks on September 14 through 16 and cleared the Westwall's two lines, heading through Mausbach towards Eschweiler where it ran into an ambush. Task Force Lovelady lost seven Shermans and a tank destroyer and pulled its remaining 13 Shermans back into cover. Halted by German attacks, General Rose, C.G. of 3rd Armored thought the checks were only a temporary hindrance but events on September 17 and 18 proved him wrong.

The corps commander ordered the division to consolidate and hold their positions. To do this, limited-scale attacks were needed to improve the division's positions. Trouble was, little headway was made. Indeed, by this time attrition had left some infantry companies with not much more than half their normal strength; armored units had been similarly weakened.

September 19 was an all-out battle. The fighting was so fierce that I, the loader, had to replace the 30-caliber machine gun barrel that got too hot to fire. The tank fired shell after shell from the cannon. Suddenly, there was a voice outside the tank! Our tank commander, Sergeant Clarence Jones, nicknamed "Red" for his red hair, was told to get out, that Lieutenant Baer was taking over.

2-Lt. Paul E. Baer, Jr had already lost two tanks in this battle. As a platoon leader, he felt he should lead another tank crew. Thus Sgt. Jones was replaced.

Here we were in the midst of a battle and a commander change happened.

Lieutenant Baer, stunned by what he had seen that day, got in and stood staring. No words, no motion, just staring! Over the radio came a voice urging Lt. Baer to move quickly as he was being shot at. Nothing happened! A second call. I looked out the periscope to see a fireball go by, shot from a German 88 tank gun. Finally, Lt. Baer said, "Driver, back up." These were his last words.

The second shell tore through the turret. The tank reared up. Ellsworth Reavy was thrown backwards and Lt. Baer fell forward. Both were killed instantly.

My commander's hatch and my nearest exit from the tank was now blocked by two dead bodies. I feared I was trapped. I attempted to move the bodies with no success. Seeing light in my peripheral vision, I escaped by going out the driver's hatch just as the second shot set the tank on fire. On bailing out, I dislocated my shoulder again, a frequent event as a result of the jeep accident during basic training.

The driver Alfred Ahrenson and bow gunner Walter Huffman had also gotten out, they had run about 50 yards back and waited to see who else escaped the tank. They asked me about Reavy and Baer and I shook my head, "No."

While standing, I became aware that my leg was bleeding. I ran to a nearby light tank and asked for a bandage. The answer was "Come up and get it." A hand appeared out of the top hatch with a bandage. As I climbed up the side of the tank to retrieve it, a burst of bullets hit the tank beside me.

This was the second time I was someone's personal target. A quick look spotted the German with a "burp-gun" under some brush. My yell to the tank of the German's position was the last time he fired his gun.

With my tank gone, I found shelter lying in a half-dug foxhole. I was trying to decide how to best protect myself. If I lay face down, my spine would be exposed; if I were face up, my heart could get hit. Luckily for me, a medic came by. He asked if I could walk. With my positive response, he gave me instructions for where to find an ambulance for a ride to the field hospital. I was taken via ambulance out of the foxhole to the hospital where I got the ubiquitous tetanus shot, a quick workover on my leg, a cot for the night, and a K-ration dinner. The next day I was taken back to E Company Command Post.

The first sergeant was close to tears upon hearing of Reavy, one of his longtime friends and the second son killed in that family. Before dinner, I was reunited with Red Jones, Ahrenson, and Huffman. Walter Ling came in as the new loader and I became gunner. We were back to the front within 24 hours, where E Company tanks were very few. I was really happy to have Sergeant "Red" Jones back as my tank commander.

Years later, after an X-ray, the doctor asked me if I had gotten shot in the foot. "No, shrapnel in the leg," was my response. The doctor noted I now had a piece of metal in my middle toe.

My first tank was gone, along with the New Testament Bible given to me by my home church. Also, I lost my musette kit which contained all the supplies I needed from grooming to smoking. Along with the rest of the crew, I learned an unintended but important lesson that day: Don't save the good stuff for later. A bottle of Belgian wine and cartons of the "good" cigarettes were lost in the tank.

On the date of this letter, my crew and I were back off the front on reserve. It was quite a treat, after all we had just gone through, to be taken by truck to a portable shower. Each man had a shower head. Stripped naked, warm water, soap and clean towel. What a treat! Everybody got clean clothes. Ralph Brill, a friend from home, was in the group to go next, but the Germans lobbed in a stray shell and the shower company folded up and left. "Too close to the front."

In the final line, I asked for socks for Christmas. The Army provided socks. I must not have seen the supply sergeant in a while. Another thought is the Army provided a pair of olive drab socks. Mom would give multiple pairs in standard black.

I didn't write home anything about what happened to me. I had just seen two people killed instantly while sitting inside the tank. Working and talking together one minute, all within my reach, and gone the next. Until this incident, I thought I was safer inside the medium Sherman tank. Later Shermans became known as Ronsons due to their flammability but I never heard this during the war, only at reunions of the 3rd Armored.[9]

My understanding of how dangerous war was going to be and what a sitting target a tank presented to the German army just became very clear to me. Survival depended on quick thinking and lots of luck. Thoughts of losing two tank crew members, surviving a burning tank, dislocating a shoulder, being wounded, shot at, and losing everything I owned in the tank swirled in my head. Not a word about it to my family, though. I shielded them from what was really happening.

---

[9] National WWII Museum, n.d., para. 2.

Tank Casualties

If a tank were penetrated by an anti-tank round, there was a reasonable chance that there would be fire. This was by no means certain and often depended on whether the ammunition "cooked off" and exploded. Many knocked-out tanks were subsequently recovered, repaired, and reused, although it was unusual for tanks to be reused after fire damage—particularly if main ammunition exploded. The main cause of fire was the stowage of ammunition. Early Shermans had ammunition storage in the sponsons with ready use rounds at the loader's feet. When it became clear that these caused most of the fires, the ready-use rounds were reduced in number and given an armored casing, applique armor was applied to the tank's sides, and later Shermans used the "wet" system of ammunition storage, keeping most rounds below the turret basket in the hull of the tank and encasing them in water sleeves.

Survey of Allied Tank Casualties in World War II[10] of March 1, 1951, looked at a sample of 841 tanks knocked out in the European Theatre of Operations. Of this

Turret penetrations would certainly kill commander and probably loader but, if the ammunition didn't cook off, often other crew members could escape. (NARA)

---

[10] By Alvin D. Cook and L. Van Loan Naisawald of the Operations Research Office of Johns Hopkins University.

If you didn't get out quickly, a burning tank was a death trap. (NARA)

sample, 48 percent were knocked out by 88mm gunfire and 75mm accounted for 40 percent. The sites of hits from gunfire were split c. 31 percent turret, c. 51 percent hull, and c. 18 percent suspension. Overall, they found that about half the time gunfire rendered the damaged vehicle unrepairable.

They looked more closely at a selection of some 275 medium and 50 light tank crews of First (U.S.) Army. This showed the percentage of casualties by crew position—an overall 51 percent for M4 crews. This means that around 2.5 men became casualties for each tank that became a battle casualty. The tank commanders had the highest casualty rate—generally assumed to be because they were most likely to be traveling "heads up" and thus exposed to the Germans' two main casualty-producing weapons—gunfire and bazooka attacks. The light tank (M5) casualty rates were, understandably, higher—around 65 percent. The 3rd Armored Division lost 633 medium tanks between June 29, 1944 and April 22, 1945.[11]

Walter's crew had lost its tank and two crew members—statistically, that was about average. It shows how versatile tank crew replacements needed to be. He ended up as gunner: but he could have needed to take any of the crew positions, other than commander which was reserved for a more senior soldier.

---

[11] *Spearhead in the West* (3rd Armored Division, 1946).

War is ugly and terrifying. To survive you have to kill the people trying to kill you. It went against everything I had been taught. The first time you know you're going to end an enemy's life isn't easy and doesn't feel natural. However, you do it or else your life might be over.

Letter #69: postmarked October 6, 1944

Dear Family,
You are probably wondering where the paper came from, it is part of a book (some kind of ledger) I picked up.

I finally got that first package you sent, and believe it or not, it wasn't in too bad of a shape. I guess I told you already, but in case I didn't I could use stuff like socks and handkerchiefs as well as candy and chewing gum. I haven't gotten that dog tag chain yet. I will let Lenore know as soon as I do.

By the way be sure and tell me when you receive the money I sent home. I sent a hundred dollars.

Be sure and have some of those canned pears when I get home. I think I could eat about a bushel myself. Lately I have been having some swell meals. I helped eat 3 rabbits, 2 chickens, and 4 dozen eggs.

Here is something else I forgot to mention. I need a razor. I think a double edge razor would be best, because I can get blades for it a lot easier.

I got a letter from Aunt Hattie the other day, and boy did I get a bawling out. She sent another of her reminders, an empty envelope and a blank sheet of paper. That fruit cake she has for me should be able to walk most of the way here.

I don't know what's wrong with me today that me makes me write so much maybe I'm getting homesick.

I want to thank Sara for writing to me, and if I can find the time, and somebody beats me over the head to make me write. I write her a letter someday.

I guess I better close now so I won't get writer's cramp.

Love
Walter Jr.
P.S. Remember me in your prayers. It's already done plenty of good.

The fighting continued until September 25 and then Task Force Lovelady moved back from the front lines to Breinig. We were there for one week. We were told it was for "complete rest, no war for a week." Then the Germans moved a company of 155mm artillery in the same area, we fired. The Germans didn't like it so they fired back. One week away from the war, didn't happen.

We took our tank onto a hillside. We ran it back and forth several times then dug the area out underneath the tank. We laid the tarp on the ground. Our plan was to go out the escape hatch and lie on the tarp at night. This would allow us to stretch out. The plan was perfect except the escape hatch was frozen shut and, having no hammer, we beat on it with our trenching tool until it finally gave way.

In my unit, there was a Native American everyone called "Chief." Alcohol and Chief did not mix. After drinking too much alcohol, Chief started shooting his gun, claiming the Germans had killed his mother and father. Nearby soldiers and I took cover and started counting shots. After eight shots, we tackled Chief, took his gun, and let him sleep it off.

After leaving Breinig, we returned to the front and moved to Stolberg. The town was half in American hands and would remain so until mid-November's Operation *Queen*. My tank was stationed next to a two-story house with most of the front blown off during early fighting in Stolberg. It was okay except for the smell of a bloated cow rotting in the field.

The left side of the tank was next to a house wall with an open area to the right, with an occupied pillbox about 150 feet away. A pillbox is made of concrete about a foot thick with a slit to shoot through. The Germans used these locations to shoot unsuspecting soldiers. The location of the pillbox

Infantry getting a ride on an M4 of 33rd Armored Regiment in Stolberg on October 14, 1944. (NARA)

Static warfare led to a range of living arrangements—here, a truck-racked tarp as a shelter beside a 3rd Armored foxhole near Stolberg. (NARA)

was the crest of a hill. They could see us and we could see them. However, at night, one could hear the German horse-carts bringing in supplies for their troops. Getting out of the tank in daylight meant risking artillery fire. They had us marked and the observers in the pillbox were very alert. Any bodily functions that couldn't be done in an orange juice can in the tank were done out of the tank after dark. Quickly!

One night in Stolberg, the tank crew heard the Germans trying to clear away rubble from a pillbox doorway. *Pick, pick, shovel, shovel.* My commander had me slowly move the gun in the direction of the sound. When the digging sounds began, I fired the gun. The next night again, the sound. *Pick, pick, shovel, shovel.* The commander commented, "Just forget it!"

There were American infantry soldiers inside the house. They had the equipment to heat up water for our coffee. Another member of my tank and I made a plan to get inside the house, heat up the water, and return to the tank with hot water for coffee. I jumped out first. The guy inside handed out the can for water, then he jumped out and we headed for the house.

Making it safely inside, water heated, the task to return to the tank was put in action. I went first, and the German in the pillbox spotted us and took a shot. I dove for the ground while the guy holding the bucket backed up against the house, holding the bucket in front of him. A chicken went flying and plaster from the house rained down. With neither of us hit, we took off on a dead run back to the tank. Coffee was served. As we got down to the end of the can, a sign of our close call was found: plaster from the house.

Germany in October was very cold. Sleeping in a steel tank was a challenge. E Company tanks were told to pick a house and tell the occupants to go to City Hall in Stolberg. Where the homeowners were sent after that was arranged by the Army. My crew and I found a house with a middle-aged couple living there and sent them on. While there wasn't much to do, we could warm our coffee, eat our K-rations, and not worry about being shot at. It was about three days of warm sleeping.

I also borrowed paper from a ledger in their house to write home. Seeing a real kitchen brought back memories of home and all the foods I loved (and still do): ham, eggs, peas, chocolate. I wanted a bushel of canned pears. It seems that maybe the K-rations weren't enough and we started eating the vacated family's livestock: chickens, rabbits, and eggs.

In the cellar, the family had rabbits and large jars with fresh eggs being soaked in water. One of the crew decided a rabbit would be good to eat. He picked up the rabbit and swung it against a metal door. The rabbit responded in turn by scratching the man. This really made him mad. He took out his knife and killed the rabbit. I didn't participate in the preparation of the animal for eating. However, I could cook and eggs are something I did rather well. The task of making eggs for everyone fell to me.

I needed things I lost when the tank exploded, like razor blades, socks, handkerchiefs. I wondered what my parents must have thought. I can hear my dad now, "Didn't we just send him this stuff?" My mom would have been more kind hearted saying I was probably sharing my things with the tank crew.

I would write to my sister and say what? War was awful. Tanks didn't protect you from fire-balls. Men were being killed. Cities were being destroyed. I was scared for my life. My world had been turned upside down. Fun times were few. Saying I was homesick was an understatement. I just wanted to make it home. The postscript at the end of the letter was the closest I came to telling my family I was not in a safe place.

New orders were given. E Company was ordered to a position on the front. Never in one place too long.

Letter #70: postmarked October 21, 1944

Dear Family,

I don't know how long this letter will be, but at least you'll know I'm alright.

If you should get a letter from Uncle Sam saying I was "slightly" wounded don't worry about it. I just got my leg cut a little by a piece of shrapnel. That happened the 19th of last month and is all healed up now.

I finally got a letter written to Aunt Hattie so she will have a request to send that "doctored up" fruit cake she's been saving since Easter.

There is one thing I'll ask for Christmas. Sometimes I have a little time and, as you know, I got that reading habit. So if you should run across a good book I would appreciate your sending it.

In a letter I got last night you mentioned my getting dirty. Dirty isn't the word for it. This mud over here is like glue and showers are few and far between. When we get a rest (usually 4 to 7 days) we get showers and clean clothes. Boy! I'll really appreciate a nice warm bathroom and a tub of hot water.

While I'm thinking about it. It usually takes your letters 10 to 15 days to get here. If you think of it tell me how long it takes my letters to get home.

I give you a good example of American soldiers. We are sitting here close enough to throw rocks at the "Heinies" and everybody is laughing and telling jokes.

I guess that is all for now.

Love

Walter Jr.

The funny thing about this letter is it was sent to Elm Grove, *Wisconsin*. I don't know if the Army told folks back home about my wounds. So, just in case, I finally told them twenty-two days after and left out the horror that accompanied the wound.

A week on the front in Stolberg with no fighting relaxed the crew. I report this as laughing "close enough to the 'Heinies' to throw rocks." "Heinies" was the nickname the soldiers gave the Germans. Where it came from is unknown to me, but it was frequently used in my letters home.

After a week on the front line, a decision was made to switch crews. We would go back and another crew would take our place in the tank. At the designated hour, we left the tank and went back toward the woods about 50 yards away. We were stopped with a call of "Halt, who goes there?" It was our platoon leader lying on the ground with a submachine gun. He asked for a password.

Sergeant Jones replied, "I only know the password you gave us last night." We were then advised to proceed. Within the next few minutes, we heard the lieutenant again. The response was fire from a German burp gun. He had just stopped a German patrol. The lieutenant fired but they found no bodies the next day.

It was over a week before my crew and I had another tank. When we entered the tank, we thought we had a new tank. The inside was painted all white. A sergeant came over and ordered everyone out and his crew took over the "new" tank, leaving us an old clunker. After the war, I learned the white paint inside the tank didn't mean it was new. When a tank had been hit, often someone's head exploded and paint was used to cover it up.

During the month of October, our crew saw little fighting. The Americans needed gas, ammo, more tanks, more crews, and more food. The quick dash to the Siegfried Line had gotten way ahead of supplies. The Germans were glad to wait, as this gave them time to set up defenses and prepare for what they knew was coming. In turn, we began receiving daily briefings about the attack planned for November.

While given a brief respite, we went back to Breinig. While in Breinig, the lieutenant went to a beer hall and got a keg of dark beer and a keg of light beer. The owner said he didn't have to give the lieutenant the kegs for free, so he paid the owner in German marks that the U.S. had printed. Worthless money.

When I was in Breinig, a tooth filling fell out. I went to a house with a government sign for dentist. When I went in, the dentist was lying on the couch. The sergeant asked what my issue was and went to wake the dentist. The sergeant pedaled a bike which was attached to the drill the dentist would use. After finishing his work on my tooth, the dentist looked at me and said, "Son, you have a lot more work that needs done, but you'll need to come back when I'm not so busy." There was no one else around. The dentist went back to his couch and laid down. Rumor had it the dentist was an alcoholic.

Not having learned his lesson the first go round, Chief began drinking again. Word through the camp was there was a girl in town who was "very friendly." Chief decided to find out. When the girl came to the door, she began screaming, frightened of a man with dark skin. Chief ran into the room and tried to get her to stop causing a commotion. The M.P. hearing the girl, came running. The M.P. stood outside the door and told the soldier to come out with his hands up. Chief responded, "I'm coming out shooting!" He pointed his gun in the air outside the house and shot off a couple of rounds. The M.P. hit the ground.

At this point, Chief came running out and back to the beer hall where we were staying. I told him, "Give me your gun." I quickly disassembled the gun and laid it out as if to clean it. The rest of the soldiers covered Chief up with a blanket. The M.P. came running to them and asked if they had seen him, using a slur for African Americans to refer to him. The whole crew said they hadn't. Luckily, Chief didn't respond. The next morning Chief moved on up the line away from the M.P. who might have spotted him.

On the return to Stolberg, a spot was found that looked good for hiding the tank. The driver had no backup mirror so Sergeant Jones got out to give him directions. A big mistake! A mortar shell landed within feet of Sgt. Jones and made his leg a real mess. I jumped out and helped him get back out of sight. Medics came quickly and after initial treatment, Sgt. Jones was taken to a hospital. He was the best commander I had, competent and very likable. I knew our tank crew would really miss him. I made a call to the company commander for a tank commander replacement. Shortly, after the ambulance left, a jeep drove up asking for Sgt. Jones. We said, "Did you pass an ambulance on the way?"

They said, "Yes."

We replied, "That was Sgt. Jones."

They said, "He has just been awarded a field commission as a second lieutenant!"

My new tank commander had been in a tank on D-Day. The sergeant's tank had caught fire and he was able to escape before the tank sank, but it left him badly burnt. After recuperating in the hospital for five months, the sergeant returned to active duty. Our tank was parked in a fire break (a path in the forest where power lines go through). A P-47 plane looked like it was coming for the tank. The bomb hit a nearby abandoned house. The sergeant got out of the tank and just kept repeating, "I can't take it." I called back to the medics that the sergeant was having a mental breakdown and was coming their way.

Battlefield Stress

It's not so much if as when—almost everyone has a breaking point depending on the intensity and frequency of the combat they see, usually somewhere between 60 and 240 days. At some stage combat exhaustion sets in: "A state of nervous exhaustion created by prolonged exposure to the stress of combat or the battlefield. A temporary condition that responds to a combination of relative safety, sleep, and relative physical comfort."[12]

Various factors can speed up and enhance the process. Fear is the obvious one. The threat to life, limb, and health versus the obligation to perform one's duty

---

[12] Leon, Maj. Robert M.: *Battlefield Stress*; Maxwell AFB, 1987.

creates an inner conflict that can lead to breakdown. Loss of comrades is another strong contributor: the experience of watching others suffer and die adds significantly to the strain of the battlefield. Data collected in World War II indicated a high correlation in units where soldiers saw close friends killed or wounded and later saw men crack up.

Physical discomfort doesn't help, nor does fatigue—General Patton said, "Fatigue makes cowards of us all." Even during the best of times most soldiers averaged four hours or less of sleep out of each 24 hours while they were in the line.

Then there's the separation of a soldier from home, family, friends, and women and the possibility that he may never see them again creates stress and the isolation of the battlefield—the loneliest place in the world.

The National WWII Museum suggests that more than half a million service members suffered some sort of psychiatric collapse due to combat. Alarmingly, 40 percent of medical discharges during the war were for psychiatric conditions. The vast majority of those can be attributed to combat stress.

The new tank commander was Sergeant John Fasula. John was a former first sergeant but had been busted back to his permanent rank for fighting. He was from Louisiana and was in the process of being divorced. He was "Old Army."

The weather got cold. Guard duty on the tank during this cold weather required getting creative. A tarp was placed on the back of the tank. The blankets were lapped, making room for four men to sleep. After doing the two hours of guard duty, the soldier kicked the next person up. The nice warm spot just vacated became the spot for the soldier coming off guard duty.

We were under observation by the Germans. Leaving the tank in daylight would bring a quick artillery shell. The loader in my tank insisted he had to get out even though we argued vigorously against it. His exit was quick and okay. The Germans were waiting for his return to the tank. He got most of his body in quickly. But an arm over his head got a shrapnel wound. The shot caused him to not be able to move his hand. The wound was miniscule, but the suggestion of taking the sulfa (sulfonamide) pill was met with "Not the Cube." It was a common joke about the size of the pill, which was large. The pill was supposed to prevent you from getting an infection. He took the sulfa and promptly left the tank to get to first aid. The crew and I were stuck waiting on a replacement for the loader.

Letter #71: postmarked October 31, 1944

Dear Family,
Here's another one of those "I'm O.K. letters".

I am in a rest area now, and Boy! This is really O.K.!! We are sleeping in a house, and it's really a treat. There aren't enough beds to go around and some of us have to sleep on the floor but even that's better than the damp ground.

There is another thing I would like to request for Xmas. I need a razor.

One of the fellows (a Sgt. from N.Y.) found one of those collapsible top hats and we are taking turns trying it out.

I guess I'm run down now so I'll sign off.

Love
Walter

The house was empty when the crew got there. Not enough beds but tables and chairs! Just like home, but unfortunately, no hot food. However, the kitchen truck knew our location so we didn't starve. The nicest part was no one was shooting at me.

The reference to sleeping on damp ground was an option you had only if we were far enough off the front line. A blanket for either a pillow or cover and the advantage of stretching out was the only reason for doing this. Inside the tank, I'd have to sit up to sleep, which was something I'd been known to do.

Inside the house, we tried to entertain ourselves to keep from reliving all the things our crew had been through. We lost two crew members and our tank in September. We'd now had three tank commanders, one dead, one injured, and one with a mental breakdown. We had to replace a driver, loader, and tank commanders. Would I be next, or would I survive? This kind of thinking caused anxiety. No one wanted to fall apart.

Looking for anything to distract us was important. Out came the collapsible top hat. I'm sure there were jokes and songs surrounding the find. Again, anything at all to make life seem normal.

Oh yeah, send a razor. I wonder how many times I requested this from my parents?

Letter #72: postmarked November 22, 1944

Dear Family,
I don't know what I will say but at least I can scratch a few lines.

I got that picture you had in the paper. I don't think I saw that picture before. While I'm talking about pictures. I would like to have one of the family. I only have those few small ones.

I don't really know what to ask for Christmas. I guess I would enjoy some candy and I can use all the gum you can send. If I don't have some gum, I'm liable to bite my fingernails off clear up to my elbow.

You said you thought I was in Uncle Howard's old outfit but you'll have to guess again.

Mother, you can do me a favor if you will. Take some (or all if you need it), of the money I sent home and buy the folks a Christmas present from me. I'll tell you now because I'd probably forget later. P.S. And Lenore too.

I guess I better sign off now. I already wrote three pages. Boy! That's a record, isn't it?!!!

Love

Walter Jr.

P.S. You weren't surprised to see Cpl. on my letters, were you? I knew if I waited long enough, they'd give me that $77 a month job.

Surprised I'm a corporal? My first letter home had an arrow on the return address pointing to the crossed-out P.F.C. with Cpl. written above it. The new rank came with the job of gunner. I didn't know it. As I was addressing the envelope for home, my commander told me I was a corporal. So, I quickly edited my title. The extra money was nice, but there was no place to spend it. Thus, I sent $100 home.

It was during this time that we decided to liberate a cow. Cliff Elliott, a lieutenant and platoon leader, always told this story at reunions. We had a rancher in our group. Using a rope, the cow was tied to one of our trucks. The truck, while moving slowly, was a real trot for the cow. When a tree with a branch high enough to reach and get the cow off the ground was found, the rancher shot the cow. He then strung the cow up and proceeded to divide up the meat. Cliff hadn't had a steak in a long time and really wanted one, so the rancher made him a steak. Cliff ate it with enthusiasm. Later that night, he was the sickest he had ever been. The meat wasn't cured enough to eat. The order came from the higher ups: no more freeing cows.

Pictures taken and received come up in my letters. The funny thing is I only have a few pictures of myself and most were in Camp Polk. A picture of my family was probably a wish and something my parents thought might put me in danger if captured.

My letters during this time keep focusing on Christmas back home. I wanted to share with my family and be present even though I wasn't there. It seems my list of what to get me kept growing to include books, razors, candy, and gum. Holidays filled with tradition were something I really missed.

I asked for gum a lot in my letters. It was the one thing I didn't share. The gum helped me when cigarettes were few and relieved tension. Chewing my nails was a sign of my anxiousness with my situation. A German out there wanted me dead. I just wanted to make it home to my family.

The First Letter #73: postmarked October 28, 1944

Dear Family,

I've got enough paper here to be able to write for a week, but I can't think of a thing to say.

I was surprised to hear that Sara is in the 1st grade! She seems so young. Has she still got curls?

Talk about rain!! I don't think it's rained as much in five years in W. Va. as it has here this last month. And it's starting to get colder too.

I am trying to catch up on my letter writing, but for me to think of enough to write is like trying to grow hair on a ping-pong ball.

I have sent money home twice now. The first time I sent 100 dollars and the second time I sent 45. So as soon as you receive the check (or whatever) it is), please write and tell me.

You ask about fellows in this outfit from home! I think I told Aunt Hattie but I forgot when I wrote home. There is only one fellow, a Sgt. who lives in Fairmont. He has been to Wheeling quite a few times so he and I talk about home once in a while.

I only got one letter from Harold Hathaway. I answered that but I haven't heard from him since. He should have a new address by this time. If he has, will you please send it to me!! I still can't get this story straight about Bill Nickerson is he going to O.C.S.??

Well! I'm finally run down. I didn't think I last this long.

Love

Walter

Plenty of paper to use to write home was once again from a ledger found in someone's home.

It was late October. We were all getting tense over the attack that was planned for early November. Writing letters relieved some of the tension. There was much I would have liked to have written to them, but the censor wouldn't have approved. Tensions grew within our group as we waited for our role in the upcoming battle. In everyone's mind was the thought, *Will I survive?*

Also mentioned in the letter was Bill Nickerson, another graduate from Lindsley Military High School in Wheeling, West Virginia. He did get to Officer Candidate School. He also got wounded.

I must have been teasing my sister Sara, as she was in eighth grade. She did have curly hair.

The First Letter #74: postmarked November 6, 1944

Dear Family,

Just a line to let you know I'm O.K.

I got your letter that had the scores on how many packages I have coming. If I get them all it will take me from this Xmas until next to eat them. I want to ask another favor of you. Please write a letter to:

Mrs. Paul Williamson

620 E. 9th St.

Kansas City, MO

And ask for Byron's (her son) address. Mac is the fellow who took that detail for me so I could visit N.Y. (remember?). Byron and I got separated in England.

There is nothing new here so I guess I'll sign off.

Love

Walter Jr.

My hometown church, St. Mark's Lutheran, had sent me a small pocket notebook. I used it to write the addresses of the people I met along the way. I still have this notebook.

In the midst of a war, outside the combat zone, I had time to think about things and people I'd met along the way. I'm sure I felt I owed Bryon something for taking my place so I could visit my mom and Lenore in New York. This was a pleasant memory and something calming to focus on.

Waiting! We spent the month of October holding the line. At the beginning of November, the entire 3rd Armored Division was to begin our attack. The officers informed the tank commanders who then relayed the plans to the tank crew. The goal was to break through the German lines as fast as we could and advance seven miles a day.

Every day a bit more of the plans was shared. Towns we were to go through and expectations of our success. Every day, the anxiety grew.

Every day, we checked the equipment to make sure everything was ready for battle. I tried to find something funny to say to help relieve the tension. Playing cards or telling jokes with the crew helped pass the time.

Letter #75 (1): November 6, 1944[13]

Hello Dick!

I guess by the time you get this letter it will be too late but I'll still wish you a happy birthday.

You are as bad as me about writing letters. As a matter of fact, I think you a little worse.

About that car of yours. I wish somebody would break down and tell me what kind it is, Willy's or otherwise.

I have a couple of souvenirs to send but I can't find the stuff to wrap them in. I'll send them as soon as I can.

Do you ever see Jim Mull anymore? The next letter you write (in answer to this one) give me the latest rumors from the home front.

I hear you started a bad habit. Mother tells me you are smoking a pipe now.

One other thing. Take off for college and don't worry about a job.

Write soon

Walter

---

[13] As I mentioned, once I was overseas my mother's numbering system became jumbled. There are two letters both numbered 75. The first is to my brother, who would be celebrating his 18th birthday.

After reading this letter, I called my brother to ask how long he smoked a pipe. He responded, "I don't think I ever did."

My brother's car was a '35 Pontiac that he paid $200 for with the money he earned working at the A&P. He wanted to enlist in the Army but was too lightweight for his age. When he got turned down, he decided to go to work at the Defense Plant at Wheeling Steel. They made gas cans. Dick was at the beginning of the line, and our Uncle Howard and Uncle Howard's girlfriend were further down the line. Uncle Howard used to say people called him "Speedy" because he worked so fast. One day Dick put this to a test. Dick worked as fast as he could. When they got to Uncle Howard, things started backing up. Shortly thereafter, the line had a rest break. Howard complained to Dick about working too fast because they didn't pay you to work any faster.

Dick didn't stay long at Wheeling Steel, as the Army called him up for a second round and enlisted him. He headed to Texas to be a cryptographer and ended up a sergeant at Camp Atterbury in Indiana.

I'm not sure I ever sent home the souvenirs. It would have been things I picked up from my wanderings around town, i.e., a belt buckle, a Nazi flag.

Operation *Queen*

While 3rd Armored's Task Force Hogan was attached to 1st Infantry Division fighting in neighboring Aachen, the rest of the division—indeed, the rest of First (U.S.) Army—regrouped, resupplied, and performed Herculean feats of maintenance. Troops were rotated and replacements trained. By early November the division was ready for the next offensive, which was delayed by bad weather until the 15th. Operation *Queen* was a large offensive that involved First (U.S.) Army's V and VII Corps, and Ninth (U.S.) Army's XIX Corps. It was planned to push up to the Rur River (called the Roer in Dutch) and to take the Rur dams before thrusting towards the Rhine. The eastern (First Army) side of the attack was through the Hürtgen Forest; Ninth Army's terrain was easier, the Rur plains.

3rd Armored's role in this operation saw C.C.A. given the task of holding the line at Stolberg, while C.C.B. was to seize the ridge northeast of the road connecting Hamich and Hastenrath before being ready to exploit any breakthrough in the direction of Cologne on the Rhine.

Task Force Lovelady, part of C.C.B., consisted of 2nd Battalion, 33rd Armored Regiment (less 3rd Platoon, Company B); 2nd Platoon, Reconnaissance Company, 33rd Armored Regiment; Company E, 36th Armored Infantry Regiment;

1st Platoon, Company C, 703rd Tank Destroyer Battalion; 1st Platoon, Company D, 23rd Armored Engineer Battalion; and Medical Detachment.[14]

The mission was carefully planned with help of aerial photography and maps. It had to secure Werth and Kottenich before being ready to send assistance to troops attacking Hastenrath. Company E was on the right flank.

A huge aerial bombardment—1,300 bombers of Ninth Air Force—opened the attack. The fighting was fierce and the Americans struggled to reach the river, let alone create a bridgehead on the German bank. And when V Corps was given the mission to go after the Rur dams, it ran into German troops preparing for the Ardennes offensive. Few advances were made and on December 16, the Germans started Operation *Wacht am Rhein* and the Battle of the Bulge forced 3rd Armored into a defensive role.

Letter #75 (2): November 19, 1944

Dear Family,

I don't know what to write about but at least you'll know I'm O.K. I haven't gotten any mail for about 4 days now so when it does come, I have plenty of reading material.

I just came from church. I am one of the best members. We have church services in a German school house.

I got one package, with a fruit cake in it but I forgot to look at the address. I think it was mailed before I made Cpl. that means sometime in Sept.

I'm just about run out of anything to say but I'm ashamed to write such a short letter. Which reminds me this is "Heinie" paper. If you want to call it paper, it's more like cardboard.

I've got another request. I need a pen. I can't buy one and I lost my other one.

I'm run down for sure now.

Love

Walter Jr.

P.S. How much money did you get from me? There should be $145.

Although written home on November 19, this letter arrived in such poor condition that the post office had to put it in another envelope. It was postmarked in Elm Grove on February 19.

It seems that I had been good at scrounging up paper. Church services were usually short, with a matching short sermon. On rare occasions, the chaplain had an assistant with a field organ who could play hymns.

Fruit cakes were always welcome, even one sent in September that arrived in November. No matter the condition, they were always shared and fully devoured. My Aunt Hattie promised me a fruit cake and generously soaked

---

[14] This and other unit information from *Spearhead in the West* (Third Armored Division, 1946).

it in rum. Knowing Aunt Hattie's thirst-quenching habits, I was sure she tested the quality of the syrup. When it did arrive, it was greatly appreciated.

There was a 16-day gap between my previous letter and this one. A lot had happened but the censor stood in the way of saying much. So my family got this rather lighthearted letter about church, fruit cakes, lost pens, and money sent home.

After five weeks of recuperating and resupplying men, tanks, and equipment, the 3rd Armored Division was poised for the big attack. My crew and I lined up on November 15 with all the tanks of E Company and waited for the appointed hour. It was now! Suddenly I heard a noise I had never heard before. I was at a panic stage. My first thought was "Germany has a secret weapon!" Sergeant Fasula, the tank commander, reassured me it was ours. I stood up and looked out and saw American rockets for the first time. They were laying down a wide cover on the forest to the company's flank. Big sigh! Then the word. "Go!" Fighting began.

The rockets Walter heard were T27 "Xylophone" 4.5-inch rockets fired from tubes on the back of a 2.5-ton truck. They were inaccurate and the launching flashes revealed their firing positions—but psychologically they were terrifying. (NARA)

A German officer had gotten in trouble with Hitler and decided the better choice was to defect. When interrogated, he advised that the minefield ahead was laid out like a garden plot, areas surrounded by wire that looked like a plant bed with bare rows between. He advised, "Run over the wires; there are no mines there." Clever plan by the Germans.

As my tank started for the minefield, I observed Fasula lining them up for the path. I pointed out the advice they got from the German officer. Fasula screamed, "I'm the tank commander!" We ran over a mine. The tank left the ground and it was time to evacuate. The rule for leaving a tank in a minefield was to go to the back of the tank and stand in tracks the tank had made.

After quickly getting out, I counted heads and saw only four. I looked around the side of the tank and saw the driver. Against all instructions, he jumped in the minefield instead of getting off the back into the tracks. I yelled, "Look at your foot." It was there that he saw the prongs of another mine! He climbed over the tank into the tracks and, along with the bow gunner and loader, took off for safer ground. Fasula and I began a slow walk back until bullets whizzing by turned us into track stars. I've commented that I wished someone had a stopwatch. I'm sure I broke the world record for 100-yard dash wearing Army boots.

We were one of four E Company tanks that hit mines. By the end of the operation, Task Force Lovelady lost a number of others to mines—in total 17 tanks had been damaged but only four were write-offs.

The front had moved on about three miles or more. All was quiet. I wanted my musette bag (backpack full of shaving equipment, socks, underwear, toothbrush, comb, etc.) from the tank, so I walked slowly toward the tank in the minefield. Suddenly I was pelted with the debris from two mortar explosions. A disabled half-track ahead, I ran looking for immediate shelter. Half-tracks, however, have no top. Not wanting to see if my assailant would try to hit the half-track, I decided to try a mad dash back to where I came from. I ran at full speed and dropped to the ground when everything went red from lack of oxygen. Two more explosions near me made the adrenaline kick in and move me. On arrival back in safe territory and completely out of breath, everyone asked what was wrong with me. When I told them about my adventure, no one believed me, saying that the area had been overrun. I replied, "Ha!"

While my platoon with Lieutenant Elliot was in a German farm field in reserve I walked over to an anti-aircraft group. A German plane was hedge hopping over the fields. The anti-aircraft crew, using the 50 caliber four-barrel machine gun, killed the pilot. His plane slid to a stop in the field. I ran down to the plane and took the pilot's fur-lined hat. It was cold and I thought the hat would be great inside the tank. The only problem was the connection for the microphone didn't work with an American tank.

My crew and I were eating K-rations. I could have told my parents how the Army had a daily diet worked out. The breakfast K-ration had a fruit bar. Not a laxative but helpful. For lunch, K-ration had a cheese bar. Intestinal tract is not too loose. The dinner K-ration had a chocolate bar designed not to melt or break. A reward for eating the first two!

Rations

The most common U.S. Army rations were C, K, and 5-in-1. "C-rats" were developed in 1938 and were provided in six 12oz tinplate cans opened with a key. Three meals provided about 3,700 calories. They consisted of stews or combinations of some form of meat and spaghetti, potatoes, noodles, or beans. They also included chocolate or other candies, gum, biscuits, and cigarettes.

Introduced in 1942, the 5-in-1 ration fed five men for a day, providing 4,200 calories, and was produced for motorized combat groups in the desert. In 1943 the 10-in-1—basically two 5-in-1 packs—superseded the 5-in-1 but so many had been produced that they continued to be used until war's end.

Replacements pick up their rations. The men are receiving packets of cigarettes. Each holds three boxes of K-rations. (NARA)

K-rations were significantly lighter and came in three small boxes—breakfast, dinner and supper units. They were developed in 1941 by Ancel Keys, a University of Minnesota physiologist at the request of the U.S. War Department, which wanted a non-perishable, ready-to-eat meal that could fit in a soldier's pocket. In the final version, the K-ration provided three meals giving 2,830 calories. This was, in reality, too little for a fighting soldier who often felt short-changed.[15]

Letter #78: postmarked November 28, 1944

Dear Family,

I should use V-mail then I wouldn't have to write so much I really don't think I can fill this page but at least I'll try.

Tomorrow is Thanksgiving Day and I'm trying to work up an appetite. They brought in some turkeys today and they really looked good.

This company seems to have the odds and ends as far as men concerned. We have one fellow who came over from Germany in 1938 and also a fellow who came from China in the same year. I borrowed this pen from the Chinaman.

Some of the fellows in this company request everything from soup to nuts, but a lot of the packages arrive in slightly mangled condition. That is one reason I don't ask for a lot of cookies and stuff like that. There is one thing I would like to have though and that is some tea. One fellow got a box of tea bags today. Naturally I helped him use them.

Boy! We are really having our share of the rain and mud. I don't think we've had over two days of sunshine since we've been here, but the one to really pity is the doughboys.

I really surprised myself by writing so much. I'll have to be careful or I'll get writer's cramp.

This is German paper I'm using (you probably guessed). When I use this up I'll probably have to use "toilet tissue."

I guess I've sounded off enough for now so I'll sign off.

Love

Walter Jr.

P.S. Is Keith Linton's address still the same?

The poor doughboys' infantry. If they didn't find an abandoned house or barn, they were stuck sleeping outside. They had tents. Just imagine trying to sink tent poles into soaking mud. Not to mention touching the side of the tent would have rain inside. The infantry was constantly on guard and, unfortunately for all of us, November had some very tense moments.

The front had moved on a few more miles and was holding. At this point, the 8th Armored Division, the unit I did basic training with, moved up to the front and the 3rd Armored went into reserve.

---

[15] *A Brief History of U.S. Army Rations*, Frontier Army Museum Fort Leavenworth, KS, 2021.

I asked for Keith Linton's dad's address. Keith was a junior like me. Many mornings, I waited for Keith to get ready to leave for school. Hanging on the wall of his house was the poem "In Flanders Fields," written in remembrance of the World War I soldiers who lost their lives. Red poppies are the symbol of this sacrifice. Poppies were worn by all on November 11 for Remembrance Day. I memorized this poem and can still recite from memory today. With all that was happening around me, I understood the meaning of this poem. I probably was thinking of writing to Mr. Linton to let him know that I not only knew the poem, but I also understood its meaning firsthand.

Letter #73 (2): postmarked November 28, 1944

Dear Family,

Forgive me for writing V-mail but it's all I can get my hands on right now. When you write regular letters will you please enclose a blank envelope, that will help a lot.

I bet I've got the world's record for having a shoulder dislocated. Yesterday I did it for the ninth time. But in spite of that I doesn't give me any trouble.

Am in best of health.

Love

Walter

This V-mail, dated November 28, 1944, found my tank near the city of Eschweiler, Germany. We survived a major hurdle of the minefield and days of Germans determined not to give ground. We then had a Thanksgiving dinner where we all overate.

When this was written, however, all was quiet. I walked into town with several others and climbed a light post to retrieve a Nazi paper flag. Nothing like a souvenir you can fold and carry in your pocket. My tank was parked next to a German farmhouse whose occupants had left. This also provided souvenirs. German inflation money stuffed in a drawer. Again, fold and carry.

As for my shoulder, I just kept putting it back in the socket. Out it went, I grabbed my wrist, pulled in, and snapped it back in place. A bother, yes. Not necessarily painful. I was in the best of health physically and mentally but this wouldn't always be true as the war to end German domination began in earnest. The tank can't save you. A stubborn commander can get you killed. One wrong decision and my life could be over.

Letter #74 (2): postmarked January 13, 1945

Dear Family

Only 23 more days 'til Xmas, but it doesn't even seem like December.

So far I've gotten 2 Xmas packages. One from Aunt Hattie and one from Mary and Eleanor. Can you still get razor blades? I am running short. As a matter of fact I'm using Heinie blades.

Boy! I wish I had a camera now. Believe it or not my hair is now long enough to comb. (With a Heinie comb).

Love

Walter Jr.

After the fiasco in the minefield, I had time to wander. I wanted to see what damage the rockets had done in the woods. With a friend, I walked to the woods that I presumed were not dangerous. We came on a German anti-tank gun and, when looking through the sight, discovered it was aimed at my tank. Again, I survived someone trying to get me. It made my adrenaline flow.

Fortunately for me, the German crew was killed when the attack began. In my angered state, I took the belt buckle, knife, fork, spoon combo and comb from one of the bodies. Only the buckle made it home.

Eventually we were given another tank and caught with the company in early December. With our tank parked next to an abandoned house and barn, we took advantage of it during the day. At night we climbed back in the tank because the Germans would drop anti-personnel bombs. The bombs were loaded with whatever they could find that would make good shrapnel, things like nails, glass, metal pieces. The house wasn't safe from these bombs.

I wanted to make it to Christmas. In the midst of bombings, soldiers getting killed, and destruction everywhere, I was trying to focus on something positive.

Letter #76: postmarked December 7, 1944

Dearest Family,

Christmas is really slipping up on me. To be truthful it does not even seem like December. One thing which that makes it seems funny is when I get letters you wrote around Thanksgiving. The last one I got was the day after Thanksgiving.

If this piece of German money was any good you would really be in the chips. At the present rate of exchange, a mark is worth ten cents. This is inflation money a whole barrel full isn't worth two cents.

The flag I picked up in a street. I looked everywhere but a cloth flag is as scarce as a gold wrist watch.

I hope you can read this writing the light isn't too good and I am getting nervous.

Love

Walter Jr.

This was December 5 in Germany. The nerves were for what may lie ahead. Losing two tanks, I knew at any time things could go wrong. Survival in war is sometimes quick thinking and sometimes just luck.

Tanks tried not to move at night to engage in battle. Letter writing was done during this time. Of course, the lighting was dim because no one wanted to show the enemy the tank's position.

Inside the tank was a small motor; if the battery was going down, you fired it up. On a perfectly quiet night and very dark outside, suddenly you heard *putt, putt, putt* and you knew a tank's battery was charging. It also gave the Germans an idea of the tank's location.

German inflation money was mostly worthless. A joke in my letter with some truth to it was a barrel full wouldn't cover the cost of needed items.

Letter #77: postmarked December 11, 1944

Dear Family,
Here's another "I'm O.K." letter. I can't think of a darn thing to write. I got four packages the other night. One from Lenore and three from home. We have been having nightly snacks of hot coffee and cookies. The sandwich spread was really good. The fellows said to be sure and ask for some more. I got the wallet from Doc.

You ask what my job was. I guess it won't hurt to say. I am a gunner. The same job I had the first three months in the army.

It's trying awful hard to snow but the snow won't stick. The people who live around here say that usually by this time of year the snow is three or four feet deep. Right now the mud's that thick.

The fellow across from me is writing a letter on a sheet of paper about 3 feet long and two feet wide. I don't know what he finds to write about. I'm run down already.

Love
Walter R
Merry Christmas!!

With the tank parked next to a farmhouse with tables, chairs, and a stove, life had a certain routine to it. I'm sure my packages were a big hit. I don't really remember the sandwich spread with little crackers, but I'm sure anything different to eat would have been most welcomed.

The wallet was from Bill Megahan's dad, Doc. I'm sure Doc put a few bills inside the wallet before sending it to me. Unfortunately, the wallet didn't make it home after the war.

Rain or snow would have made little difference inside the tank. However, walking around weighed your boots down with mud, making excursions around town more time consuming as you picked up your feet to keep from getting sucked down into the muck and getting your uniform caked in it.

I didn't speak any German at this time. Talking with town folks meant they either spoke English or I had someone with me who could speak their language. Talking about the weather was probably the safest conversation to have. I often wonder if the people of this village had any idea what was about to happen to Germany. Were they really followers of Hitler's ideology or just helpless in the face of a dictator?

Being in the house and visiting the town had its advantages, but someone higher-up was planning another move. Hitler just wouldn't call it quits. There would be one more letter before the Battle of the Bulge.

Letter #79: postmarked December 16, 1944

Dear Family,
This is really going to be a short letter. I can't think of a thing to say.
I've gotten six packages from home so far. Last night I got a package from Aunt Hattie.
I got a letter from Mrs. Williamson last night and there is a slim chance I may get to see Byron.
Boy! Pennsylvania is really represented in my tank. Three of the crew are Reading, P.A.
Love
Walter Jr.

Once again, I counted on my mom and Aunt Hattie to replenish my stock of candy and fruit cake. Mom even wrote Mrs. Williamson a letter, and sweet Mrs. Williamson wrote me back. Unfortunately, I never did get to see Byron.

We were still next to the house and lazing around, trying to stay warm. Living in the house in the daytime was fine; there were beds and chairs. At night, it was back to the tank. The Germans kept dropping their anti-personnel bombs. Naps by day were possible and allowed for stretching out; at night sleep came while sitting up inside the cold metal tank. This wasn't the most comfortable way to get a good night's sleep but it beat the alternative of getting killed by a bomb.

Letter #80: postmarked January 9, 1945

Dear Family,
Please forgive me for not writing sooner, but I have been busy, and among other things I got my head in the way of a piece of shrapnel. I didn't get hurt too bad and I'm having a rest now. I'm sorry I couldn't write around Xmas but I was busy then too.
Thanks a lot for giving Lenore that present from me, she said she really likes it.
I think I got most or all of my Xmas packages. I lost track of the count. The fudge was in good condition and I could go for some more.
I guess I'm about run down now so I'll sign off. I'll try to write again soon.
Love
Walter

One wonders what my parents and family thought when they read "my head got in the way of a piece of shrapnel."

I wrote this letter after two weeks of bitter fighting during the Battle of the Bulge. On December 19, C.C.B. had been detached from 3rd Armored and hurried to Spa assembly area to fight with V Corps. Once at Spa the orders were changed and instead C.C.B. was attached to XVIII Corps (Airborne) and sent to the La Gleize-Stavelot area on December 20.

Taskforce Lovelady was attached to 30th Infantry Division and comprised: 2nd Battalion, 33rd Armored Regiment; B Company, 36th Armored Infantry Regiment; Platoon, Reconnaissance Company, 33rd Armored Regiment; Platoon, B Company, 23rd Armored Engineer Battalion; and E Company 120th Infantry Regiment (from 30th Infantry).

The task force shot up an enemy convoy and then had its first major engagement in Trois-Ponts. E Company's lead tank shot up a German 88mm anti-tank weapon that stalled progress for an hour as the truck towing the gun burned. As we sat and waited, the noise from the turret traverse bugged me, so I turned it off.

Eventually the four tanks ahead of me went around the burning tank. I had forgotten I had the traverse mechanism turned off and as a result the tank's gun barrel rotated left as we dipped into the ditch, burying the gun into the dirt. We had to back out of the ditch and stopped to make sure the barrel wasn't filled with dirt. Dirt in the barrels would cause the gun to not fire correctly, which could kill people inside the tank.

The four tanks ahead went through Trois-Ponts, under a railroad overpass, and planned to turn towards Malmedy. At this point they became victims of a German ambush. All four tanks were destroyed, many of the crews, and the platoon leader, 1-Lt. Albert W. Hope, were killed. There was grief for those who lost their lives, and a realization that my stupidity saved my life and the crew.

Lovelady left a unit as a roadblock under Major G. T. Stallings. While we waited for action, restlessness with the troops was apparent. One day, I spotted a German off in the distance, with his pants down in a fire break relieving himself. After getting out of the tank I ran across the street and insisted an infantryman give me his rifle. I fired four quick shots. The infantryman took four more shots. The German didn't even recognize there were bullets aimed at him. He pulled up his pants and wandered back into the woods. After thinking about this, I realized the German soldier was too far away and bullets weren't landing anywhere near him. Lucky for him. He lived to see another day.

While in Trois-Ponts, the company bugler went flying by in a jeep. He didn't know how to drive. The higher-ups figured a quick lesson on brake and gas would suffice and sent him on an errand by himself. As he was careening by, he lost control of the jeep and slammed into a tree. Rumor had it he was so badly injured that he lost both legs. Years later at a reunion of the 3rd Armored Division, he came walking in. He had broken both legs but fully recovered. The rumor mill is still intact, much like it was in basic training.

My tank was put into Lieutenant Elliot's platoon, which held Trois-Ponts for several days and then moved back to nearby Petit-Coo.

Then the *Panzergrenadiers* of *Kampfgruppe Peiper*, commanded by *SS-Obersturmbannführer* Jochen Peiper, spearhead of *1. SS-Panzer Division Leibstandarte SS Adolf Hitler*, attacked Petit-Coo with a determination to move from there to Trois-Ponts and secure the bridges they needed to cross the river with their heavy Tiger IIs. My tank and a light tank next to mine held our ground for hours, killing over 50 SS troopers. Our force was cut off. With no infantry support, the tanks were very vulnerable to being hit with the Germans' *Panzerfausts*. It was decided the best move was further away from the center of town. We held this position for three days until, finally, Task Force Lovelady had another 30th Division company attached and relieved the position. When the infantry arrived, Kampfgruppe Peiper destroyed their armored equipment, took what was left of the troops, and slipped back through the American lines back to Germany.

It was Christmas Eve, and Taskforce Lovelady moved southwest out of the front line. On New Year's Eve Colonel Lovelady was moved to 45th Armored Medical Battalion with influenza. Major Stallings took over and Task Force Lovelady became Task Force Stallings, just in time to start the Allied counterattack which got underway on January 3, 1945. The northern arm, of which 3rd Armored was part, headed towards Houffalize and a rendezvous with Third (U.S.) Army coming up from the south and Bastogne.

It was cold out and staying warm wasn't easy. Our column of tanks had stopped to refuel. So you can imagine the excitement when I saw a woman carrying a steaming pan in our direction. My first thought was *hot coffee*. I grabbed my cup and went out to meet her. She poured me a steaming cup of chicory. She then turned to the elderly man beside her and introduced him as a general in World War I. I reached out to shake his hand when he grabbed me by both shoulders and kissed me on both cheeks! I was not at all familiar with this custom. I stood there stunned. I'm not even sure I thanked the woman.

I warned the crew, "Beware of the general. He'll kiss you!" This was the same crew that lost the tank in the minefield. There were five of us and we had now been together for about six weeks.

For the offensive, Task Force Lovelady comprised: 2nd Battalion, 33rd Armored Regiment (less 3rd Platoon, Company B); 3rd Battalion, 330th Infantry Regiment; 1st Platoon, Company D, 23rd Armored Engineer Battalion; 1st Platoon, Company B, 703rd Tank Destroyer Battalion; 2nd Platoon, Reconnaissance Company, 33rd Armored Regiment; 1st Platoon, AT Company, 36th Armored Infantry Regiment; 391st Armored Field Artillery Battalion.

In Malempre, I heard my first "Screaming Mimi," which is what we called the 150mm *Nebelwerfer*. It made a high-pitched squealing sound. A truck driver bringing supplies to the troops had just gotten out of his truck when the Screaming Mimi hit it. It was like the 4th of July as the truck exploded along with all its supplies. The driver kept saying, "I'm not an infantryman!" The infantrymen, who were staying in a nearby barn, took the driver with them. As they waited for another supply truck, a grandmother living in the house came out, went to the corner of the barn, lifted her dress, and peed. The shocked soldiers remained quiet for once!

A day later, on January 7, the battle reached Fraiture. A group of infantrymen from the 83rd Division were following my tank. Their leader had been wounded earlier in the day. All these men had been flown from the States and this was their first day in combat. They had yet to fire a shot in combat. Moving into Fraiture, we received lots of small-arms fire. These eight men stayed close to the back of the tank, which protected them.

Inside the tank, everyone was focused on survival. Helmets were not worn because they only got in the way. As we approached the city, Sergeant Fasula ordered me to put a high-explosive round in the second-floor window of a house. Then he ordered the driver to pull up as close as he could to the house, whereupon Fasula tossed a hand grenade in the window. This had a positive effect. A German infantryman came running out the front door and ran towards a nearby barn. We shot him with the machine gun.

Our tanks moved forward across the road and over a small stone fence. My next target was far to the right, where we received machine-gun fire from a house. It was at this point that German infantry fired a Panzerfaust at our tank and missed.

The first round missed the tank but injured several of the infantrymen. They kept yelling, "There he is, there he is!" They were so new to battle they didn't shoot at the German. It takes a lot to shoot someone, and these new recruits hadn't learned that their survival depended on it.

My command was "Gun left." I started traversing the turret to the left to line up the target for a shot. A second Panzerfaust round hit the turret. I was leaning forward when a blast hit, spraying shrapnel across the top of my head. That round killed Sergeant Fasula. He slammed into my back with his fists, knocking the breath out of me and pushing me into the periscope. The driver and bow gunner were able to get out of the tank. Fear gripped me and I was anxious to get out but I was trapped by the commander's body pushing down on me and the loader as well. I just knew the third shot was coming and it would be the one to ignite the tank. Slowly Fasula's body rolled onto the floor. I quickly escaped through the commander's hatch. The loader climbed over Fasula's body and followed me out of the tank.

With the death of the tank commander, I became the senior officer at the scene. I screamed for the infantrymen to follow me into the nearby house. Inside the house, I began having the soldiers patch each other up and take the sulfa pill the Army issued for soldiers who were wounded. I felt cold on my head. When I reached up to touch it, I pulled my hand back and found it covered with blood. I asked a nearby G.I. how bad and the standard answer came back, "Doesn't look bad." A soldier in the group had a serious leg wound.

At this point there was no tank or means of transportation. I had the most wounded soldier climb on my back. I carried him for about 100 yards to a road. We moved up into the woods to avoid becoming a German target.

An American jeep came by and picked us up. In the front rider's seat was Major George T. Stallings, a man beloved by us all. He had been shot by a sniper in Règné. He had a chest wound. As we rode along, I could see how every time the Major took a breath, the bandage moved.

The jeep arrived at an aid station or triage center. Here, a doctor made quick decisions as to who would move on for further treatment, who could be patched up and returned to combat, and who had given their all here on earth. An ambulance driver arrived and told the doctor in charge he had room for one more. The doctor looked at me and told me to go. I argued that the infantryman's leg was bad. The doctor yelled, "I said you!"

"Yes, sir." And off to the ambulance I went.

Once we arrived at the field hospital, my treatment began. The doctor removed the larger obvious bits of shrapnel from my head. I asked for a piece of the shrapnel which I brought home with me. For years after the war, I felt tiny pieces of shrapnel coming out of my scalp.

Casevac

By the time of World War II it was understood that medical treatment should start as close to the front as possible, that casualties should see a doctor as soon as possible, and that the wounded should be quickly evacuated for treatment at a safe distance from the front.

The chain of evacuation started with combat medical units—the battalion medical detachments, company aid men, litter bearers, etc. The casualties were carried—usually by ¼-ton trucks or jeeps crewed by two aidmen—to the battalion aid station if it had been set up. (Sometimes the speed of advance would mean that this wasn't an option.) Here the wounded would have their first encounter with a doctor. Each of the combat commands had a medical company attached and would treat casualties evacuated from all the aid stations of the units assigned to the command.

The next step was a collecting station from where casualties were sent to the clearing station which was further back and had more equipment.

From here casualties traveled to field hospitals (400 beds) where surgery could be performed on the most severe cases or evacuation hospitals (400/750 beds) that treated illnesses and less urgent surgical cases.

From these, the casualties were sent to fixed hospitals in the Theater, which made it easier to return the soldiers to duty, and only sent back to the States if return to the lines was unlikely.

I was told to go lie down on a cot. Thinking I would be there for the rest of the night, this soon changed when the sergeant ordered, "Get your ass in the truck." I was taken to the company headquarters.

As for Major Stallings, he survived the chest wound but he did not return to the division—his war was over.

Unbeknownst to me at the time, this was my last day in combat. I had been in combat from July 1944 to January 1945. I had survived the loss of three tanks and been wounded twice. I had been the target of the enemy numerous times, just missing me by inches. I had been inside a tank with three men who were killed instantly. I had five tank commanders, two who were killed. I had seen more men killed, both Allies and foes, than anyone would have wanted to. I was just twenty years old.

3rd Armored in 1945

Walter left the division as it fought its way southeast towards a rendezvous with Third (U.S.) Army forces around Houffalize. Task Force Lovelady had become Task Force Stallings when Lovelady was hospitalized. After Stallings was wounded, Captain Ronald K. Bacon took command briefly until Lovelady returned. The heavy fighting continued towards Cherain where the task force sustained serious casualties.

By now, the First and Third (U.S.) armies had met outside Houffalize on January 16. St. Vith was recaptured on the 23rd but by that time 3rd Armored had been pulled out of the line for much needed replenishment and refitting. They were able to train their replacements, enjoy two weeks of peace, U.S.O. shows and Red Cross donuts, and even some passes to Verviers and Paris.

Their next battles were back in the Rur River area from February 26. Advancing swiftly, the division reached Cologne by early March and cleared the city by March 7.

Two weeks later, 3rd Armored crossed the Rhine and were part of the encirclement of the Ruhr that saw the capitulation of what was left of German Fifth Panzer, Fifteenth, and First Fallschirm armies by April 18. One of the casualties was the divisional commander, General Rose, who was killed on March 30 (see p. 96).

3rd Armored's war finished at Dessau on the confluence of the rivers Mulde and Elbe in eastern Germany on April 24, after which it became part of the occupying forces until deactivation in November.

3rd Armored on the Manhay–Houffalize Road on January 7, 1945, the day Walter was wounded. (NARA)

CHAPTER 5

Hospital to Home

Letter #81: postmarked February 4, 1945

Dear Family,

I'm sorry I haven't written sooner but I haven't had enough time and ambition all at one time.

I am really living the "Life of Riley" now. I am in a hospital between two nice clean sheets with (believe it or not) a pair of pajamas on. I am not in the hospital for being wounded. I just had some trouble with my stomach and intestines.

Just keep writing to the same address and my mail won't get scattered all over.

Love

Walter Jr

My last letter had been written 15 days earlier with news that my head "got in the way of some shrapnel." How they must have waited for more news only to find out I was once again "living the life of Riley." In truth, I was taking it one day at a time.

After returning from the field hospital, I loafed one day at the company command post. Diarrhea had me up all night long. The next day, the first sergeant came to where I was lying and said, "I'm sending you up as a tank commander."

I turned it down. "I want to be the gunner. I've had five tank commanders. I want to be a gunner." At that point, I sat up and immediately passed out.

I quickly came to and tried to get up, but my legs were wobbly. They called for medics who helped me walk across the street to a Belgian house where a dear lady put a warm brick at my feet. An ambulance came and took me to a large hospital in Liège, Belgium. I was on a steady diet of bismuth, to stop the diarrhea, and paregoric, to calm my gut.

From there I went to a hospital in Paris for several days. I met with a psychiatrist. He asked me to explain my experiences. I kept focusing on my shoulder coming out of joint. I did, through our conversation, tell him about the horrors I had experienced in combat. I believe he thought my arm was my excuse for not returning to the front but understood I was traumatized by all that had happened. The recommendation was to get further treatment.

My next stop was a hospital ship to take me to England. While aboard, the filling fixed by the alcoholic dentist in Breinig fell out. I made a trip to the dentist's office on the ship where I encountered the dental assistant. He wondered if I had any souvenirs. I gave him a Deutsch mark. In turn, he gave me a carton of cigarettes. I made out on this deal. The tooth got fixed and hasn't bothered me since.

My final destination was a hospital near Bristol. The diagnosis was extreme fatigue from combat. My personal diagnosis: I was tired of war and my shoulder wouldn't stay put.

Letter #82: postmarked February 13, 1945

Dear Family,

Please forgive me for not writing sooner but as you can see I've done some moving around.

I hope I didn't scare you when I wrote the last time and said I was in a hospital. It's really not as bad as it sounds. They're going to try and fix my shoulder, it has been giving me some trouble.

I guess it will be alright to use this address now.

I'm running out of paper so I guess I'll have to quit.

Love

Walter

An American hospital was where I stayed for about one month. I told my family I was hoping they would operate on my shoulder. Instead, it was to determine I had battle fatigue. So much for my constant complaining about my shoulder. My shoulder continues to pop out of joint in everyday activities. It was disappointing that I couldn't get it fixed during my hospital stay.

Battle fatigue was treated with a shot of insulin. We all then promptly returned to bed where our candy was hidden and indulged. This went on for a while until the doctors determined we were okay.

While here, I became friends with an English soldier who was admitted with a badly smashed toe. A 50-caliber gun had dropped on his big toe. There was no room in any of the local English hospitals, so he got stationed with us. Unable to walk due to a large cage over his big toe, I helped him with getting food and drink. Coffee was the only drink served. I inquired with the nurse if there were tea bags available and she found some for us. The English chap and I became tea-drinking buddies. Every mealtime I would put on enough water for two cups of tea.

Finally able to walk, he gave me instructions on how to shoot darts but was working with a poor learner. As I left, my new friend gave me his sister's address and suggested I stop by for a visit. I never made it.

Letter #83: postmarked March 17, 1945[1]

Dear Family,

Here is that long letter I promised to write. There are lots of things I would like to tell you but, I'm afraid the censor wouldn't pass it.

You remember the letter before last I said I was wounded? Well it was too bad and I went back to the company. About a week after that I got sick. I had a high temperature and was too weak to walk so they sent me to the hospital. I would like to tell you how I came back and some of the places I saw but I can't anyway. I ended up in England. I came to England to get my shoulder fixed but it's just the same as usual. The Dr. claimed I had combat exhaustion so I got treatment for that.

I have been reclassified and am now in limited service. This means I won't go into combat again.

I think I got all my Xmas packages. I got enough anyway. I got the razor but it got in the way of a German shell before I could use it. (I've got another one now.)

I sent Sara a bracelet the other day so tell when it comes.

I guess I run down for now, but I promise to write oftener.

I'm feeling fine but still wish I was home.

Love

Walter

P.S. Tell Lenore I said Hello!!

My parents must have been confused by this letter. I said my wound was "too bad". I meant to write "it wasn't too bad" and I went back to my company. Then I got sick and ended up in England, but I was feeling fine.

During the day, the hospital would let us out for a couple of hours. It was on one of these releases that I found a bracelet for my sister. She kept it until a couple of years ago when she decided to give it to my daughter.

At the hospital to pass the time, we played cards. A beautiful young nurse came in and asked if anyone wanted a back rub. We all said no at first, and finally one fellow said he would take one. Soon we were all wanting a back rub after seeing the young nurse rub her hands all over his back.

The censor wouldn't want you to know what I've been through. More to the point, I didn't want to write what I'd been through. I was exhausted by war and I just wanted to make it home.

As this letter was arriving at my home, I had just arrived at my next stop: a replacement depot for the ground forces. I had a new outlook on my future:

---

[1] Mom stopped numbering my letters at this point.

no more combat! Anywhere the Army sent me where there would be no more killing would be welcome. When I said I was "feeling fine," it was a gross understatement.

Letter #84: postmarked March 25, 1945

Dear Family,
I don't know what to write about but you'll know I'm O.D. at least. I've got one request to make. It's the same old story, I need a fountain pen. I guess this is about the hundredth time I've asked for a pen but I feel lost without one.
I told you this was going to be short.
Love
Walter Jr.
P.S. Thank Mrs. Jarrett for the Easter card.

This short letter spent time with the military postal service. The envelope was censored and then dated March 25, 1945. A subsequent date was stamped on the back of the envelope by the Wheeling post office on June 18 and the letter itself bore a stamp from the Elm Grove office, also on June 18. Seems no one in Wheeling was going to take the blame for the late delivery.

I had money, but I couldn't find a place to buy a fountain pen. I wasn't in a major metropolis and the availability of things was limited.

Mrs. Jarrett attended our church. Her son was also in the service. I guess without an ink pen I would have been unable to write a thank you note. Besides, my mom would let her know I got the card.

Another holiday passed and I was still alive. I was looking forward to my next assignment outside of combat.

Letter #85: postmarked March 26, 1945

Dear Mom,
I just got some mail from home and I will try to answer some of your questions. No doubt your first question is what does G.F.R.P. stand for. It means "Ground Forces Reinforcement Pool." In my other address the Det. of Pat. Stands for "Detachment of Patients."
You asked about the Purple Heart. I have gotten two awards. Instead of a second one you get the Oak Leaf Cluster. I'll send them both home soon.
It was my left shoulder which was bothering me. The doctor says I will have to suffer with it the rest of my life, there is nothing they can do for it.
I got the package with the New Testament in it, but haven't gotten the one with the fountain pen. I think I got all my Xmas packages.
I had a short furlough and guess who I met in Bristol? I doubt if you know him but Dick will. It was Eddy Majors. There is a fellow here with me from S. Wheeling who is related to the Saunders on Paxton Ave.

I guess I'm about run down for now so till later,
Love
Walter Jr.

Detachment of Patients was the medical service I received during my stay in the hospital. I'd been placed on limited service, which meant I was away from combat for the time being. The Ground Forces Reinforcement Pool was after my stay in the hospital.

I was back in a British barracks near Birmingham, England. This meant three meals a day and a bed to sleep in.

At roll call, the sergeant had a routine. He would name the chore to be done and call out the names assigned to complete it. This routine never changed. Your name was called, you left ranks walking past the sergeant into the tent behind him, signed the book, and did your assignment. I had an idea that I shared with a friend. As the last names were being called, we would walk past the sergeant like we were assigned, go on through the tent, and hustle to the British P.X. for tea and biscuits (English for cookies). It worked the one time I tried it!

Passes were not hard to come by, usually for 48 hours. Asking for one depended on how much money you had. Got money? Ask for a pass. On one occasion, six other G.I.s and I went on a pass together. Before leaving the train station we made a pact. We would stay over by one day and when we got back, we would claim we thought we had to return the day after the pass was up. We all agreed. We all came back one day late. We anticipated a check by the M.P.s, but there were no M.P.s!

Emboldened by that experience, a friend and I decided to try it again. However, on alighting from the return train there were M.P.s! My friend was in a state of panic. "We're in trouble!"

I came up with a plan. "When I get up to the M.P., push me and I'll start a fight." As planned, I was pushed.

Before I got past yelling "hell" and "damn," the M.P. yelled, "Keep moving!" Plan A worked. This learning experience kept me from trying this again.

From the depot by train, it was only a few minutes' ride to Manchester. A couple hours to London or Bristol. When the money dictated, I was off!

As for the Purple Hearts, they were not given to me until after the war. It was documented on my paperwork that I had been wounded twice and should receive the medal and Oak Leaf Cluster.

Here it was the end of March and I was still getting Christmas packages. As far as the people mentioned in the letter, it was just in passing that we met, and no crazy antics were done.

Please send the camera! I was ready to take pictures again. I know I got the camera because I have two pictures of my Quonset hut and the wheelbarrow used for moving kegs.

Letter #86: postmarked April 5, 1945

Dear Family,

Well! As strange as it may seem I am now in the Air Corps. I don't know what kind of a job I am going it get but when I find out I'll let you know.

Today was the third Easter away from home but it doesn't seem that long. This morning I had two eggs sunny-side up. Boy! They hit the spot. For dinner we had chicken.

I guess I run down now. At least you'll know I'm O.K.

Love

Walter

By early April, I was on my way to the 95th Bomb Group in Horham in East Anglia. During World War II, the Air Force was part of the Army and was officially named the U.S. Army Air Forces but many called it by its older name, the U.S. Air Corps. My destination was described as "some air base." The Army wasn't always that specific with information. It was going to be another adventure in my Army career. But I didn't feel any anxiety having just dined on "two eggs sunny side up," a meal missed very much in my six months of combat.

I had been away from home for many holidays. Easter Sunday would have started at St. Mark's Lutheran Church. We would have all walked together. Then mom would have made a special luncheon meal. It wouldn't have been uncommon to have some of my mother's sisters and children there, as well. Being with family was something my mom cherished and I truly missed during my time in the service.

Letter #87: postmarked April 23, 1945

Dear Family,

I hope you'll forgive me for not writing sooner, but I just couldn't get started.

I really got a break being transferred to the Air Corp. It is really swell here. I have had to work pretty hard for the last few days, but a little work won't kill anybody. We really have good meals too. They have ice cream and we've had fresh eggs for breakfast quite a few times.

I am going to be an armorer. That's the short work for cleaning guns, but that's about all I'm qualified to do, except drive a truck (which I refused to do).

If you will send me the address of some of the fellows which are in England (I think you said H. Hathaway was here) I may be able to see them.

There are three things which I could use now if you want to send them. That is a pen, my wrist watch (If I have one) and my camera (If I have one). I can also use some home-made cookies. If you send the watch and camera you had better insure them.

While I'm in the mood for writing I'll tell you some of the places I've been through. Paris and London for one. I've been in Aachen and Düren in Germany, Charleroi in Belgium, Cherbourg and St. Lo, as well as Paris in France, and Cambridge, Bristol and Birmingham as well as London in England. But the one place I really want to see is Wheeling, W.Va.

I guess I'm run down for now so I'll sign off.

With Love

Walter

I had a new address: 334th Bombardment Squadron, 95th Bombardment Group. I wondered what my family thought of this assignment. I was pleased with any placement that kept me from being in combat and the threat of being shot or killed and having to kill people to stay alive.

My move was to East Anglia near a small village, Horham, which was close to Diss, which had a station on the line to London. I anticipated my next job as an "armorer" would be with guns, but I got a surprise. Armorers loaded bombs. The gunners on the B-17s took care of their own guns.

I indicated I could not lift my left arm over my head, so I was assigned to the catwalk in the bomb bay to winch up the bombs and attach the shackles. On one occasion, my hand slipped off the wench and a 500-pound bomb went back down onto the cart. At the loud bang, I dove backward and banged my head. The fellows watching me laughed, adding, "Walter, do you think if that bomb went off diving backward would save you?!"

Two incidents stood out in my memory of those days. I helped load napalm that may have been dropped on Dresden. I also took great joy in having loaded boxes of food that were dropped in a soccer field in Holland. The Dutch were starving.

Climbing in and out of the plane caused my arm to dislocate twice. I decided I needed another job. I went to the major, who made assignments, to make my case. My new assignment was at the P.X. as a "clerk non-typist." The title of the job doesn't really explain what the work entailed. I was a salesperson in the P.X.

I just wanted to be home. I had seen so much senseless death.

334th Bombardment Squadron

The 334th was assigned to the 95th Bombardment Group, in the USAAF's Eighth Air Force. It was based at RAF Horham a large field located next to the village of Horham, some 4 miles southeast of Eye in Suffolk, and flew B-17Fs. The 334th attacked enemy troop concentrations during the Battle of the Bulge from December 1944 to January 1945 and bombed airfields to support Operation *Varsity*, the airborne assault across the Rhine in March. The unit's last bombing mission was on April 20, 1945. In May, it dropped food to the Dutch as part of Operation *Chowhound*, losing one aircraft that had to ditch into the North Sea after engine problems. Thereafter, until it returned to the United States, the 334th transported freed P.O.W.s.

Letter #88: postmarked April 30, 1945

Dear Family,

I don't know what I can say to fill this page but I promised I'd write more often so here it is.

I just had a pass and went to London, I stayed two full days. I could have stayed longer but I ran out of money. I have to laugh when I think about it. I was wandering around the second largest city in the world with only 1 shilling & 6 pence, which is the same as 30 cents!!

I slept in till 9:30 this morning then went to church. We had cream chicken on toast, peas, mashed potatoes, and coffee for dinner, and then I went to the show.

I have been trying to write a thank you letter to Mrs. Johnston but I can't seem to get past the first line.

Yesterday I got three more Xmas packages. All from home. They were full of cookie crumbs and flat cig but the candy was good. I got the one with dog tag chain from Lenore.

Send me the address of that little girl Sara writes to and I may be able to take her some candy and gum. I think I remember to ask for the addresses of any of fellows in England.

I'm running out of ink so I'll quit now.

Love

Walter Jr.

Getting a pass was no trouble. You could get one any time. It depended on how much money you had. I was always smart enough to buy a "return" ticket. Stuck in London and low on cash was no problem if you had the ticket back to the base.

My friends in the 334th Bomb Squad and I had a favorite pub in London, The Lion's Head. It was just a short distance from the Opera House. The pub was divided by a screen allowing women on one side and men on the other. Ironically, there was no dart board and no arguments.

G.I.s arriving in London went to "Rainbow Corner," where they were sent to an available hotel. The cost was two pounds. On my first solo trip to London, I arrived at night. Taking the subway (the underground/tube), I came to the surface in the dark at Piccadilly Square. A Bobby (police officer) gave me instructions to find the Corner with the assurance "You can't miss it."

I walked several blocks and asked for directions from another Bobby who headed me back in the same direction I had just come from. He too assured me, "You can't miss it."

On the walk back, I ended up meeting the first Bobby. Having pity on me, he took me right to the steps of the hotel. While I thanked him for his help, I silently said to myself, "Ha! Can't miss it. It's totally black!"

The base offered a Protestant service I attended. They also had a show, sometimes live and sometimes just a movie. I fell into a routine and felt lucky to have this assignment.

It was April and I was still getting Christmas gifts. The long-awaited dog chain from Lenore arrived. Is a flattened cigarette still smokable? The answer depends on how desperate you are.

My sister said she really didn't know what to write to the little girl in England so she didn't. Sounds like a family trait. So, there was no visit to the little girl.

I supposedly had a reason to write to my landlady who lived next door to my parents, but I couldn't think of anything to say.

Letter #89: postmarked May 22, 1945

Dear Family,

Please forgive me for not writing sooner. I have been pretty busy and I have been moving around a little. I have a new job. (Second since I've been here). My shoulder is giving me quite a bit of trouble and I asked for a transfer to a job where the work was light. I am now a clerk in the P.X (Post Exchange) I think that if I work hard enough I can kick out the top Jew and take over.

I have gotten quite a few packages lately as well as back mail. I got the package mailed to the hospital and also the one marked 13. The pen works fine.

We have been having beautiful weather. Especially around VE Day. Which reminds me. I spend VE+1 and VE+2 in London. Boy! Did I have a time. I met one of the Sgts. Who gave me my Basic Training back in the states. He is also from West Virginia.

My new job is just like being in civilian life. I go to work at 8:30 and work till 10:00 then I start at 11:30 and work till 4:30. I get two days off every two weeks and I will probably spend them in London.

I think my relations are trying to get me married off to some English girl. Eleanor and Aunt Hattie both ask me if I'm going to get married over here. Aunt Hattie says she likes to hear Englishmen talk. I have been to several dances but I haven't seen one yet that could beat the American girls. But…I would sooner go out with a Limey girl than the bags the Red Cross sends over here. The only one's that will talk to privates belong in S. Wheeling and the one's that do speak to you go out with the officers. So you see you go with the Limey's or you don't go out.

Well! Here I am writing four pages!! I guess I'll have to quit. I'll send you my Purple Heart soon. Incidentally I have been given the P.H. two times. It's worth 10 points toward demobilization.

P.S. I have been thinking lately (I have plenty of time for it now and I may go to school after the war. The Army will furnish my tuition and pay me 50 to 75 dollars a month.)

I guess I'm run down now. I hope you can read my writing. (I am pretty nervous).

Love

Walter Jr.

My relatives teasing me about getting a war bride was met with a rather colorful description of the Red Cross "bags". South Wheeling had many bordellos in a four-block square. During the war, these were supposedly closed down; in reality, they just moved around. One can only imagine my young sister reading this letter asking for an explanation!

On the lighter side, I really enjoyed my new job as a clerk in the P.X.. I also found a new friend, Roy Ferguson from Rossmore, West Virginia. We found a vacant room within a few feet of the P.X. and were allowed to move in our beds and stay there.

One night, we saw a light in the P.X. after hours and quickly went to investigate. We found two men, both in military dress, filling a duffel bag with rationed cigarettes, gum and other items. We asked, "What do you think you are doing?" They claimed they had permission to do what they were doing and they were keeping track of all they were taking. Roy and I made them put it back and leave. The two guys didn't want to find out how things would go if they didn't.

The next day when Roy and I told the other clerks what happened, we got a surprising story. There was an overweight man who on a regular basis went into P.X. to get supplies, with permission from the lieutenant in charge of the P.X.! He would take the goods from the P.X. into London and sell them at a generous markup to a buyer he had arrangements with. That money was used to buy liquor for the base's Officers' Club, at another markup. They claimed that this man had more money in the Horham bank than anyone in the village. It was also claimed the lieutenant owed him lots of money. This only happened one time when Roy and I were there. But that wasn't the end of the story! One night there was suddenly a large commotion in the corner around the pool table. I investigated. There he was, running a game of craps where he took a rake-off!

While working at the P.X., I decided to ask one of the laundry workers, Rose, for a date. She suggested we go to a movie in the next village. Sounding like a fun date, I asked what time I should pick her up. The reply caught me by surprise, "Knock me up at about six." Back home, this had a totally different meaning and it had nothing to do with the time to pick someone up for a date.

The night of the date, my only method of transportation was a bicycle. I pedaled about a mile to her house. She on her bike and me on mine, we pedaled another couple of miles to the next village where the only movie showing was a cowboy saga. When I suggested I wasn't much interested in the show, the young lady suggested we go to a carnival in the next village. Back on the bikes, we set off another couple of miles. The carnival was fun.

Finally, we pedaled home to her house. After dropping her off, I pedaled out of sight and promptly got off the bike and walked it home. This was my only date with Rose. Too much exercise for a young soldier for a second "knock up."

Roy was dating a girl off base. She had a younger sister, so Roy invited me to come along. He decided to bring the family an American ice cream treat. We got on our bikes, excited for the family to try it. It ended up being very disappointing. They didn't like it. It was too cold!

Roy and I made friends with the mess sergeant and cook. We provided them with good cigarettes. In return, if we didn't feel like rising early for breakfast, the cook would make us a special-order breakfast. The question was usually, "How would you like your eggs?" One day I needed a pair of socks. The supply sergeant, whom we also supplied with better cigarettes, gave me a whole package of socks. I insisted I only needed one pair; the supply sergeant insisted I take the whole package.

I had been in London and was returning to the Base on VE (Victory in Europe) Day. I went to sign in, as was the procedure. The sole person in the Day Room was a G.I. sweeping the floor. He asked me what I was doing there. Like a smart aleck, I answered, "I'm supposed to get a pass!" The sweeper went to the officer's desk, took out a pass, stamped it with the officer's signature and handed it to me. I immediately told the fellows in the armorer hut how to get the pass. The officer in charge of the armorers came looking for someone to do some work later on VE Day. Confused when he couldn't find anyone, he learned that thanks to the G.I. working the day room, everyone had gotten a pass off base.

It should come as no surprise I had to borrow some money, and it was back to London on VE Day with three friends.

One of the guys in the group knew where to get some whiskey on Windmill Street. A knock on the door, money exchanged, and a bottle of whiskey was shared in an entryway. I took one slug; whiskey was not my drink of choice. The bottle was passed around, when along came a Bobby. One of the fellows asked if he would like a nip. With a big smile on his face, he replied, "I don't ordinarily drink on duty, but on a day like today," and tilted the bottle back and took a long swig!

I moved on from my friends to explore on my own. My description of Piccadilly Circus was "if your hands were in the air, you couldn't get them down, or vice versa." I left the crowd and went to Leicester Square.

Before the war, Leicester Square was where you went to the movies or theater. When the lights came on after six years of blackouts, a woman near me was holding her young son's hand and she began to cry. What a moment!

No more bombs! No more running to air-raid shelters, no more bodies coming home! I must admit, I joined her with a few tears of my own. The war in Europe was over, and my life was forever changed by it. After the loss of friends and comrades, again the saying went through my mind, "To lose a friend is to die a little."

Later I found myself in Green Park. Someone had started a huge bonfire. There appeared to be park benches in the fire. I moved on to my favorite pub. The next day, it was back to the base. I was glad I went and content to know now there would be no more fighting in Europe.

After VE Day, I had a new assignment. I was given the job of Manager of the Enlisted Men's Beer Hall! Roy was assigned there, too. Getting the beer for the P.X. meant Roy and I had to go to the railroad tracks and pick up the kegs. We were told by the lieutenant that if they made any money, we could keep it. Interesting! We never made any money. When our friends came to the club and didn't have the funds for a pint of room-temperature beer, we helped them out. This was a job I took very seriously, testing all kegs to make

Piccadilly Circus, London, on VE-Day—some party! (NARA)

sure the beer was of the highest quality room-temperature beer. Sometimes it even required a second test.

In closing the letter, I admitted to still being nervous. Battle fatigue doesn't stop when the soldier is no longer fighting. A sound or a smell can trigger a flashback to a battle experience. While the war in Europe was won, the Japanese had not surrendered.

Letter #90 (The Final Letter): postmarked May 19, 1945[2]

I celebrated my 21st birthday in England. The flyers and plane crews soon left the base. The future was back home for a 30-day furlough. I had not been home in over 29 months. My next assignment was in the South Pacific.

I was riding the train through McConnellsburg, Pennsylvania, when my traveling companions and I learned that Japan had surrendered. Relief flooded through me; I wouldn't be going back to war. Arriving in Pittsburgh, I left the Pennsylvania train and asked the police officer where I could get a cab. "Son, you'll never get a cab tonight." He asked where I was going. I told him to the B&O station. He told me to keep walking about a mile straight down the street.

Nearing Wheeling on the B&O, I asked the conductor if the train stopped in Elm Grove. He replied, "Not usually, but today it does!" I got off the train and walked home to find no one there. My family, having waited for everyone to exit the train in Wheeling and not seeing me, figured I missed the train. On arriving home my mother questioned Walter Senior why he hadn't turned off the lights. Assuring her he had indeed turned off the lights, they walked into the kitchen to find me eating, having made myself an egg sandwich.

I enjoyed my 30 days at home. I broke up with Lenore, which was not all that happy an occasion. Marriage wasn't in our cards. She was a devout Catholic and I was a devout Lutheran. Neither of us was converting to the other's religion, so we moved on from our relationship.

The 30 days went fast. I was off to Sioux Falls, South Dakota. My shoulder continued to cause problems for me. The Army doctor didn't want to do surgery. My argument was I had 78 points and could be discharged tomorrow. Soldiers were getting discharged with only 20 or 30 points. Everyone was assigned points; you got additional points for time overseas and medals awarded.

[2] It contained postcards of London's famous sites prior to the War and a bulletin of the 95th Bomb Group [H] 300th Mission Party "Horham 300 Jamboree." I didn't include a letter and I had to add extra postage to send it.

The lieutenant ordered an X-ray of my shoulder and decided to schedule surgery. The surgery was performed by a surgeon from the Cleveland Clinic. My arm was in a sling for a brief period. I was given exercises to improve mobility. I spent another month in the Army to recuperate.

While recuperating, an incident occurred which was funny (if you were there) but had interesting repercussions. A bedfast patient's wife came to visit almost every day. When she bent over to kiss him, she would slip a pint of whiskey under his pillow. After she left, a patient in a wheelchair with a blanket over his legs would leave and come back with Cokes. This made for great convivial times in the day room with, of course, a portion shared with the original provider. Empty whiskey bottles in the trash raised a concern with the head nurse who told the hospital chief of nursing, a major. The major came with a lecture about what would happen if this continued. Then she observed a burn spot in the white blanket covering the card table. We received another very angry lecture about smoking and destroying government property. As she walked away, a patient, with little modulation in his voice, expressed an opinion often used by enlisted men: "Chicken shit!" Majors do not take kindly to this sort of comment. The ward was restricted, meaning we couldn't do any activities out of the ward.

A day or two later, pushing a book cart, came a lady from the Red Cross. I inquired if she needed any help. She asked if I knew how to run a 16mm movie projector. I assured her I had done so on the church's machine to help the pastor. I got the job, but not until I was interviewed by the hospital director where I claimed innocence as to who brought in the whiskey! I had observed that when the pastor ran the machine, there were directions on the inside of the opened door. No problem running the projector and now I was free to go into every ward, including the infectious disease ward.

One day after showing *Buffalo Bill* in my own ward, the refreshment provider motioned me over to his bed and in a whispered voice told how, during the film, his wife had climbed into bed with him. He wondered if they could have a movie the next day. How could you refuse a request like that! I set up a movie for the next day. The men were excited because they rarely got a movie two days in a row. They set up their wheelchairs and chairs and then howled when it turned out to be *Buffalo Bill* again. My response was I knew they would like a movie and it was the only one I had.

On her next visit, the Red Cross lady asked me if I would be interested in working in the base movie theater. I was and quickly learned the routine. Upon arriving at the projection booth, the sergeant there explained how to work the machines with the advice that if anything caught on fire, "Knock over the fire extinguisher on your way out." It was a paying job. A dollar for the projectionist and $1.25 for the chief projectionist. The sergeant suggested we would alternate as chief projectionist. I did this until released from the hospital and discharged from the service.

To get discharged, I had to report to Sioux City, Iowa. It was here where it was determined that I didn't have my summer khaki hat on a cold November day. A newly ranked second lieutenant was doing the inspection. He wasn't going to let me go until I accounted for the missing hat. My explanation of having been shot out of three tanks and lost more than that hat didn't satisfy him. As he continued to rant, someone in the back of the room yelled, "Chicken shit." This really fired the lieutenant up. Luckily an older, wiser major came out of his office to resolve the issue. Being sent along to the next officer, it was determined I never received my good conduct medal. While he couldn't put it on my discharge paperwork, he handed me the medal.

November 30, 1945, was my last day in the service. Then it was off to home for good. Wiser to the ways of the world!

Acknowledgements

A big thank you goes to my mother, who saved everything. Without those letters, none of this would have been as in depth. Those letters spurred my memories.

To my daughter, who found the letters and encouraged me to write a book and hounded me until I did, thank you. My son, who loves to read, told me to give more details. My brother and sister don't remember much about my time in the service but encouraged me to write the book.

My son's daughter-in-law and my granddaughter, Dr. Jessica L. George, the English teacher, gave me critical feedback and encouragement. She was the editor extraordinaire who helped this book reach publication. Jessica is currently an English language arts teacher at South Point High School in South Point, Ohio, and her students help keep her editing skills sharp. Jessica earned National Board Certification in 2015 and a doctorate in educational leadership in 2022. She lives with her wife and four rescue animals in Huntington, West Virginia.

For all those over the years who told me to write a book and tell about the funny things that happened, thank you. I finally did commit those things to paper, along with things I don't readily share about the tragedy of war.

Thank you to all who were involved.

Bibliography

Ancheta, A. (2022, March 27). War Bonds. *Investopedia*. https://www.investopedia.com/terms/w/warbonds.asp.

Blakemore, E. (2020, June 16). "How PTSD went from 'shell-shock' to a recognized medical diagnosis." *National Geographic*. https://www.nationalgeographic.com/history/article/ptsd-shell-shock-to-recognized-medical-diagnosis.

Citino, R. (2017, July 11). The Louisiana Maneuvers. *The National WWII Museum: New Orleans*. https://www.nationalww2museum.org/war/articles/louisiana-maneuvers.

Cole, Lt. Arthur L. (1945, May 8). *Canadian soldiers celebrating VE-Day, Piccadilly Circus, London, England, May 8, 1945* [Photograph]. BiblioArchives/LibraryArchives. Canada. https://www.flickr.com/photos/28853433@N02/6924693312.

Guise, K. (2019, December 7). Mail call: V-mail. *The National WWII Museum: New Orleans*. https://www.nationalww2museum.org/war/articles/mail-call-v-mail.

History.com Editors. (2009, November 9). Jubal Early. *History* [A&E Television Networks]. https://www.history.com/topics/american-civil-war/jubal-a-early.

Lewis, R. (n.d.). combat fatigue [sic]. *Britannica*. https://www.britannica.com/science/combat-fatigue.

National WWII Museum, (n.d.). The M4 Sherman Tank. https://www.nationalww2museum.org/visit/museum-campus/us-freedom-pavilion/vehicles-war/m4-sherman-tank#:~:text=Notorious%20for%20their%20flammability%2C%20Shermans,well%20as%20bolstering%20defensive%20positions.

Savage, J. (2011, Oct. 26). "Pop at the pictures: Wartime London dances to America's tune." *The Guardian*. https://www.theguardian.com/music/musicblog/2011/oct/26/1940s-london-rainbow-corner-swing.

"War pigeon." (2022, December 28). *Wikipedia*. https://en.wikipedia.org/wiki/War_pigeon.